COMPLIMENTS FOR HABITS TO BENEFITS

DR RICH ALLEN
greenlighteducation.net
Green Light Classrooms
High-Impact Teaching in the XYZ Era of Education
The Rock 'n Roll Classroom
Humane Presentations
New Shoes.

This in-depth examination of how to create helpful habits will be a life-saver for parents struggling to understand their children and help them lead happier, more successful lives.
For those interested in the science behind habit formation, the first section offers a theoretical framework for thinking about the influence parents can have in early childhood.
The rest of the book is a treasure-trove of 56 practical habits that will help parents to create resilient human beings. Readers will return again and again to seek inspiration for becoming better parents.

DIANNE MCCABE
Corporate Organisational Change Consultant
Devoted Mum | Change Coach, Facilitator, Speaker at the happy path.
Sydney, Australia

Ha-Le Thai's book HABITS TO BENEFITS is a fascinating read. Ha-Le draws you in with her wealth of knowledge and experience yet strengthens her approach to parenting with education and scientific research.
As a parent, I instantly saw habits I can work on with my child in a practical way. I feel this book will be a reference manual for many parents, one of those books that you go back to again and again, depending on the circumstances you find yourself in with your child/ren.
I highly recommend this wonderful book as it is a life-line for parents who may feel they are struggling or who just want to reinforce positive habits
HABITS TO BENEFITS helps you create a strong foundation for your child's life and will give you the added benefit of strengthening the bond between parent and child.

MIKEY LAI
Business owner, Stock trader, High-performance coach, trainer, mindset mentor, facilitator of growth at MENTORING YOURSELF. Father of 2, and loving husband, an impactor.
Perth, Australia

Ha-Le's book is a must read for any parent looking at nurturing their kids to have a bigger and brighter future. Ha-Le goes deep into the science and workings of the human mind and how it operates before she gives us practical tools that will help parents assist their child's development. There are detailed explanation of each habit, why it's so important to develop them and all the different benefits you'll gain from them from intellectually to socially to help your kids thrive in this world. How we are as adults are from the habits we establish as a child.

LEANNE SHELTON
Business Owner, Wife, and Mum to Gabrielle and Indiana
Sydney, Australia

As a mum to two young daughters, I'm constantly reflecting on my parenting style and attitude. With the first seven years being the most crucial in their development, there's a lot of pressure to get it right! Habits to Benefits has given me confidence in some areas and tips for improvements in others. Everything is broken down into easy-to-understand intellectual, emotional, social, and physical benefits, making the book a fantastic resource for building two positive, resilient, and well-rounded individuals.
Highly recommended!

SHARON MUSCET
*Expert Authority,
Speaker and Author-A
devoted Mum to her
two young men.
Adelaide, Australia*

"Habits to Benefits – Building a Brilliant Child" is a must read for all parents wishing to raise happy, confident, compassionate and kind children with a bright future. Ha-Le is a source and wealth of knowledge in her experience as an Educator. I was blown away by her words and practical tips.

There are so many habits that I have learned that I will apply to my parenting and I am confident will positively impact my children and their future.

Ha-Le is a true gift.

PHUONG PHAN
*Success Mindset
Coach
Radio Host
International Speaker*

A practical guide to helping parents understand the importance of keeping good formed habits in our child/children and why it's important when you as a parent must shift with the right mindset. As adults we must lead by example no matter what.

This book provides 56 techniques and are broken up so we can read direct to hat situation with easy step by step guide. Books are for any paen especially if you are starting on or are busy. There are a lot of valuable new golden advices and clear simple takeaways.

The book is awe inspiring and handy to help under to become better parents and to help us build stronger resilient child/children.

ROWENA DITZELL
Graduate Transition Consultant
CEO and Founder Graduate Advantage.
Sydney, Australia

Habits to Benefits' is an amazing parenting guide for all families, but especially those with young children. Ha-Le's experience, passion and knowledge shine throughout the book. Ha-Le explains the relevant psychological and theoretical frameworks in an approachable and easily understandable style. She then guides the reader through 56 Habits to help bring out the best in our children. The content is rich and easy to implement. I wish I had 'Habits to Benefits' when my children were younger!

PHUONG HOANG
A loving mother of Many and Heli-Former Owner and Director of BIRRONG -SAIGON PRESCHOOL.
Vietnam

This is A marvellous book that I really need for my two precious son and daughter. I am so glad that I've had a privilege to read it when my children are still young. Ha-Le's book, HABITS TO BENEFITS, will be my guidebook under my pillow every day and my compass for doing and equipping right things for my children. I can't wait for HABITS TO BENEFITS to be translated into Vietnamese for parents. We need right guidance very much for being successful parents in the socially ever-changing context of Vietnam and the world. We can't be wrong in our parenting with HABITS TO BENEFITS in our hands. Thank-you so much Ha-Le for your dedication and love for children.

IAN COOMBE
#1 Bestselling Author of WIKID POWER and Creator of the Decision Quotient.
Sydney, Australia

What a delight to read a book about early childhood development that mentions decision-making so often! Ha-Le's book, Habits to Benefits, is a decidedly invaluable and insightful resource for parents.

Make the decision to read Ha-Le's book and take action to learn Habits to Benefits. Use it as a practical guide by prioritising the areas you think more important (priority setting is a critical process in decision-making).

May parents decision to improve their parenting habits return enormous benefits!

KIKI WONG
Mother of two boys, Director at The Silent Company Voice over talent, Professional backing vocalist.
Hong-Kong

This is not a just any parenting book. It's a book to guide and teach you to become the best version of yourself for your children. It helped me understand myself and what I can do to be the best parent that I can be. With the ever-changing world we live in, facing all kinds of challenges, it is important to understand the deeper meaning of good parenting. This was exactly what Ha Le's book was able to deliver to her audiences. Parents! What a joy to read!

ACTIONABLE - ENGAGING - FACTUAL

HABITS TO BENEFITS
Vol. 1
BUILDING A BRILLIANT CHILD

ESSENTIAL IDEAS FOR PARENTING

A Step by Step Guide of 55+ HABITS FOR CHILDREN OF ALL AGES

HA-LE THAI
International Bestselling Author

The first edition was published in 2019

Copyright © 2019 by Ha-Le Thai

All rights reserved. This book or any portion thereof cannot be transmitted in any form or by any means; be it electronic or mechanical, including photocopying, recording or by any information storage and retrieval system. The book may not be reproduced or used in any manner whatsoever without the express written permission of the publisher except for the use of brief quotations in a book review.

The Australian Copyright Act 1968 (the Act) allows a maximum of one chapter or 10% of this book, whichever is the greater, to be photocopied by any educational institution for its educational purposes provided that the educational institution (or body that administers it) has given a remuneration notice to Copyright Agency Limited (CAL) under the Act.

Printed in the United States of America

First Printing, 2019

Cataloguing-in-Publication details are available from the National Library of Australia www.trove.nla.gov.au

ISBN 978-0-6484486-7-9

Edited by: Dr Minh Duc Thai, Olaniyan Damilare Julius, Abigail Summer
Proofreading and line editing: Dr Minh Duc Thai
Cover design: Ha-Le Thai and Leb Raingam
Interior design: Leb Raingam (Nonon Tech & Design)

Published by: Waratah Publisher
Address: 67 ROWE DR Potts Hill, NSW 2143
www.briliantchildren.education
www.halethai.com.au

ACKNOWLEDGMENT

I want to thank my beloved daughter, Hong-An, who taught me the games of life through trials, pains, hurt, and failures until I became triumphant and most of all, became a good mother. She was the one who indirectly inspired me to write HABITS TO BENEFITS to parents.

Thank you, Minh, for believing in me and encouraging me to share what I knew to parents. His constant words into my ears for so many years, 'Put down all knowledge you have into a book to be read through parents' eyes', became a burning desire in my heart to write this book .I am indebted to Minh for spending much of precious time reading, commenting and editing HABITS TO BENEFITS despite his full-time work.

I also thank my four beloved brothers, Hiep, Hien, Hung and Hai who shaped me and made me into a good sister and an Educator through their lives' successes and failures.

I am humbled and grateful to Dr Joe Subino, Brian Tracey, Dr Bradley Nelson, Dr Steve G John, Sharon Pearson, Joe Pane, John Assaraf, Herman Muller, Marie Muller, Dr Tad James, Dr Adriana James, Arthur Bablis, Linda Thackray, and Sean Jason who have been my teachers, my masters, my coaches and have taught and inspired me in many ways directly and indirectly, and who have motivated me and encouraged me to write and complete the book HABITS TO BENEFITS.

Special thanks to DR Rich Allen, Dr Minh Duc Thai, Andrea Virginia Sanchez Aguilar who is Psychologist specialized in child development and existentialist psychotherapist, Dianne Mccabe, Sharon Muscet, Ian Coombe, Rowena Ditzell, Kiki Wong, Leanne Shelton, Phuong Phan, Phuong Hoang, Olaniyan Damilare Julius, and Michael Lai, who were patient enough to read HABITS TO BENEFITS and provide their comments and reviews of it.

I'd like to express my deepest gratitude to Leb Raingam (Nonon Tech & Design) who spent so much time and a considerably huge effort in formatting, internally designing and materialising this book from a raw word document. Leb didn't mind going back to the manuscript countless times to insert, remove and adjust for the book to come out in such a beautiful form as it looks now.

Thank you to all of my precious clients who shared with me their childhood experiences with their boldness. These inspired me to devote my time to research and write HABITS TO BENEFITS to encourage parents to do the right things to their beloved children as early as possible.

Lastly, I thank all the parents who have believed me and encouraged me to share my knowledge with all parents all over the world. I also thank all parents who were willing to share their true parenting stories with their courage. I am particularly grateful to all children whom I had worked with and met in my life. They helped me to love children dearly and motivated me to make my best contribution to their world.

On a final note, I would like to express my thankfulness and gratefulness to Simone Feiler Clark of Brisbane Audiobook Production for choosing the right person for the voicing over of HABIT TO BENEFITS, and her patience in waiting for the completion of the book which took a longer time than expected. I also thank Simone for her dedicated effort to make the audiobook of HABITS TO BENEFITS reachable to all parents the world over.

Ha-Le Thai

FOREWORD

Simply stated, the decisions we make every day define us – who we are to ourselves, who we are to others, and how well we achieve our personal and professional goals. Yet many decisions are made on an unconscious level, without careful, mindful, considered analysis as to possible outcomes.

To maximize our success – and the successful of those around us – we need to develop patterns in how we make choices, patterns that allow us to consistently realize our true potential. The earlier in life we cultivate these patterns, the better. As we grow up, this ability to make high-level choices become a part of us, our daily habits. They serve to strengthen us, deepen our understanding of ourselves and others, and help us achieve our life's ambitions.

This book will be both an excellent starting point for anyone interested in undertaking this highly rewarding journey of self-development, as well as a wonderful constant companion every step of the way. It offers an in-depth examination of how parents can guide children to create helpful habits, and lead happier, more successful lives. Readers will return again and again for the next idea, and each time they will discover further inspiration for helping their children – as well as helping themselves on their own journey.

The practical nature of the book is its greatest strength. The in-depth investigation of the science behind how we develop habits will certainly intrigue many readers. However the 56 practical habits that emerge from this understanding will be a true treasure-trove for everyone – especially parents seeking to guide their children towards becoming resilient and positive young adults.

Dr. Rich Allen
greenlighteducation.net
Green Light Classrooms
High-Impact Teaching in the XYZ Era of Education
The Rock 'n Roll Classroom
Humane Presentations
New Shoes

THOUGHT AND REFLECTIONS

There is a saying about leadership that you can start tough and soften up, but you can't start soft then toughen up. The same goes with parenting because parenting is about providing leadership through example — for decades! Starting with the tough decisions in parenting makes life much easier for everyone in the long run than starting soft. Tough decisions need to be made from the start. Once you start parenting, you can't decide to quit — no matter how tough it gets!

Yet, Ha-Le quite rightly says, "Parenting can be hard. All it takes, however, is a shift in perspective — a move toward exercising determination in the preparation you give to your child/children.". This requires some thought about parenting from the outset and Ha-Le's book provides a terrific foundation for parents to work out their perspective and approach to their children. Working on and mastering Ha Le's habits requires a disciplined approach to parenting — over decades!

Research shows that whilst they might not readily say, children feel more loved and cared for when parents make tough decisions and set boundaries than when they don't! Children look to exploit any inconsistencies in their parents' approach as they push boundaries to discover their own identities.

I like to say that discipline is about being consistently persistent! Discipline is like a constellation of decisions — all forming a recognisable pattern.

Developing discipline requires developing habits — ones that are hard to break. Like washing hands, saying thank you, daily hygiene, cleaning dishes, putting on the traffic indicator, eating the right foods and exercising.

Good discipline and habits deliver enormous benefits. In parenting, the benefits from good habits last several lifetimes as they are passed down through generations.

Developing those habits takes change. Change is not easy but it's easier for people to change when the benefits outweigh the effort. Rest assured, they do when it comes to parenting!

My passion is to help people make better decisions for a better life and world. Your decision to change your parenting habits will be one of the best decisions of your life! The benefits will help your children make better decisions too! I counted over six dozen references to decision-making in Ha-Le's book. What a delight to read a book about early childhood development that mentions decision-making so often! Ha-Le's book, Habits to Benefits, is a decidedly invaluable and insightful resource for parents.

Make the decision to read Ha-Le's book and take action to learn Habits to Benefits. Use it as a practical guide by prioritising the areas you think more important (priority setting is a critical process in decision-making). As you start out, simply work on one area at a time – maybe choose one per day or week to work on. To reward yourself, make an assessment of each habit before you start and then again every few months to track your progress!

May your decision to improve your parenting habits return enormous benefits!

Ian Coombe
Parent
Multi award winner and multi #1 bestseller on decision-making
Former CEO of Playgroup Queensland
Former State Government Adviser on Early Childhood Education
IanCoombe.com

TABLE OF CONTENTS

Acknowledgment ii
Foreword iv
Thought and reflections v

PART ONE THEORETICAL FRAMEWORK 1

1. Introduction 2
2. Parenting made easy 8
3. The Mind 12
4. Classical Conditioning, Anchoring in NLP & Habit Building . 23
5. The Mind and Its power 31
6. Belief and Self-Concept 40
7. Importance of the seven years of life 47
8. Importance of equipping young children with The right habits during The Early Stage 50
9. Message From The Author To Parents 53

PART TWO HABITS TO BENEFITS 56

1. Love and Life appreciation 57
   Habit One Enjoy all the little things. 58
   Habit Two Work on family culture 62

Habit Three Home is the best place to come back 66
Habit Four Relax living environment. 71
Habit Five Enjoy free thing around: sun, flowers, parks, nature, and wild animals. 75
Habit Six Enjoy the good music. 80
Habit Seven Having a good dinner with the whole family. 84
Habit Eight Work on the appreciation of nature 89
Habit Nine Start the day with a happy mood. 94
Habit Ten Celebrate good behaviour, and achievements 98
Habit Eleven Read good books. 103
Habit Twelve Having a music background for studying and works. 108
Habit Thirteen Appreciate and look up to great persons. 113
Habit Fourteen Be kind 117
Habit Fifteen Having compassion 122
Habit Sixteen Work on Sharing and caring 126
Habit Seventeen Make physical contact with trustworthy and loved ones .. 130
Habit Eighteen Self-entertainment 133
Habit Nineteen Finding passion 138

2. Resilience 142

Habit Twenty Turning Problems into Opportunities. 143
Habit Twenty-One Letting go of the Past 147
Habit Twenty-two Ability to respond to stress. 151
Habit Twenty-three Ability to find a solution for challenges. 156
Habit Twenty-four Recovering from a stressful time. 161
Habit Twenty-five Recover emotional balance after challenges. 166
Habit Twenty-six Ask for help when needed 171
Habit Twenty-seven Accept mistakes as a chance to be better. 176

3. Self-discipline 182

Habit Twenty-eight Obtain abilities to tell right from wrong. 183
Habit Twenty-nine Follow a regular bedtime routine. 188
Habit Thirty Engage in physical activity 192
Habit Thirty-one Talk openly and calmly even when you're upset 197

Habit Thirty-two Possess a good study routine 202
Habit Thirty-three Use active listening skills 207
Habit Thirty-four Allow the right amount of TV 212
Habit Thirty-five Eat healthy food 217
Habit Thirty-six Be cooperative 222
Habit Thirty-seven Be able to admit to the mistake. 227
Habit Thirty-eight Be emotionally open and quite sensitive. 231

4. Self-worth 236

Habit Thirty-nine Take pride in self 238
Habit Forty Have Integrity. 242
Habit Forty-one Allow the past mistake to go 247
Habit Forty-two Believe in him/her 251
Habit Forty-three Retain a great breakfast 256
Habit Forty-four Enjoy dinner/ meals with the guests. 260
Habit Forty-five Obtain a sense of being him/her 264
Habit Forty-six Maintain self-love. 269
Habit Forty-seven Carry out good personal hygiene. 274
Habit Forty-eight Keep the body safe and safety awareness. 279
Habit Forty-nine Know when to say NO. 284
Habit Fifty Have Courage 289
Habit Fifty-one Drink plenty of fresh water 294
Habit Fifty-two Eat fruits and vegetables 299
Habit Fifty-three Develop the interest 303
Habit Fifty-four Obtain a hobby 307
Habit Fifty-five Have bravery 312
Habit Fifty-six Know how to stand up for rights 317

PART THREE CONCLUSION 322

REFERENCES 325

Part One
THEORETICAL FRAMEWORK

1. INTRODUCTION

► **CHECK YOURSELF**

- Have you ever felt stuck or struggled through a hard time with your child/children?
- Have you tried your best, but the best you truly want for your child/children doesn't seem to be happening?
- Have you ever had concerns about what the future of your child/children might be like?

arents, nowadays, often say that children are so hard to manage. In my research, I have found the blame does not fall solely on the child/children. Parents are facing challenges in raising their children because they lack the essential skills needed for good parenting.

Believe it or not, all successful people achieve their goals based on productive habits. While unsuccessful people don't achieve their goals based on unproductive, non-effective habits.

I would ask you to consider why two doctors who are the same age and graduated from the same medical school, live totally different lives? One may be very well known as a successful doctor, while the other may be undervalued and not recognized.

I encountered twin sisters at my preschool. I was totally fascinated by the ways they responded to the world. They were both the same age (just born a few minutes apart) and looked almost identical. However, one was labelled 'devil,' and the other one was called 'angel' by their parents. Since they both attended my preschool full time, I observed them and realised some exciting things about them. Each of the girls had different habits which led to different lives, despite the fact that they had so many similarities. I will get into this in greater depth later in the book.

> 95% everything you do is the result of habit
>
> Aristotle

▶ ALL HABITS ARE LEARNED AND UNLEARNED

Early on, Michael Jordan had a habit of missing the basket each time he threw the ball toward the target. Despite this unwanted habit, he built up a routine of continuous practising and self-discipline. Sticking with this over time he achieved his goal and it became his golden habit. Finally, that developed habit helped Michael Jordan get the ball on target accurately, successfully and repeatably. In the end, he became one of the world's greatest basketball players ever to play the game. This, after he has missed more than 9000 shots and lost almost 300 games! Habit comes out of what you think, and what you do all the time. Successful, wealthy people achieve their goals in life through their thinking and their doing. Consistent thinking and doing results in habits.

Habits can make the poor rich and the rich poor. They can direct you throughout your life. Once learned they can help you do what you should do, when you should do it, whether you feel like doing it or not. Habits are foundations on which choices can be made more easily. Once a habit is formed, recognizing a situation and anticipating the outcome becomes a big help in determining how to act. Habits take some of the guesswork out of your life.

▶ TIME TO TAKE CAREFUL NOTICE OF YOUR CHILDREN

There are many self-help books available which are mostly eye-catching, with persuasive titles. Some Gurus try to show and advise people about developing healthy habits for a contented and fruitful lifestyle. Some books recommend excellent new habits for you to learn yourself. But the bottom line is: *How many people are really willing to change for the better?* Is it possible for people to change and achieve their goals when the old habits are so deeply rooted in their lives? Research shows that a great majority of people, who read self-help books, attend programs, seminars and study workshops fail to change. The reason is simple: they are comfortable with the old habits they have already developed.

> Bad habits are like a comfortable bed,
> easy to get into, but hard to get out of.
>
> **Proverb**

I have a friend who joined me in a training on Body and Mind learning. He really wanted to move on in life and get rid of things he no longer wanted as part of his life. Sadly, he has been dealing with depression, and still hasn't been able to change the habits which he has had for his whole life.

The importance of habits in parenting is a huge and critically important topic. Believe it or not, you are in the process of building or ruining your child/children's life through the habits you have now. Whatever your child/children's age, they have developed many habits based on the way you raised and taught them. Who your child/children become in life is being identified through habits.

Children are always affected by their surroundings. They are like a sponge which sucks in everything—good or bad. It's vital to start building up healthy habits for your child/children at a young age. It's important for parents to remember that bad habits can be hard to break. The sooner you establish healthy habits in your child/children, the more likely these habits will stay for years to come.

> "If you are going to achieve excellence in big things, you develop the habit in little matters. Excellence is not an exception; it is a prevailing attitude."
>
> **Colin Powell**

▶ MY EXPERIENCES AS AN EARLY CHILDHOOD EDUCATOR:

I worked in the early childhood field for more than 25 years and connected with many parents, children and clients of all ages. My career experiences and life-long learning have inspired me to write **HABITS TO BENEFITS**... for parents. I felt an intense desire to get parents to know the power of habits in their child/children's lives. I wanted parents to know how much children would benefit from parents who knew how to equip them with the right habits.

I was saddened to meet children who had been healthy and happy while attending my preschool only to later in life turn into depressed adults, lacking in hope. Some had developed incredibly low self-esteem and were unable to remain employed. I couldn't help but wonder why these children had turned into different adults with depression, desperation and low self-esteem. Did it have to do with negative habits formed inside them with the passing of time? I asked myself, "Is that what gradually changed them and geared them to become the people they are today.

The mother of one my former student's told me, "He kept playing games and failed at school, year after year, and couldn't get into university."

Then, I met another former student, a young lady, who had this to say: "I can't find a permanent job because I don't have any skills." I felt heartbroken for my former students but I could see the responsibility fell on their parents who didn't have the skills guide and equip their child/children well! I believed my former students' parents probably felt guilty and had regret for what their children had become.

The fact is, they can't do anything now for their child/children. These grown children have already formed their habits and become the person in charge of himself/herself. Now you can understand why some people are not able to achieve their goal of a better life even though they would like to at the conscious level. This happens because what a person learns during their childhood period becomes rooted deeply inside and this runs a person's life in almost every aspect.

On the contrary, my heart sang when seeing my former students thriving with great success in work and family. The answers were quite apparent to me. These students achieved great habits that were taught by their parents. They had been equipped throughout their childhood period and at different stages of their adolescent life!

I would conclude that hardly anyone could excel in a job without doing the work over and over again until it becomes a habit. To become a great speaker, a person needs to practise speaking over and over again until they master the process. To become a good doctor, a doctor needs to deal with and handle many cases and treat many various illnesses. Similarly, looking into the future of a child who will grow up and cope with the many demands of life such as personal needs, work, spiritual needs, relationships and family's needs etc, he/she needs to be taught, guided and equipped with appropriate habits and essential skills by parents to become a competent and confident adult.

From my life journey, I have learned so many valuable experiences that are related to habits. My parents didn't teach me how to care for myself and they spoiled me so much as I was their only daughter. I had the habit of having fun with life and with whatever I wanted. I could ask my family members to help me with whatever I needed instead of doing it by myself. These habits made me pay a large price when I left my country, Vietnam. I was so incompetent to care for myself and my newborn baby. I was so clumsy in a lot of things because of inexperience. Then I found myself trying to deal with depression since I couldn't cope with the challenges of being a new mother! When I came to Australia to begin a new life, I suffered from a lot of setbacks. I then got three types of cancers one after the other. To my understanding, after many years of researching and studying, I understand the causes of those cancers might have been triggered by the lack of abilities and endurance to cope with adversity. Since I had never developed the habits of bearing challenges and hardships when I was young, my body was not equipped to deal with the great stress I found myself unable to escape. According to Dr Deepak Chopra, it is well known that stress negatively affects the body's ability to maintain good health. Luckily, I realised that I needed to obtain the necessary habits and skills for survival. Now, I have a magnificent life with confidence and competence for facing and coping with whatever life brings to me. Through this, I could assure you that everyone can change old habits whenever we wish. Realising all of these things, I got inspired to write this book to help parents gain a good understanding of habits and know how powerful they are to the future of your child/children. And from this, you would know why children need to be equipped with good habits. You need to know, what good habits are, and how to build good habits for your child/children as soon as possible. Most people have heard the well-known proverb:

 You will reap what you sow!

Furthermore, when writing this book, I became quite fascinated with the Biggest Loser Television Show. This show helps illustrate the power of developing habits.

In the very first week, some contestants were eliminated. The number of participants kept getting smaller as the weeks went by. In the final week, there was only one winner.

What was so interesting to me was to see the power of habit and how it affected people's lives in several different aspects. The ones who were eliminated first were the ones who had the lowest scores for the ability to change old habits and replace them with new ones. The winner was the one who shook off all the old unwanted habits which caused him to become overweight.

My point is to stress, one more time, how powerful habits are to human beings. Therefore, instil good habits in your children and you will reduce the unnecessary stress and pain they will experience later, when they grow up. Now more than ever, we need to equip our children to be resilient, to be able to navigate change and bounce forward from challenges, difficulties and anger in life. This book aims to give you tools to do just that. I believe that you never want to witness the failure of your grown-up son and daughter, don't you?

▶ RAISING YOUR CHILD/CHILDREN

Raising and teaching your child/children should bring joy. How powerful would your child's life be if you have a daughter/son who was not afraid to take risks, who was not afraid to think creatively, and everybody loves and adores him/her? Every child deserves the best from his/her parents. The type of parents who never give up on bringing the best to their child/children and who understands the power of good parenting. Is this job tough? Yes! It is tough, but it is not impossible. You *can* do this. You are the parents. You brought your child/children into the world and you have the responsibility to raise him/her rightly for a happy life.

2. PARENTING MADE EASY

Parenting can be hard. All it takes, however, is a shift in perspective — a move toward exercising determination in the preparation you give to your child/children. This requires hope, confidence, and an understanding that parenting skills and children's lives are profoundly interwoven.

As an Early Childhood Educator, Trainer and Life & Health Coach, I have learned many valuable lessons to pass on. As a mother, a long-life learner and a healer to myself, I have always known that making parenting easy is far more than just going with the flow. You must be intentional about the way you parent. It's also about being strong emotionally, spiritually and physically, and having a depth of knowledge about parenting.

Acknowledging the deep connection between your beliefs and your knowledge of parenting is a first step toward truly making your parenting easier.

This book, **HABITS TO BENEFITS**, is your Owner's Manual for making that happen — for bringing a wholesome, joyful and prosperous life for your beloved sons and daughters.

There is no magic wand that will transform your parenting skills. Yet, this book is written to ensure that you have a complete guide for parenting in the right way. You may have to make changes. But, when you align your knowledge with your parenting, you can move mountains, and your child/children's life will be a successful one. You'll gain access to guidance that will take you in the right direction of becoming the parent you want to be. Whatever you want to achieve for your child/children will flow from your understanding and determination to do it right, for the sake of your child/children.

HABITS TO BENEFITS is a book which will provide you with the necessary skills you need to equip your child/children at an early age.

▶ EXCELLENT PARENTING

This is a book about excellence in parenting, and more importantly, how to make your child/children's future excellent.

This book includes the principles and lessons I have learned from great parents who raised their children to be successful adults. It also includes the lessons I've learned from observing the children who came to my preschool and from my clients who came for life coaching and wellness. I've utilised all that information, and brought my real-life experiences to this book. These are the same principles and lessons I have used in teaching and coaching many parents. These principles are designed to help you gain great confidence and successes in the mission of parenting.

In many ways, this book is the outcome of my experience throughout this magnificent journey of teaching and learning. It represents the collection of the education I have attained and wish to give to those who aim for parenting excellence and who want to become more so they can give more.

Human growth and development happen through experience. It is based on the experience of the stories in your life, the school you attended, the people you have met, and the books you have read and everything else—starting from childhood.

Furthermore, this book is packed with science-based theories and skills laid out for parents and children exercises. It will help you, as parents, in touch with new understanding of the power of habits and how they affect your child/children's lives now and in the long term. This book also shows you how to apply essential habits for your child/children in practical, easy ways.

Wherever you are right now, as parents, the content of this book and its practical applications can benefit you and your child/children. Each part of the book, each habit and its benefits will take you and your child/children down the road to success. You will learn new skills, new practices and you will be able to see your parenting in a more comfortable light, Your child/children will grow better in many ways. You are going to learn what is best to put into the "skills bank" of your son or daughter. Besides, your skills for parenting will be sharpened through learning new knowledge, new understanding about habits and their benefits to your child/children's lives now and in the future.

When you reach the end of **HABITS TO BENEFITS**, you will be better able to understand your duties and responsibilities as parents. You will gain insight into the growth of your child/children at a deeper level. The feeling of guilt, frustration and anger will be replaced by joy, confidence, and a sense of accomplishment.

Parenting is hard and very demanding work and **HABITS TO BENEFITS** will help you do the job with certainty and contentment. I would not expect that you - parents will take all the information in this book on-board in one reading. I encourage you to think of this book as a resource that you will return to again and again to support your child/children in any situation, or any need you may have.

▶ AN EXCELLENT CHILD COMES FROM EXCELLENT PARENTS

Excellence is staying at your best when it means the most – every point and every day. For parenting, it is being at your best in every single circumstance. A great philosopher, Aristotle said: "We are what we repeatedly do. Excellence, then, is not an act, but a habit" That is a vital principle you will experience in reading this book.

▶ PARENTING CONDITIONING'S PROCESS

Parenting conditioning is a process in which you search within yourself to see what you have as a parent as you raise your child/children. What are your strengths? What are your weaknesses? What is your motivation? The answers to those questions and challenges live inside you. As you go your way into this book to discover new skills for parenting, you will find out what motivates you to begin this journey by continuously reflecting upon your attitudes, knowledge and actions. While reading this book, you will recognise self-discipline and the changes you must make to access all the untapped and endless potential that resides inside you as a parent. Tapping into your thinking and analysing potential is crucial for peak parenting. This book also will teach you to have the best parenting performance by coaching you to follow instructions and search the power from within you to raise your child/children to their best of your ability. My life's purpose is to help you open the excellent parenting that lies within you and to coach you to develop the tools to accomplish that goal. You can improve your parenting by taking new actions and applying new knowledge to your parenting approach. And no matter how good you may be, we all need improvement in one area or another.

▶ FOR SUCCESSFUL PARENTING- THE GOAL IS ACTION

Everyone wants to be successful parents and **HABITS TO BENEFITS** provides you with strategies and ideas that will give you the best opportunity to accomplish any task and duty you desire as parents.

As you continue on your journey through this book, employ each of the habits listed for your child/children to achieve your process-based goals along the way. This is how you recognise and build your skills and knowledge, to facilitate the steps of this process in your parenting journey. It is your job to enable each habit to turn into benefits in your child/children's life. It is the purpose of this book to provide the information and knowledge to facilitate habit formation step by step, so that you may achieve the results you desire to achieve for your son/daughter. You can take one habit a day, from now on, to achieve successes in parenting. It all comes down to taking the first step and then another and another until you reach your best parenting. Be patient in the process and enjoy the journey.

3. THE MIND

Through all the trainings that I have had and research I've studied, I have come across several famous men and women, from all around the world, talk about the power of our mind and specifically, the power of our subconscious and unconscious minds. Brian Tracey, Dr. Tad James and Adriana James, Dr Steve G Jones, Dr Kanzas, Dr Bruce Lupton and the well-known life coach, Anthony Robins, Hypnotherapist Marisa Peer to name a few.

These famous masters and teachers mentioned a lot about the conscious mind, subconscious mind and the unconscious mind in their books, their talks, their teaching and in their seminars. They offered how to change people's minds and help them get rich in physical, mental, financial and many other ways. They brought out the undeniable truth about the power of our mind which can make a mature person become a prince, princess or a beggar depending on what they think about their lives. They tried to fix the already fixed mindsets of the grown up in different ages, but not everyone received a good result because they couldn't or wouldn't change their habits which had been set deep in their internal world.

I have been very fond of the following quotation:

> ❝ It is easier to build strong children than to repair broken men. ❞
>
> **Frederick Douglass**

I totally agreed with him!

As I mentioned before, there has been a lot of famous and well-known masters, teachers, scholars who have tried to fix the adult's mind for attaining success, happiness and prosperity, and the outcomes have been limited. You and I have experienced the undeniable truth— that we are facing more and more problems every day. We witness a lot of wealthy and well-known people get into mental, physical illnesses, commit suicide and so on through many books, articles, WHO's statistics etc. They couldn't rescue themselves even though they have a lot of money!

For that reason, I felt motivated and passionate to bring parents the concepts of the mind for successful parenting!

I think the theories on the conscious mind, subconscious mind and unconscious mind are still very new to a lot of parents. Therefore, I have the desire to address these concepts in this book and maybe in my next book on parenting. To me, these concepts are fundamental, and when you get to know them, your understanding of your child/children's growth and development would be shifted. Your parenting job would be much easier and more enjoyable!

Before studying positive Psychology, NLP, Hypnosis and the other modalities, I had a simple thought that the mind is the brain and the brain is the centre of our thinking.

After a training with Brian Tracy, I came to understand more about what the mind truly is. I've learned that we have two minds in one, a conscious mind and a subconscious mind. And then, after more studies and research, I found out that our mind has three in one, a conscious mind, a subconscious mind and an unconscious mind. You may wonder why I bring this topic of three minds to the **HABITS TO BENEFITS** book.

Let me tell you that what I am about to explain to you is critically important. It contains the essential knowledge you need to know for raising and teaching your child/children properly.

I am fascinated by understanding the power of our mind. And wherever I interact with parents, I ask them if they know anything about the conscious mind, subconscious mind and unconscious mind. To my surprise, I've found more than 99% of parents I meet don't know anything about this subject. And then, when parents feel frustrated about the results they have with their child/children, I know the root cause. This gives me motivation to try my best to convey and explain the power of our mind: the conscious, subconscious and unconscious. I hope parents, including you, will gain awareness of what to teach your precious children; now and later. I will help you look at these three minds and how to use your new-found knowledge to change your child/children's unwanted habits and insert healthy, vital habits to create a happier little human and a more successful and confident adult in the future.

▶ A QUICK UNDERSTANDING OF THE HUMAN MIND

This is an area that people have debated for many decades. My purpose of bringing this message to the art of parenting is to help you to have the right perspective on why your children are doing what they are doing. This will also explain why some parents are successful with parenting, but some fail despite their enormous efforts.

Three minds in one is not a new concept in the area of mental health especially in Psychology and Hypnosis. A lot of research studies have been carried out, and many psychologists, psychiatrics, doctors and philosophers have shared their discoveries in this area such as Carl Jung, Lev Vygotsky, Ivan Pavlov, Milton H, Ericson, John Grinder, Michael Hall, Dr Bruce Lipton, to name a few great Scholars. had theories about three minds in one was Sigmund Freud, a world-famous Psychiatrist from Austria. He stated that our mind is made up of three components- the conscious mind or ego, the pre-conscious or subconscious mind and the unconscious mind.subconscious mind and the unconscious mind.

The clearest and easiest way I have found to demonstrate the concept of the three minds is by using an iceberg. If you assume at the very tip of the iceberg is our conscious mind. It probably represents about 5- 10% of our brain function.

Below this is a somewhat extended section that Freud named the pre-conscious or subconscious. It is much bigger than the conscious mind and represents about 50-60% of our brain capabilities.

The part under this is the unconscious mind. It holds the entire diameter of the bottom of the iceberg and fills out the other 30-40% of the whole.

See the illustration of Picture 1

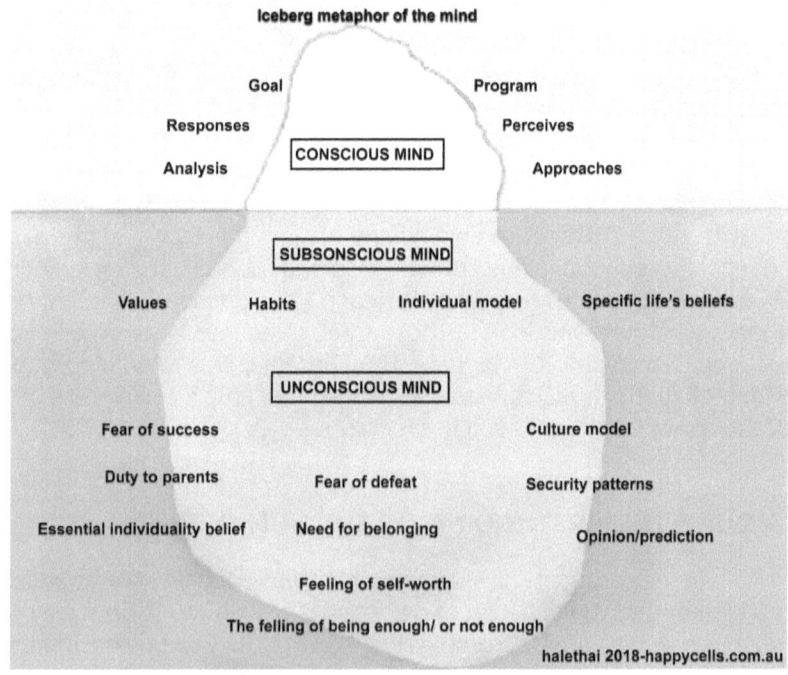

Picture 1 -Iceberg metaphor of the mind

▶ THREE MINDS IN ONE

This book is a concise guide to developing good habits in your child/children. As a result, I am not going to bombard you with a lot of theories which are related to the mind. I hope in the scope of my explanation, you will understand why you are doing what you are doing and why your child/children are doing what they are doing.

▶ THE CONSCIOUS MIND

If you seek an answer to clarify what the conscious mind does, you'll get varying results. Some say what differentiates it from the subconscious/unconscious mind is consciousness.

Another opinion holds that the conscious mind is where you do all your thinking and logical reasoning. Yes! These are parts of the conscious mind's work.

Through further study of NLP (Neuro-Linguistic Programming) and Hypnosis with Dr Tad James and Dr Adriana James and the book 'Your Unconscious Mind- Unravelling of greatest mystery of the human brain' by John Murray, I have come to understand that the conscious mind has the most powerful functions, and those the other two minds can't perform. That is a capability to conduct your focus. Its capacity to perceive that which is not true.

When the habits formed by the conscious mind work through the experiences that repeat over and over again, the work is not done there. I want to explain further that when habits are stored in the subconscious mind, this will direct the decision making of a conscious mind. We express it this way: the conscious mind is a goal setter and the subconscious mind is the goal getter.

Let me explain further.

Habits are something we repeatedly do; every day. These will control the conscious mind. This explains why some people are successful and some fail in their work, despite having the same age, degree and responsibilities at work. Why some people are so sad, miserable, and bitter while some are happy, perseverant and optimistic when both of them are faced with the same situations. Things happen like that because each person has different habits that are rooted deeply in their subconscious mind and people use what they have inside to respond to the world.

Just imagine your child gets loaded up with good and positive habits at an early age and through their adolescent years. That child will reap the benefits for the remainder of their lives and are destined for good fortune!

▶ THE SUBCONSCIOUS/UNCONSCIOUS MINDS

These are the terminologies. In the fields of Psychology, Psychiatry, Body and Mind connection, philosophy and so on, they use concepts of the subconscious mind and unconscious mind and their functions to explain things. I bring them here with simple explanations for you to have an idea of what they are about and how they function in our lives.

The subconscious and unconscious minds are separated but carry out the same function of storing all the experiences, memories, emotions and so on that have happened in our lives. I put them into one group to help you understand them easier. We discuss this topic for building habits for children, not going deeper into the philosophy of human growth and development. I don't want to bombard you with a lot of complicated information. My main purpose is to lead you to a new area of how to raise and guide your child/children's learning and growing.

Our subconscious/ unconscious mind is like a vast memory bank. The potential is practically limitless; it forever collects everything that ever occurs to us (see Picture 1). The role of our subconscious/ unconscious mind is to recollect and recover data. Its job is to make sure that we react exactly the way we have been formed. Our subconscious/ unconscious mind informs everything we speak and do to implement a model logical with our self-concept. Our control program of the subconscious/unconscious mind is subjective. They do not think or reflect alone. They only follow the instructions they get from our conscious mind. This is our conscious mind; it can be related to the gardener sowing seeds. The human subconscious/ unconscious mind can be used as a metaphor of a garden in which the roots form and grow. Our conscious mind acts, and our subconscious mind follows. Our subconscious mind is an unquestioning dependent. It operates 24 hours a day to make our behaviour a model compatible with our emotionalised awareness. Our subconscious/ unconscious mind supports flowers, fruits or weeds in the garden of our life.

This is a concept that can also be related to the concept of Procedural Memory. Procedural memory is a type of long-term memory that involves how to perform different actions and skills, which are stored in our subconscious mind. This type of memory involves all the acts we perform on a daily basis, such as walking, eating, tidying our shoes, etc. They are basically habits we have formed since we were little. As these actions and skills are stored in our subconscious mind, we actually don't need to remember it when we perform them. Our bodies immediately do it, same thing that happens with habits.

This could explain how people with, Alzheimer's, Senile Dementia or some sort of Amnesia, can remember how to do certain things or perform certain actions such as playing the piano or painting, even though they can't remember the day they were born or where they are at that moment. It's so because these are actions they have been performing for their whole lives, or a really long time, and they don't need to use their conscious mind to do it. These conditions, mentioned above, are all affected by the conscious mind.

In other words, by keeping us thinking and working in a way similar to what we have done and said in the past, all our habits of thinking and acting are stored in our subconscious/ unconscious mind. They have recorded all our pleasurable experiences, and they work to keep us in our subconscious/ unconscious mind. We feel emotionally and physically uncomfortable whenever we try to do anything new or complex or to replace any of our learned models of behaviour. Our subconscious/unconscious mind performs like the detectors holding us in balance and on track based on the data and instructions that we have stored from the past. We can feel our subconscious/unconscious mind dragging us back toward our comfort zone each time we try something new or challenging.

Even thinking about doing something unusual from what we are accustomed to will get us feeling anxious or uncomfortable. It's part of the reason we feel uneasy when applying for a new job. It happens if I'm driving in a hurry but I'm not sure of where I'm going. I get agitated and can't sleep sometimes as my body reacts to new things. This happens as my subconscious mind struggles to follow the command of my conscious mind. It didn't store enough of the skills I needed for driving which I was not very fond of doing. This is an example of getting out of the comfort zone.

On the other hand, the logic of these two minds is that if things worked in the past and you've survived, then they will help you go through related or similar situations by the same means. It doesn't matter how confused, uncomfortable, and unhelpful the results may be to you personally in the outside world. This links so well with the concept of habits. The subconscious or unconscious mind keeps them, and when something happens in the outside world, those habits will be used either for better or worse, depending on what habits we have installed inside the subconscious/ unconscious mind. We now clearly understand that each of us has been made by our life experiences. This also well explains why we have had so many issues in our society such as committing suicide, depression, anxiety and even cancer.

▶ HOW THREE MINDS WORK WITH ONE ANOTHER

Conscious mind is what most people see when they look at us. This is picture we portray as we live day to day with our actions and decisions.

Many people use the metaphor of a captain of a ship to indicate the conscious mind. He/she is taking a role of standing in the control room and giving out orders. The people around represent the subconscious and the deeper unconscious minds that carry out the orders from the captain, the conscious mind.

▶ MORE DETAIL OF HOW THE THREE MINDS WORK

The *conscious mind* reaches the external environment and the internal self through language, images, writing, physical actions, touching, thinking, and beliefs.

The *subconscious mind*, on the other hand, is in the assessment of our recent memories, thoughts and is in constant connection with the stores of the unconscious mind.

I mention, again, that the subconscious/unconscious minds are the storehouse of all memories and past experiences. Both those memories and experiences have been kept through wounds, shocks, challenges, difficulties including those that have merely been consciously forgotten and are no longer relevant to us. It's from these memories, thoughts and experiences that our beliefs, habits, and behaviours are formed.

The unconscious mind continually interacts with the conscious mind via our subconscious mind. It gives us the sense of all our intercommunications with the world, as refined through your beliefs and habits. It carries through awareness, emotions, thoughts, feelings and fantasies.

The subconscious or unconscious minds keep them, and when something happens in the outside world, these beliefs and habits are used either for better or worse, depending on what we have retained inside our subconscious and unconscious minds. To put it simply, we can call them our memory bank.

In other words, our outside world corresponds to our internal world. What happens to us depends to a significant degree on what is happening inside us.

Our outside experience of the world is a reflection of our inside thought models created over time as we live our life. Furthermore, our thinking about life represents our personal beliefs about ourselves.

We know story after story of great men and women based upon their experiences and lives. We are all amazed by the regular thread that works through all of them. They all appear to have or to acquire an unchanged belief and habits in their strength to overcome all barriers and reach outstanding outcomes. This belief and habits arise to give them capabilities not possessed by an average person. They go on to achieve remarkable things, often against unbelievable odds. And they regularly overcome the resistance of predictions people around them have made.

When we go deep into the research of all successful men and women we find the commonality is in the events that led them to who they are today are their childhood's experiences. These events were stored in their minds as habits and these people use what they have in their minds to cope with what life brings to them. Without skills and experiences they received during the time of their growing up, they wouldn't have had what it takes to become outstanding individuals. In general, we can use our subconscious/unconscious mind for victory or defeat, gaining or losing. We can be rich or poor depending on the way we use our subconscious/unconscious minds to reach our potential.

Here's an example to help you to better understand the conscious mind and subconscious/unconscious mind. There is a simple example to help you see more of our three-in-one mind, how it works, how we can manage its functions and what they can offer to our life. I want to analyse the functions of the mind, of both the conscious and subconscious/unconscious mind to see how powerful they are, and I will also explain how habits are formed through these functions.

First, the conscious mind identifies incoming information. The function of the conscious mind is to collect data through any of the five senses: sight, smell, hearing, taste, and touch. Our conscious mind is continuously watching, analysing and classifying what is going on around us. For example: when hearing an approaching noise on the street, the conscious mind knows that a vehicle is coming. The subconscious/unconscious mind brings up all stored data through all the experiences of the past. It may tell us what kind of vehicle is coming, how fast it's going and what we should do to protect ourselves. I'm sure you all have had similar experiences and reactions of the human body. With that in mind, you can begin to understand why our body is doing what it's doing. This also helps you find answers to why your child/children are doing what they are doing!

Furthermore, one of the functions of the subconscious/unconscious mind is to store information which is collected by the conscious mind. Do you have a memory of driving your car for 30 minutes and then realising you had passed many streets and got home safely without remembering how you got there? This happens because of our driving skills obtained through repeated practice over time. These skills are stored in the unconscious mind which will then send conscious commands for driving. The subconscious mind takes on the job. What we store in the subconscious mind will decide the quality of our performance. We carry a lot of information subconsciously — all the skills which are related to how to operate the car and drive it to our destination are stored in the subconscious mind. It didn't happen in one act. We need to repeat the action over and over again until it becomes our habit. When we send commands from our conscious mind to our subconscious/unconscious mind, all essential nerves and muscles are coordinated and put into action in a single instance to obey our decision. All the continuously performed actions form life-long habits.

Another example of the conscious mind and subconscious/ unconscious mind is threading. You can do this task more easily and quickly after repeated practice. We use our conscious mind to get the thread through a needle with a lot of concentration and effort. After drilling, the habit is formed and you can put the thread through the needle more quickly. The same thing happens with wearing shoes, operating a machine, cleaning our teeth, cooking, cleaning etc. Whatever we practise and practise, over and over, will become skills and habits that are stored in our subconscious/unconscious mind. This means that the subconscious/unconscious mind decides the outcomes of our lives. The conscious mind gives out the command and the result of the command depends on what we've stored in our subconscious/unconscious mind.

▶ **THE CONSCIOUS MIND, SUBCONSCIOUS/UNCONSCIOUS MIND AND YOUR CHILD/CHILDREN'S FUTURE**

I've explained the power of the human mind and how three minds work together as one. Through this, I want you to think of how the subconscious/unconscious mind is connected to your child/children's future. Whatever you repeatedly do and teach your child/children, will be stored in your child/children's subconscious/unconscious mind, not a single thing is left out. When your child aborts whatever life brings, he/she will keep acting it out as one of the old habits. This way is sometimes called self-hypnosis or autosuggestion, and it's incredibly useful in two areas. Your child can use whatever he/she stores in his/her subconscious/unconscious mind to overcome fears and build confidence in life for relationships, social and emotional development, studying, achievement, health and other activities. They can even help to solve problems such as reluctance, fear of public speaking or nervousness in dealing with any challenge in their daily life.

Later your child/children can use habits to accelerate the development of motor skills and sports ability in areas such as tennis, golf, skiing, hockey, skating, football and basketball. Habits are considered forms of mental rehearsal. Your child/children practises movements, thinking, acting, doing all sorts of things over and over in his/her practices, hands-on experiences, using imagination and visualising perfect performances. Everything will be programmed into your child/children's subconscious/unconscious mind. When the subconscious mind accepts the mental picture, skills, and thoughts, these will be the commands to guide future actions for your child/children. The next time your child actually performs an activity, he/she will be much more relaxed and confident. Your child will be noticeably better than they were before.

For example, have you seen the latest version of Karate Kid? I bet you have. In the movie we see how Mr. Miyagi takes a simple action of our daily life to teach Kung-Fu to Xiao Dre, even when he doesn't get it at first. By making him put on his jacket, taking it off, throwing it on the floor, picking it up and then put it on the coat rack over and over again, he is actually teaching him Kung-Fu movements that he would later use in fights. Why? Because with the help of his subconscious/unconscious mind, the body immediately remembers how to respond and make specific movements.

Most gold medal-winning Olympic athletes use this technique, or something similar, to become experts in their field. Business people use it to give themselves psychological advantages in meetings, negotiations or confrontations.

Skills work better and better when your child/children practises more and more, until they become habits which are stored permanently in your child/children's life.

One crucial thing that I want to mention is the subconscious/unconscious mind never knows what is right and what is wrong. It absorbs everything that happens in your child/children's life. Therefore, you need to be extremely careful about which habits are being formed in your child/children.

A promising future needs a lot of great attributes including the habits that will form who he/she becomes. So, it is time for you to start building the future with your child by encouraging and installing right habits right now.

Before going on, I have an exercise for you to practise good habits with your child/children. Through this, you will see the power of the subconscious/unconscious mind in helping to form healthy habits.

Here's an exercise for you to do. Take a sheet of paper and make a list of all the things that you want to see in your child/children's life. Write down everything that you can think of, i.e. happiness, good health, good friends, financial security, travel, prosperity, popularity, recognition and respect from others. Let your imagination run freely about how you would like to see your child/children's future develop.

Here's the next challenging part. In the next three days, talk only about the things on your list for your child/children. Check if you can get through one entire day without criticising, condemning, complaining or getting angry or upset or worried about anything. See if you have the willpower and strength of character to think about only what you want for your child/children. Do it for one whole day and then the next day. This exercise will give you real insight into where you are in your development as a parent. It will also be a test for you to check how far you need to go. In the next section of the book you will learn how to help your child/children get the right skills for success. You will also learn how to achieve any goal you ever set for your child/children in preparing a solid foundation for the future.

4. CLASSICAL CONDITIONING, ANCHORING IN NLP & HABIT BUILDING

To further understand the power of habits, in light of current theories and scientific research, I will provide two more approaches to help you. The first one is a famous experiment conducted by Pavlov called classical conditioning and the second is a newly-found Anchoring from NLP (Neuro-Linguistic Programming) which came out as a result of various research and analyses of Pavlov's theory. Through these explanations, you will gain more insight into why you do what you do and why your child/children does what he/she does as well as all the people around you. It will also assist you in understanding the concepts of the conscious and subconscious/unconscious minds.

When I studied and researched Classical Conditioning and Anchoring with NLP, I began to think of habit formation. Classical Conditioning and Anchoring, to me, are another expression of habit building. I bring these concepts to you, as parents, to deepen your knowledge on how the mind works according to different science-based research. To me, you can apply good techniques to teach, raise your child/children, but if you don't know how things work, the outcome of what you want to bring to your child/children can be very limited. Theories need to go hand in hand with practice for the best benefits in your parenting.

▶ PAVLOV'S THEORY

Pavlov's Classical Conditioning theory views learning as habit formation and is based on the principle of association and substitution. Therapists also use Classical Conditioning to reduce and eliminate many types of unwanted habits. This includes addictive habits. My purpose of using Pavlov theory to link to the habit building. Before we go further, I want to show you some examples of Classical Conditioning.

Aversion therapy: is a form of Classical Conditioning. In Aversion Therapy, people intentionally form a paired association between an unwanted response and an unpleasant happening. For instance, you can administer a drug that causes someone to become nauseous and vomit if he/she ingests even a little bit of mint oil. This intentionally forms a paired association between mint oil and vomiting. Before the Aversion Therapy, a person would ordinarily associate mint oil with positive feelings. Because your subconscious/unconscious mind does not know what is real and what is unreal, a new habit can be formed by mental rehearsal and repetition. Most great athletes and actors use mental rehearsal to improve their performance in many ways. Mental rehearsal is vital to learning how to change your habits without needing to repeat the new pattern over and over again physically.

The key thing to remember is that Classical Conditioning involves automatic or reflexive responses and not a voluntary habit. What does this address? For one thing, it means that the only responses that can be elicited out of a Classical Conditioning model are the ones that rely on responses that are usually made by an animal (or a human) that is being trained. Dog training is an example of Conditioning.

▶ HOW CLASSICAL CONDITIONING PLAYS A ROLE IN OUR DAILY LIVES

Our conditioned stimuli can be derived from different aspects of life that have evolved over the years. Here are some applications of Classical Conditioning that we may or may not be aware of in our everyday lives.

▶ ADVERTISEMENT

Advertising techniques are also heavily associated with Classical Conditioning. Some businesses even research the behaviour of the people within their target market. Companies employ different personalities for advertising to aid in conditioning their target's brain. For example, an animated character with a lot of strong, interesting sounds is often used as a commercial model for children's products to get their attention. When seeing lollypops on TV, your child/children may desire to have a lollypop to satisfy their craving. Some people when seeing Coca-Cola in advertisements, may go to the fridge for that drink or drive to the store to get one.

In the advertising field, you can also use specific daily scenarios as a way to classically condition the market into purchasing a product. For example, a child or adult having a terrible cough is shown in advertisements for cough medicines. In return, the target market decides to buy the product when they suffer from that kind of cough.

► ALCOHOL OR DRUG ADDICTION

Rehabilitation centres also use Classical Conditioning in their treatment of drug and alcohol addicts. Addiction is a simple example of Classical Conditioning as people are addicted to a particular substance to feel relaxed or euphoric. For instance, caffeine addicts may experience ease upon smelling or thinking about coffee.

► FEELING RESPONSES

Two types of feeling responses can be produced through Classical Conditioning: negative and positive reactions. Negative responses, like fear, can be stimulated by connecting it with what the person hears or see. E.g., if they are afraid of snakes, a nearby sound of the bushes moving can make them afraid of snake bite, even if they don't even see a snake yet. Phobias like fear of heights can also happen to some people when they go to the mountains or high places. Positive responses such as leisure can also occur when a person thinks of someone, some food, or some favourable thing. Excitement is also based on Classical Conditioning. When you feel something good is about to happen, like seeing your child/children after work, cooking a meal you love or watching a television program that you like, you are quite likely to feel excited.

► WANTING FOOD

Wanting food is one of the by-products of Classical Conditioning. People become hungry when they think of a dish they yearn for, resulting in its instant purchase or preparation.

Their yearnings happen as they are able to experience something filling when they ate the dish out of pleasure or hunger in the past. Some people walking or moving around a town can feel hungry after they spot an eatery or a popular fast-food chain. This happens because people are trained to believe that restaurants provide the food they want to eat.

► REMEMBERING PAST EXPERIENCES

People can also associate anything with an experience either positive or negative.

A soundtrack that you heard during your travels might make you remember those sweet memories whenever you hear the music on the radio. The fragrance of perfume similar to what your partner wore during a memorable date can make you remember those sweet memories as it flashes in your mind again. A smell of food from a shop or a restaurant may make you remember a lovely memory of having that food with your loved one.

It's that very understanding that sometimes, our feelings are the product of past experiences. We remember experiences better because we remember how we felt in the past. Particularly when the environment indicates or spots a trigger, it will produce a chemical reaction.

Post-traumatic ailments are also a by-product of Classical Conditioning for people who had a traumatic experience. The anxiety generated by PTSD may occur if a soldier, who returned from war, hears fireworks during a New Year's or Australia Day, Independence Day (USA). Even though they may have enjoyed fireworks before going to war, the loud sound now triggers horrible memories. In some extreme situations, the soldier may become enraged or hysterical when they hear fireworks.

▶ CLASSICAL CONDITIONING IN SCHOOL AND WORKPLACE ENVIRONMENTS

Strict teachers, bullying, and school rules and regulations can induce fear in children when they attend classes. A stern teacher who hates noise can silence the whole class once she gets in the room. It's because they might have encountered a teacher's scolding or punishment when one or more students made unnecessary noise during class.

Workplaces can produce more disciplined workers by implementing strict compliance and attendance policies. Friendly work environments or workmates close to you can induce a feeling or attraction and desire to be prolific at work.

▶ DRUG AND FOOD INTAKE

Drugs can also cause a modified response to our bodies and minds depending on how we felt when we first used a medication.

For example, a bad tasting medicine can cause vomiting the next time you take it.

In some cases, vomiting can be caused when the patient merely hears the name of the drug or sees the drug. This happens a lot in children or in people who are allergic to the medication. However, some patients may feel relaxed when they are about to take a medicine that reduces the symptoms of their ailment.

The same conditional response is also applicable to food. A child who doesn't like vegetables may feel nauseated or have uncomfortable feelings when seeing or even hearing about them. However, the need to eat and hunger may occur to a person when they hear about their favourite meal.

There are many examples of Classical Conditioning used in our everyday life. The ones mentioned above are the generally experienced ones. For sure this will help you be alert as far as Classical Conditioning is concerned.

▶ CONDITIONED BEHAVIOURS AND HABITS

We all have a lot of these accustomed responses. The way we react to things today is very similar to the way we reacted to them yesterday, and the way we will react to them tomorrow; even if there isn't a great reason for it. Think of Pavlov's dogs salivating without a tangible reason; the remains of once good habits (salivation aids eating and digestion) became wasted effort. Habits, for all beings, tend to become anticipated over time. We may not even be conscious of our automatic responses to stressors in our lives. Do you know what your habits are? If not, ask a close family member or friend about your habits.

Moreover, they can tell you how your performance changes based on your stress levels. Remember, you can't tell when your child/children are tired and whining?

In every second of our everyday life, we are nurturing our current behaviour and responses, for better or worse. This may hit you as bad news – every time you keep up a bad habit, it becomes more inherent. This is true (and a good reason to take action now), but there's quite an upside, too. The good behaviour you choose today will continue to become more natural with time, and, as Pavlov showed us, new habits can be learned with a little voluntary effort. This is great news and hope for you as parents who want to change habits for your child/children at any age.

▶ ANCHORING

Anchor metaphor:

When thinking about Anchoring, we automatically think about a piece of equipment that is used to join a vessel to the bed of a sea to prevent the ship or boat from turning away from its course due to wind or tide. When the boat or ship starts to switch from its proposed location, the anchor helps guard it by tightening its spot and not allowing it to stray too far away. When you reflect on it, some of our behaviours serve as anchors for us. When we start to stray away from where we want to be, there is specific behaviour you can begin doing that will help bring you back to your centre and your intended direction.

Anchoring in NLP:

NLP, which stands for Neuro-Linguistic Programming, is a process by which you use a gesture, feeling, thinking, action either in oneself or in someone else. In other words, NLP is the language of the mind which helps you understand where you are now and where you want to be. Anchoring is one of the techniques of NLP to help people insert or activate a desired state. The supposed anchored state can then be revived or re-activated by reapplying the gesture, feeling or sound. The stimulus may be totally neutral or even out of conscious awareness, and the response may be either positive or negative. They are capable of being formed and augmented by repeated stimuli, and thus are analogous to Classical Conditioning as mentioned above. For example, there is a comedy which made you laugh so much that when seeing that comedy again, even just seeing the packaging of the DVD, you automatically laugh again. It anchored the deep feeling that you experienced before.

Another example of Anchoring is when you pass by a cake shop, the aroma of the cake can make you remember your grandma or your mother who baked the cake for you before. The pictures and sounds or smells and maybe the feelings are brought to the surface. Linking this with habits formation, people may say, "He has a habit of thinking about his mother when he eats that kind of cake." This can help you to understand why some people are successful and some fail. The experiences which have been anchored in them decide the outcomes of that person's life.

Basic NLP Anchoring involves reality, the elicitation of a strong congruent experience of the desired state, while using some notable stimulus such as touch, word, sight or sound at the time this is most fully actualised. In some cases, repetition of the stimulus will re-associate and restore the experience of the state.

▶ THE WAY ANCHORING DEVELOPED

Anchoring is developed when you keep doing an action, having feelings or thinking over and over again with the high pitch of your emotions. Anchoring is also the way to establish a new habit. Anchoring is used as a reminder which is stored in the subconscious/unconscious mind. Anchoring may bring success or failure to our lives.

Moreover, Anchoring is also formed when both of the two of events happen together on a routine basis for a specified number of times. For example, if every time your child/children eat while watching television, they may find themselves becoming hungry when watching television. Some very young children, when they have a dummy in their mouth, need their blanket or soft toys to hold in their hand for comfort.

Below are more examples for Anchoring that children have in their lives:

Every day after I wake up, I brush my teeth.

After going to the toilet, I wash my hands

Great anchors are things your child/children already regularly do each day or each week.

Waking up and going to bed are good daily examples. That's why morning and evening routines are so important.

There are many more:

- Showering after school or early in the morning
- Getting Dressed
- Having breakfast
- Packing lunch
- Playing game after school
- Having an ice-cream when it's hot

In NLP there are several criteria to check the power of an anchor. The primary one is the intensity of the state the person is undergoing. The more compelling the state, the more probable the anchor will work later on. For example, if a child has a sensation when drinking coke and eating a Big Mac, this will anchor in the child's mind. Later, when seeing the advertising for MacDonald's, the child may have a desire to have what has enjoyed so much. This sounds very much familiar with the Classical Conditioning concept of Pavlov.

In this same sense, the famous philosopher, John Locke, also had a theory. He said that when we are born, the human mind is a complete but receptive "Tabula Rasa." Meaning our minds are a blank slate, where we imprint knowledge through our experiences. So, by taking this theory into consideration, when kids are young, parents are the ones with the responsibility to provide them with learning experiences that can work to start positive habit building. Knowing what you want to teach to your kids and looking for interesting ways to teach these habits, you will find Anchoring an amazing tool to assist you in that effort.

▶ ANCHORING AND HABIT BUILDING

Now, I believe that you have a general understanding of how Anchoring works in our lives. This should help you understand how powerful it is in your child/children's life. The only way you can build a new habit for your child/children is to perform it consistently. To make something a healthy and helpful habit, you, as parents, need to help your child/children repeat that action over and over again at a regular time or moment. The important thing about using Anchoring is that it helps your child/children remain faithful and serves as a warning for each stage of life to keep them on the right track. Anchoring can help you maintain old and new habits which are beneficial for your child/children's life. Anchoring practices can be compelling in getting your child/children to where you want them to be in life. So, anchoring good habits as early as possible can also be useful when you're trying to teach new habits for them. If your child/children build up new habits with a solid anchoring of a habit, it can often be simpler to make that habit permanent. Just imagine you help your child/children to anchor a lot of good habits in his/her subconscious/unconscious minds, they would handle their life later with the courage, confidence and conviction without your concerns. I think this is the biggest fulfilment that all parents want to achieve on the journey of raising up a successful and happy adult!

5. THE MIND AND ITS POWER

▶ WE EXIST AND FORM OUR LIVES WITH A LOT OF HABITS

A habit is a thing we do continually without consciously realizing much about it. It is a natural cognitive (mental) and behavioural response. Habits make it possible for us to do tasks without using unreasonable mental or psychological effort. They carry out everyday life activities- that are either positive or negative.

Habits are essential to each of us, and no lives without them. The question is what kind of habits have we developed over the years. Our habits run consciously and unintentionally automatically with many routine tasks and movements. Due to habits, our mind is capable of additional ideas, programs, and the ability to concentrate on the new significant, necessary work and building of new habits. For example, when a man has developed a habit of swimming, his body automatically recognizes its coordination after practising. Once obtaining this, this person then gets an opportunity to create a new habit of swimming with quicker acceleration and longer distances. In other words, the implementation of the man's actions opens up the potential that can be used to focus on new tasks. Habit works to his advantage!

▶ HOW HABITS ARE FORMED

Habits are formed through the experiences we receive in sound (hearing), taste (gustation), touching (tactile perception), sight (vision), smell (olfaction) and the sense organs dedicated to each sense. In simple words, we all know that ears are for hearing; eyes for seeing, noses for smelling; tongues are for tasting and skin is for feeling. The nervous system must take in and transform messages about the outside world in order to react, communicate, maintain a healthy body and remain safe. Regularly, this information shows up through the listed sensory organs. To put this into perspective, we receive a great deal of data throughout the day. Research suggests we process 400 billion bits of information a second through our brain and our five senses. But we merely pay attention to 2000 of those. I explain this to reiterate that through five senses and the brain, whatever action is repeated will develop into a habit. Our nervous system is searching for a pattern of recurrence to establish an automatic process. This relates directly to the previous information related to the 3 minds, Classical Conditioning and Anchoring.

Some habits demand that we think before acting and some don't. For riding a car, putting food in our mouth, we carry these activities automatically, whereas drawing a picture, composing a song, washing a car demand that we use our reasoning for these actions. The subconscious mind/unconscious mind is doing the work as they keep the information and help to allow work to be done automatically. This is a great way to explain why habits are so hard to change. It helps explain why people do what they do. And why children also do what they do. It also helps to explain why parents so often fail in raising and teaching them good habits!

It sounds scary, doesn't it? But realise with the knowledge presented in this book, you can produce useful habits that benefit all concerned. We can also eliminate undesirable habits which may lessen your quality of life. Applying this to parenting, everyone can see that habits will have long-term effects on your child/children's future.

▶ THE IMPORTANCE OF HABITS

Research reveals that more than 40 per cent of the actions we perform each day aren't actual conscious decisions, but habits. If we observe the lifestyle that takes place in most of the big cities of the world, we will realize that in them there is no time for rest or for relaxation. Even leisure must be programmed. This busy lifestyle leads us to live running from home to work and other places where different social activities take place. We often don't take the time to understand this rushing around has been unconsciously organized by the members of our society based on habits that have evolved without conscious thought, and certainly not for our benefit.

As a result, habits play an extremely crucial part in our lives, and it's truly significant in the process parents use to raise and teach their children. Your habits will form a fundamental foundation for establishing who your child/children is and who they become.

Habits save time and energy, but still, can create enormous problems between you and your child. For example, if you have the habit of patience, and when your child/children throw a tantrum, you can successfully handle the situation. Through this, you could teach your child/children many excellent moral lessons. In contrast, if you own a habit of yelling loudly when trouble arises, you will both get disappointed, annoyed or discouraged. The worst thing is your child/children may download all of your inappropriate habits and retain them for future use.

It is evident that positive habits lead to a healthy routine, guidance and competency in your parenting and your child/children's life. It is sad to say; bad habits have the opposite effects on you as you parent. They can trap you into negative, inadequate or rigid patterns of behaviour that negatively affect your child/children. Bad parental habits such as yelling, spanking, labelling your child/children with negative words and not having enough time for your child can affect his/her happiness mentally and physically. Remember that you, as parents, are the most important figures in your child's life. Everything you do, regardless of your intention, will definitely have a direct impact on them. In other words, every child/children's future depends on the habits of their parents— whether they are healthy or unhealthy.

Illustrations of habits:

He always does homework at 4 p.m.

She cleans her teeth before bed.

Helen has no sugar in her coffee.

Michael yells at his son when he asks for a lolly.

Anna comes home very late after work.

Joanne goes to the toy area straight away every time when shopping with her mother.

He gets up early every day.

She always closes the door softly.

He eats chips every time at McDonald's.

Anna cries every time her mother leaves her at the day care.

▶ BRAIN AND HABITS

As I pointed out previously, the conscious, subconscious, and unconscious minds and our brain are extremely powerful and are continually searching for patterns that take place in our lives. Then those patterns can be turned into habits which is something we do daily without thinking. You probably have a habit of exercising at a set time, brushing your teeth every night, and perhaps making a phone call to your child/children after school every afternoon. Habits become such a part of your routine that they become part of who you are. Sadly, our unconscious mind does not distinguish between good or bad habits. Whatever is repeated over and over will have the potential to develop into a habit and these habits are kept in the subconscious/unconscious mind. When a trigger occurs, the habit appears (see Illustration Picture 2:). But, luckily, we are able to take the lead in this process through the conscious mind. It serves as an instrument that helps us decide which thoughts, actions and behaviours we prefer and which ones we will allow to grow into forming our habits. This is an excellent way for parents to create a successful plan for their child/children.

▶ PARENTING AND HABITS

All parents want to have great children and search for how to raise them successfully. I need to say your child/children are great already. The job you need to do is to activate all the fundamental skills your child/children are capable of learning.

Putting this example into perspective, consider the goal of driving well. In order for that to happen you need to take on a series of lessons and a driving test. You need to memorise all the rules of the road required to pass the test. You also need to practise until you get a good habit of driving. By then, you will gain the confidence to take the test. To raise a brilliant child requires the same approach. You need to store in your child/children a set of right habits for them to get used to in becoming brilliant children. There is no shortcut to success. You and your child/children need time and practice, over and over, to develop the right and good habits to become a well-adjusted, happy child. Luckily, children do not grow at one time. They develop with time and you have enough time to practise and teach the right attributes for them. When children own better habits, they will manifest them naturally, and these habits gradually become part of their nature. This is the essence of success in life.

> If we keep doing what we are doing,
> we are going to keep getting what we are getting.
>
> **Steve R. Corey.**

▶ CHILDREN AND HABITS

A recent study done at Brown University in the United States reported that routines and habits in children will be built permanently by the age of 9. For most children, this forms firm roots by the second or third grade. The research carried out included surveys of 50,000 families.

As mentioned above, a habit is a behaviour or performance that your child/children carry out over and over, almost without realizing it. Habits will decide who your child is and set up a foundation for his /her life. Since habits become part of the child, the habits that your child/children develop will follow and establish their character for their entire life. I think you can relate to a similar reality in your own life. If you have a habit of attending to your child/chidren with a pleasant demeanour, he/she will turn into a cheerful person. If you form a habit of eating vegetables with every meal, your child is likely to imitate a healthy eating habit from you.

In the book *THE POWER OF HABIT,* Charles Duhigg, uses a habit loop to represent how habits are established.

Illustration Picture 2

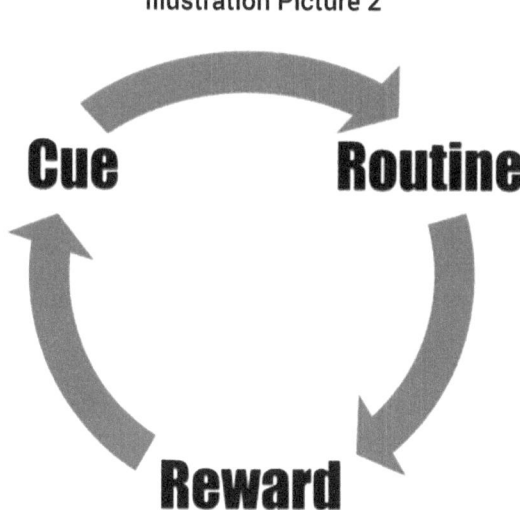

Let me quickly explain how this habit loop works.

Cue: : For a habit to form, it won't only require an action, but you also need a cue to set off a behaviour. The cue is a cause that informs your brain to move into the automatic system and tells it which habit to use. A cue can be something visual, a particular place or a moment of the day, an emotional state, and an arrangement of thoughts or a company of specific people. You can have multiple cues which increase the likelihood of the routine taking place.

Routine: is an action that repeats. For example, time for dinner, rubbing nose, shaking legs, watching TV, drinking milk as well as many others.

Reward: is a benefit, which supports your brain to figure out if this specific loop is worth repeating in the future. Again, it can be a physical sensation, an emotional outcome, such as feelings of pride that accompany praise or self-compliment.

Loop is a self-boosting process that, over time, becomes conditioned. Habit is formed from here and encoded in the structure of the brain. The skill is established and saves a lot of a child's energy as he/she doesn't need to re-learn everything he/she does.

Here is an example for the loop:

Cue: there is a boy who is watching television and sees an ice cream advertisement. This is the cue that triggers his desire to have some ice cream.

Routine: He gets to the fridge for a bowl of ice cream.

Reward: He feels satisfied and good after eating ice cream. If the boy keeps having the cue, then eating ice cream, then feeling good, this will become his habit of eating it.

The above example illustrates clearly that any habit such as smoking, exercising, eating a favourite food or drinking can become ingrained in a child or an adult, for that matter.

Understanding how habits form, you can encourage your child/children to develop healthy, helpful habits early in life. Those habits will bring permanent benefits. As a parent, you can supervise your child to help him/her make positive choices, activities, movements, and thought processes. Children learn from mistakes, and when guided properly, grow into more capable and flexible individuals. When you understand the influence of habits, you can facilitate your child/children's positive development.

 We are what we repeatedly do.
Success is not an action but a habit

Aristotle

▶ WHY PEOPLE DESIRE TO COME BACK TO OLD HABITS

I want to explain a bit why people are so hard to change for the better. It all depends on how they take control of their lives, how they guide their mind so they get extraordinary success and how they achieve stable growth. As an Early Childhood Educator, Therapist and Life Coach, I find it most frustrating when I am helping my students, parents and clients to change. The thing we come up against, over and over, is something gripping, something that keeps coming back to my client's mind or something that keeps giving up what is already gained.

Is this correct? Can people benefit? Why would some people ignore excellent outcomes for their lives? Why would somebody discard fame or reject wealth or affection? The answer is because our brain is hard-wired to respond to what is a habit and to dismiss what is not habited. Through this, you can see how powerful habits are, and now you have a good understanding of why you are faced with the problems you encounter with your child/children. They get inserted by your habits at an early age. Your child gets used to them unconsciously.

▶ PEOPLE ENJOY HABITS THAT HAVE BEEN SET

And you'll see with very young children, why they like the similar or same things. They like the same meal, the same TV programs and they love what is familiar. They don't like new food or even new clothes or new blankets because they're stored in their mind to feel safe with the familiar. They also never move too far from the family, they don't want to be too far from mum, dad or brother, sister. When they're little, they don't desire too much that's new and different. So, it is natural because we're made to love what is familiar at an early age. That's why some people actually refuse success, wealth, relationships or holidays. If it is not falling in the same routine and people are not used to something, they often will reject it.

When I watched a Weight Loss show on TV, I saw participants being given everything: a trainer, exercise machines and their own chef. And while some of them did incredibly well and became 1st, 2nd and 3rd winners, others didn't do well and were exited in the very first round. This has a lot to do with the long-standing habits that have been formed inside them.

▶ WHAT INFLUENCES HABITS IN CHILDREN?

There are several factors that decide the habits in children. These factors can be external. Why children behave the way they do is determined by a number of social, personal, psychological, environmental, religious, cultural and even political factors. Factors that affect habits in children include:

a. Biological factors:

A child's biological structure may be a deciding factor in how they embrace good habits. A child who is overweight may likely eat a lot, especially junky and fatty food. So, it is understandable when biological and health factors affect certain habits in children.

b. Physical factors:

Age and body structure play major roles in the habits of children. Children who have an abundance of energy may normally want to convert that into some form of habit. While these habits may not always be healthy for them, it is the responsibility of the parents to ensure that they are able to engage in habits that are useful and productive for them.

c. Psychological factors:

Research shows that children tend to behave in accordance with how they feel at any point in time. In matters of nutrition, a study reveals that 48.5% eat because of loneliness, 53% eat because they are nervous, 53.8% eat till they are full, 62.1% eat uncontrollably while 59.1% eat because they feel bored.

d. Social factors:

Loneliness affects habit formation in children. Children are social beings and they should be exposed to as many social interactions as possible. They learn through observation and engagement in social environments. By being close to friends and family members, they are going to develop habits faster.

e. Economic factors:

Depending not only on the financial status of the family but also on the opportunities presented, children will behave differently. Children who grow up in a low-economy home are likely to behave differently than others who have the luxury of their parents' income. It affects the food they eat, the school they attend and often their hobbies.

f. Environmental factors:

Where children live matters. Children will naturally adopt the lifestyle of their environment. The impact of environment on children cannot be overemphasized.

g. Religious factors:

Muslims fast during the period of Ramzan or Ramadan. Christians celebrate Christmas and Easter. Religion affects habit formation in children.

Even though these are all factors that can affect the habit building process on any child, they are not necessarily what determines their future's personality and lives. Many of these factors are out of the parent's control, however, it is their responsibility to ensure that they put the proper system in place to reward good behaviour and remove unhealthy habits in their children. With proper information and motivation to do things right, you can build good habits in your child/children regardless of the environment in which they are developing.

▶ WHY PARENTS FAIL TO RAISE A YOUNG CHILD INTO A SUCCESSFUL ADULT

There are many reasons why parents fail to raise a young child to become a successful adult. Many new parents assume that parenting comes naturally, so they go into parenting with a belief that they will 'instinctively know' how to best raise their own children.

Many of these 'instinctive' parenting techniques are often inherited from our parents or our reaction in opposition to what they had experienced in the past. They may work, but do not always work well, to your currently desired or intended outcomes. Not only are we raising children in an entirely different era but so are there a lot of external forces from the media and the society around that make it necessary for parents to do more than just automating their previously learned parenting techniques and responsibilities.

According to many experts, parents continually make errors when raising their children. Sadly, these errors predispose children towards feelings of insecurity and limit their chances of becoming successful and responsible in society. Later in the book, I will be focussing on 56 habits that both parents and children together can begin to adopt to raise successful and responsible children. If you want your son or daughter to be successful, it's imperative that you implement these habits.

6. BELIEF AND SELF-CONCEPT

▶ **BELIEF:**

> 💬 Your chance of success in any understanding can always be measured by your beliefs in yourself.
>
> **Robert Collier**

I can't continue without introducing the concept of belief to you which has a significant and powerful link to habits. Again, I will explain, as simply as I can, this concept so you can build good habits in your child/children.

▶ **WHAT IS A BELIEF?**

A belief is something that you have accepted as being true. This belief might be based on facts, opinions or just an assumption. You don't necessarily have to have direct knowledge of a subject or idea before you believe in it.

Your belief doesn't always hold true, so you have to constantly challenge the truths that you have received in your life. We are all driven, in some form, by our beliefs and we all seek evidence and experiences that will cement our beliefs as we do not wish to be on the wrong side of the truth. The beliefs you carry are usually your understanding of how things are and what you know to be true. However, you can't be right all the time.

When you hold a certain belief, you will naturally accept it as true and rarely ever ask questions to challenge these beliefs. Our beliefs begin to form from quite an early age through what we experienced. These beliefs are very dependent on the environment we grow up in, the things we hear, the things we observe and our experiences. These beliefs are almost like conclusions reached from all of these experiences. Our beliefs revolve around what we think of ourselves, other people and the world in general.

People will hold onto their beliefs even if they tend to hold them back and in the face of contrary evidence. It can be very challenging to reason logically when it comes to the faith that drives beliefs. These beliefs are not usually based on solid logic or any scientific data. In this sense, there are two types of beliefs: the rational ones and the irrational ones. Rational beliefs are realistic thoughts, which provoke more balanced emotions, a more adapted and productive behaviour. Irrational beliefs can be distorted, exaggerated, catastrophic thoughts, unsubstantiated claims and assumptions. Those types of beliefs disturb us, causing very uncomfortable, intense emotions, depression, anxiety, physical discomfort and therefore, maladaptive behaviour. Commonly, but not always, our bad habits are based on irrational beliefs.

A lot of people do realise, on some level, that their beliefs do not make much sense and they acknowledge contrary evidence, but from neurological studies, we have found that beliefs are not consciously or intentionally challenged and they often triumph over logic based in scientific data and reality.

Our beliefs are formed both consciously and unconsciously and we tend to be attached to them. We try to find ways to reinforce these beliefs both consciously and unconsciously. This is partly because they tend to fill up certain gaps in our minds and give us a sense of safety. Your brain needs to believe in something to feel safe and we create complete systems of belief that help us navigate the world we live in. Without this direction, we tend to feel lost and alone.

This creates a kind of map in your brain and it guides you in the day-to-day activities. As Johann Wolfgang von Goethe said, *"Man is made by his belief. As he believes, so he is."* Nobody wants to be wrong, so we never want to admit that we have the wrong mind maps. So, we find many ways of defending our mind maps and proving that we are on the correct path.

▶ BELIEFS – BENEFICIAL OR JUST IN THE WAY OF SUCCESS?

The issue here is succinctly described by Frank Lloyd:

> The thing always happens that
> you really believe in;
> and the belief in a thing makes it happen.

Your belief maps will be mostly influenced by what other people have to say and their own biases. Your maps were formed more likely without any real intentional effort on your part. So, there is a real possibility that your map is wrong and leading you in the wrong direction. This is why it is very vital to constantly question your beliefs and stay updated with the times. Try to make sure your map gives you the guidance in the direction that aligns with your own goals and desires. Constantly re-evaluate and reinterpreted the experiences that were responsible for forming your beliefs.

> To change your life, change your beliefs.
>
> Aung Pye Tun

▶ HOW YOUR BELIEFS EFFECT YOUR CHILD'S FUTURE

How adults feel, children feel the same!

One of the things we have to make our children understand is that beliefs are really just habits. Your child/children will develop and grow when they discover new realities about themselves and the world in which they live. They will learn some vital lessons about how they live, but you can help them understand better the power of their day-to-day habits and how it can mould them into better versions of themselves.

Sometimes, we as humans, are reliant on actions and words to turn our lives in the direction we want it to go, and it is often frustrating when we don't get the desired results. This is mostly because the words we speak and the actions we take are sometimes contrary to each other. Children experience the same thing! Children need to understand that after they have been able to put their goals and wishes into words, they need to take the required steps to bring it into actions and this is what should inform their habits.

Practice, they say, makes perfect. At the root of this belief is the fact that with much exposure to a certain problem, confidence begins to grow on better ways to approach similar problems in the future. This does wonders for self-belief. When your child/children are in the habit of working hard at good things, they begin to form very good habits that will spur them on to success in whatever endeavour they pursue. Success comes from those good habits.

> We are what we believe we are
>
> **C.S LEWIS**

▶ SELF-CONCEPT

> Imagination builds the image of the self and thought then functions within its shadows. From this self-concept grows the conflict between what is and what should be, the conflict in duality
>
> **Jiddu Krishnamurti**

Who are you? What makes you unique? These questions are familiar to you, aren't they?

You probably haven't really thought about this before, but you should have an idea of how to answer them. Some people might say: 'I'm a father, I'm a chef, I am a doctor, I work in IT, I am a plumber." Others will say: "I am good at teaching or I am a successful business woman." Other answers might be: "I'm kind hearted, I'm considerate, I'm a sympathetic person, I'm very fussy about noise," etc. All of these responses are rooted in an understanding of the kind of person we are. This understanding starts to form very early in our lives and it is constantly re-evaluated and adjusted as we grow up.

With children, when you ask who they are, you will get some interesting answers, and you probably will get some shocking answers.

" I am Joe, and I am good at swimming, my name is Helen and I am dumb at mathematics, I am Vincent and I am simply chubby!"

Children are honest with their self-concept. They will tell you who they are, what they are thinking and what defines them. This is their self-concept which is very close to self-identity. Children have their self- concept through the experiences that they've been through, over and over again and that forge a self-definition. The self-concept may be changed or may stay permanently for the rest of a person's life. This is also why, sometimes, we may witness a significant transformation in someone's life leading them to astounding success. In that case, a person transitioned to another person whom he/she thought they could become. To the contrary, someone can continue to have low self-esteem from the time they are young until the time they become an older person. Let's look at this further in the next section.

▶ WHAT IS A SELF-CONCEPT AND HOW IS IT FORMED?

Self-concept is an extended idea of our understanding of self, physically, emotionally, socially, spiritually and in terms of any other aspects that make up who we are. Self-concept is the image we have created about ourselves. Not simple a visual image, of course; but rather a set of ideas that we believe defines us, at conscious and unconscious levels. We develop these self-concepts as we grow up and this is rooted in our knowledge of self. It is multifaceted and it can be distributed into various individual aspects. Self-concepts are similar to self-constructs that we are all familiar with such as self-esteem, self-image, self-efficacy and self-awareness. This self-concept is a personal view on ourselves and a response we always have to the question, *who am I?* This is more about understanding your own tendencies and proclivities, thoughts, habits and preferences.

▶ THE MEANING OF SELF CONCEPT THEORY

There are some assumptions about the actual meaning of self-concept and how it is formed, but generally, scientists have come to an agreement on these points:

* On a general level, self-concept is the overview idea we have about who we are, and this includes cognitive and affective judgments about ourselves.

* Self-concept is multifaceted and it infuses our views of ourselves in terms of various individual aspects such as social, religious, spiritual, physical and emotional.

* It is learned and not inherent by default.

* It is influenced mostly by the environment we grow up in, and other biological factors. Social interaction also has a major role to play here.

* Self-concept forms all through our childhood and this is when it is more easily modified and changed.

* It can also be changed in your adult years, but it is much more difficult to achieve since you already have an established idea of the kind of person you are.

▶ PUTTING HABIT, BELIEF AND SELF-CONCEPT TOGETHER

I put these three elements together to stress how vital habits are to belief and then self-concept. This will help you understand many attributes that your child/children may have. Habits, beliefs and self-concept are interwoven and play a critical part in each other as well as a significant part in your child/children's life. Understanding these elements, one by one, and how they blend together as a single unit will give you a new lens for your perspective in raising and teaching your child/children. He/she deserves the best from you as his/her parents. You are the ones who are taking serious responsibilities in deciding the future of a human being!

Let me lead you to a better understanding of the blending of habit, belief and self-concept.

Let me give you an example. When I drive on big, busy roads, I feel nervous. The feeling has happened for a long time until it becomes my habit, a habit of feeling nervous and anxiety when driving on big, busy roads. Time after time, the same thing happens, and in my mind, it has formed a belief that I am not good at driving. Then I see myself as a bad driver on a big road. The good thing is, soon after that, I know how to overcome it after being annoyed by the nervousness. My conscious mind tells me that it is not a healthy habit and I need to change it. Then, I determinate to achieve good skills on how to control the car on busy roads. I then keep practising and practising, driving as much as possible, and shortly after that, my habit is changed. I can drive with more alertness and smoothly on the road. My belief gets shifted from not being confident on the road to trusting in myself. Then I am able to see myself as a good driver. I've become a successful person who has conquered a fear that was disrupting my life!

Similarly, in a child's world, many habits have been formed through their life's experiences and by a good deal of repetitions over time. These become their beliefs and self-concepts. Your children can see who they are now and this picture of themselves comes from what they have experienced so far. This picture is made up from their habits, beliefs and then self-concepts.

Let me bring in one more example. If a child is a shy boy or girl, he/she finds it hard to make friends. This makes the habit of making friends unsuccessful. Then the child would develop the belief that making friends is hard. He/she then forms a self-concept of, "I am a lonely person - or nobody likes me." This also partly explains one of the causes of depression in children and teenagers nowadays.

The sad thing is when your children see themselves as who they are, the world may have the same responses to their view. No one would like to approach a sad girl, an angry manager or a moody co-worker.

I hope this is helping you understand who your child/children are now.

In summing up, habit, belief and self-concept go hand-in-hand. I'm sure you would agree with me that habit is fundamental and it can help build a future or ruin it. The good news for parents is that habits that your child/children have can be changed at any time, then their belief and self-concept, of course, will be transformed as well.

> Your concept of yourself is everything you believe to be true. Everything you believe to be true about yourself has landed you precisely when you live and breathe every day of your life. Your beliefs about yourself are like the ingredients in the recipe that you use to create your self-concept
>
> **Dr Wane Dyer**

7. IMPORTANCE OF THE SEVEN YEARS OF LIFE

The first seven years are the most essential in the life of every human being. They establish the foundation for overall success or failure in that person's future. They are also very essential for every society as this is the best chance to influence future accomplishment, inclusiveness, and social stability. The early childhood developmental period is regarded as the most important stage to address inequities and a chance to provide opportunities for all children to maximise their full potential.

The first seven years of life are the years in which the personality of the child is formed. In these years you learn more than in the rest of your life. We learn to walk, to speak a language, to control sphincters, to eat, to chew, to read and write, etc. But the most important thing is: we learn how to live.

It is stated by child psychologists that the period between 3 years and 11 years is a signature period. This suggests that childhood encounters within these years are expected to influence who that child will become, how they will think, believe, perform and interpret the world to themselves.

This is why it is essential for a child to be provided with a chance to experience their own characteristics and emotions, which will lead to healthy self-concepts about himself/herself. Failure to do so could cause the child to feel that he/she is unable to ever achieve their full potential when they grow up.

Because children's brains are still developing rapidly, early life experiences have significant influences on their understanding of themselves and their ability to regulate themselves.

When things keep being addressed and repeated in children's lives, they are likely to stay with the habits when they get older. Habits will form a person with courage, experience, success at work, a healthy lifestyle and good relationships. Or, the wrong ones are very likely to produce a person with anxiety, depression, ailments, poverty or difficulty in relationships.

We all know how important a good childhood is. In infancy, we form patterns of behaviour that we carry for the rest of our lives. If we were lucky to have been brought up in a loving and supportive environment that would take us far in life even if later we face adversities. However, if we were brought up in unsupportive and challenging conditions, we can carry the mark of those experiences into adulthood as well. The first seven years of a child's life are spent absorbing the world around them. They see, hear, and absorb what is said to them, and what is not. These seven years set the foundation for the rest of their lives. Children who enjoy a loving, healthy, warm, caring and supportive life have a fantastic foundation for living healthy with the potential for robust growth.

▶ MORRIS MASSEY THEORY

For you to have an understanding of the importance of the first 7 years of life, I will introduce to you the theory of Morris Massey, a Professor and Sociologist. He named three significant groups of years during which benefits are developed. One is called The Imprint Period. He stated that from the age of one to the age of seven, we are considered sponges absorbing everything around us and taking much it as real, especially when these things come from our parents. The important thing here is to learn and discover the knowledge of right and wrong. This is a human development process in which strong evidence, patterns of behaviour and observations have become imprinted.

▶ ERIK ERIKSON THEORY

Another theory which is worth mentioning is Erik Erikson's theory of Psychosocial Development. Erik Erikson is a world renowned Developmental Psychologist and Psychoanalyst. I have been so fascinated with his approach since the time I was at college and university. I've applied this theory to my work with children. Erikson suggested that we are driven by the demand to reach capacity and competences in some area of our lives. According to Psychosocial Theory, we go through eight stages of development across our lifespan, from childhood through late adulthood. At each stage, there is a trial or responsibility that we are required to resolve. Achievement of each developmental task will result in the sense of capability and good character. Inability to manage these responsibilities leads to perceptions of incompetence. Erikson presented a total of 7 stages in a human's lifespan. I only bring to you the first two stages of development as they relate to the content of the first seven years of life. This also gives you an understanding of how important it is to have good habit building for your child/children as early as possible.

▶ AUTONOMY VS. SHAME/DOUBT

As toddlers (ages 1–3 years) begin to examine their environment, they discover that they can manage their activities and act on their surroundings to produce outcomes. They start to expose particular favourites for some appearances of the circumstances, such as people, food, drinks, toys, and clothes. A toddler's primary work is to decide the subject of autonomy vs. shame and doubt by managing to build self-confidence. This is the "me do it" stage. For instance, we might see a developing understanding of autonomy in a 3-year-old boy who wants to choose his socks and shoes and put them on by himself. Although his socks and shoes might not be a wrong pair from his choosing, his input in such crucial choices affects his feeling of independence. If we dismissed the chance to work on his circumstance, he may open to doubt his skills, which could head to low self-esteem and feelings of shame.

▶ INITIATIVE VS. GUILT

When children enter the preschool stage (ages 3–6 years), they are capable of opening actions and supporting control over their environment by social interplays and performance. According to Erikson, preschool children must solve the task of initiative vs. guilt. By getting to form and score purposes while mixing with others, preschool children can understand this responsibility. Action, a thought of dream and duty, happens when parents permit a child/children to examine, within boundaries, and then help the child to choose. These children will grow self-confidence and develop a sense of direction. The children who are failing at this stage—with their lead misfiring or suffocated by over-controlling parents—may create guilt responses and feelings.

In summing up, the first seven years of your child's life should be seen as very significant! During these periods, children will learn and absorb everything very quickly, and the most important issue is what your child takes in by this time, will stay with him/her for the rest of their lives. Therefore, building good habits during this stage is a must! Your child/children will use all the resources you provide to do their business in life later. They become rich or poor; depending on the possession of habits they acquired in their early years.

8. IMPORTANCE OF EQUIPPING YOUNG CHILDREN WITH THE RIGHT HABITS DURING THE EARLY STAGE

For this part, I will share with you more theories on how your child's brain functions during their early ages. This will help you understand how powerful habit building is for your child/children at an early age. I have to say, 'as early as possible!' You can also refer to Picture Illustration 1 for further understanding of the functioning of subconscious/unconscious mind and conscious mind that I've addressed earlier in The Mind section.

▶ **HOW THE BRAIN FUNCTIONS AT THE EARLY STAGES OF LIFE**

A lot of the information we receive from the environment, through our senses, when we are young, is recorded and stored in our subconscious/unconscious mind. As we receive and process this information, we also start creating beliefs and expectations according to our experiences that are also recorded in our subconscious mind. As we grow up, much of this information, expectations and beliefs remains with us and will have a considerable influence on our behaviour.

According to different specialists, depending on our age, or the stage of development we are in, our brains have different levels of activity, or brain waves. For example, newborns have a slower level of activity or slower brain waves. As they grow up and start taking in information from their environment, the speed of these waves increases; their brains work faster. Meaning, they start to use that information recorded on their subconscious/unconscious mind, to bring it to their conscious mind and perform different activities.

From birth to 2 years of age, the human brain works mostly with brain waves of less frequency. Thus, children at this age function mostly from the subconscious. They just censor, correct or judge the information received from the outside world. At this age, the activity of the "thinking brain" or the conscious mind, is extremely low.

From 2 to 5 or 6 years, children begin to have slightly higher brain waves, although they are mainly connected to their "inner world." The subconscious/unconscious mind continues to predominate, absorbing all the information and stimuli they receive from their environment, and storing it there. They live in the world of the abstract and the imagination. They have developed little critical and rational thinking. For this same reason, young children tend to believe everything they are told.

This then becomes the ideal stage to start forming good and healthy habits in children. Everything a child sees and hears is consolidated in the form of beliefs, and those beliefs are what will determine his/her behaviour and his/her way of interpreting reality in adulthood. This is a stage where we, as adults, need to be particularly careful with what we say to them, or in front of them, especially if we want for them to have good habits as they grow up.

For example, if you have a child this age, and every time he makes a mistake you say things like, "you always do the same thing, you're a bad boy, you're a failure," etc. These statements go into the child's subconscious/unconscious mind to then become beliefs, and from there, form habits.

How does it show? As he/she grows up and has to face new situations, he/she will usually try to avoid them. He/she will feel anxiety when doing activities that trigger them and even before, or he/she will fail in the first attempt and will not try again. The child's belief that "he/she is a failure" will have created this habit of feeling anxious or that things always go wrong. In time, with repetition, the child will validate this belief and store it as true.

This is exactly how habits are formed in childhood. Knowing this, will give you a better notion of how to speak and with your child/children, and how to teach and guide them into good habits that will form their personality and help them become successful adults.

> Children are like wet cement.
> Whatever falls on them makes an impression.
>
> Haim Ginott

CHILDHOOD IS THE BEST TIME TO PRACTICE AND DEVELOP GOOD HABITS

This is entirely because children have a really good ability to grasp and learn when they are younger. They can easily learn what is told to them and put it to use. A child's learning power is approximately 25% more than an adult. His/her mind is like a giant sponge which absorbs whatever you provide to him/her. Therefore, it is easier to inculcate good habits in them while they are young and agile minded.

A child's mind is pure and innocent. He/she believes his parents do everything for his own good. He/she looks up at you and trusts you to lead their lives with no question. To inculcate good habits in your child/children, you should show them the right way to behave at the right time, in a pleasant way. This can be done in various ways, for example, performing activities along with them, showing and explaining both the good and the bad sides of acting in a certain manner, in a particular situation etc.

Some teenagers tend to become rebellious, owing to the hormonal changes in their bodies. Also, it is important to develop good habits in them before they reach their teens. The earlier they are taught good habits, the better it is for them. Moreover, it can take a lifetime to develop good habits, but it takes just a second to fall prey to bad habits. Hence, children should be taught to discriminate between what's right and what's wrong.

In other words, before a child starts picking up any unhealthy behaviours or showing any signs of a bad habit, equip them with the right manners and behaviours and make it a habit for them to follow through every day. Also, be a good role model for your child /children by being a well-mannered parent, and your child/children will do the same. It is never too early to begin bringing the best to your child/children and if you build good habits now, as early for as you can, then he/she will have countless benefits later.

In conclusion, I addressed the importance of the first 7 years of life and the importance of habit building for these years of your child/children's life. It's never too late to bring the best to your child/children's life and you can start at any time. With your love, care and commitment you will get the benefits you want your child/children to have.

> I think of a child's mind as a blank book.
> During the first years of his life, much will be written on the pages.
> The quality of that writing will affect his life profoundly.
>
> **Walt Disney**

9. MESSAGE FROM THE AUTHOR TO PARENTS

To recap, a habit is something we do every day without thinking too much about it. It's the same for children and adults. However, it is better to form good habits when children are in their early years of development. Habits are activities and behaviours children perform subconsciously, and they're very difficult to disassociate from, because when children form and repeat habits, a chemical called dopamine is released in the brain, causing a sense of satisfaction and that strengthens the habit.

Habits are very important, and it would be difficult to run our lives without them. They automate many of the regular activities in our lives and free up our minds so that we are capable of focusing on higher level activities.

Habits serve to create routine, order, and efficiency. However, bad habits have the opposite effect and can lock us into negative or rigid patterns of destructive behaviour. Bad habits such as eating junk, smoking or driving too fast can be very dangerous to our health and well-being.

Children's brains are very powerful, and they regularly scan for patterns in their lives or things that can turn into habits. However, their subconscious mind does not discriminate between good and bad habits and anything that is repeated over time can become a habit.

▶ BAD HABITS AND WORLD PROBLEMS

Recent events have caused us to pay rapt attention to the current situation in the world. Newspapers are filled with bad news, and prisons are full of criminals. Society is corrupt, people are suffering from ailments, joblessness, poverty, and we are riding an economic rollercoaster.

There are a lot of smart and kind people who have tried to fix these problems, but everywhere we look there are more problems. We are our own worst enemies. The leading causes of death can be associated with bad habits, including smoking, depression, poor diet and a lack of exercise, according to a recent survey. Everyone has bad habits whether they are chronically late, have a bad temper, tap their feet, chew gum too loudly, eating sloppily, oversharing on Facebook, or eating junk food. And everyone knows that bad habits can impede our happiness, health, and social relationships.

Just imagine that your precious child will enter the big world with his/her unhealthy habits. What would happen to his/her life? Would he/she have enough skills to survive with the higher and higher demands of today's world? Imagine if your child is involved in drugs, becomes a victim of bullies, depression or commits suicide or even experiences a serious illness such as cancer, has problems with his/her relationships because of lacking the strength needed to fight for survival through the difficulties and challenges that life brings. I believe you must equip your child/children with right habits as early as you can, if you want them to stand on their feet firmly in whatever he/she faces in the future.

▶ HOW TO USE THIS BOOK

How to use this work

This book consists of three parts:

    Part I: Theoretical framework of child development and habit formation

    Part II: How to build up 56 habits in your children

    Part III: Conclusion

I suggest parents reading the first part thoroughly to get a full understanding of how a child grows and develops in intellectual, emotional, social, communication, physical and moral areas, then glancing through the 56 habits. You can pick up a habit or habits which is/are appropriate to your child regarding his/her age, needs or any areas of your concern or focus and follow up instructions for building that/those habit/s for specific outcomes. I also state clearly why each habit is important to your child's development, then recommend practical ideas of how to achieve each habit in order to reap all its associated benefits.

Once again, I would not expect that you- parents will take all the information in this book on-board in one reading. I encourage you to think of this book as a resource that you will return to again and again to support your child/children in any situation, or any need you may have.

Have a go and I wish you will achieve what you desire to achieve in your child.

▶ RIGHT PARENTING- BRIGHT FUTURE FOR YOUR CHILD/CHILDREN

Develop right parenting and you will bring a bright future for your child/children! Right parenting is built on the feeling of positive thoughts and learning new things every day. Not now and then. Not for a little while. Every single day. Effective parenting is built with daily right actions by your child/children. When you are doing the right things for your child/children with your best, you will have no more room for negativity and regret later. No room for doubt, worry or anxiety.

Right parenting is built with goals to give you a reason to try your best, to do the right and necessary things for your child/children to prepare them for whatever challenge the day may bring to them. A right parenting is built from knowing you are responsible for your child/ children's lives, their results, their success and their failures. Right parenting is building through learning. Learning new things every day, on topics that expand your mind and develop your parenting skills as you are in charge of someone's future.

The football legend, Pelé once said that success is no accident. It is hard work, perseverance, learning, studying, sacrifice and most of all, love of what you are doing or learning to do. Live your parenting with the determination to learn. Learn new things every single day to bring the best outcomes to your child/children. Develop good parenting and you will provide a bright future for your child/children.

Growth is the key to right parenting as you challenge yourself, every day, with your parenting roles. You will lead a happy life and so will your child/children. If you don't, your child/children will suffer.

Your mind is like a muscle that gets stronger when you embrace the challenge as a parent and you push it to its limits. When you learn what works and apply it to your parenting skills your child/children will reap the benefit.

Right parenting is one that surrounds itself with the right parents. Right parenting does not let an opinion alter its course in your parenting style. It follows its own path for the best benefits for your child/children's life no matter what! Right parenting is the type that visualizes success of your child/children's future and is prepared to work to make that picture come to life. Right parenting does not let fear, frustration, or anger get in the way of raising successful children.

Right parenting- Bright future for your child/children!

This is the purpose of reading **HABITS TO BENEFITS**.

Part Two
HABITS TO BENEFITS

1. LOVE AND LIFE APPRECIATION

▶ **LOVE AND LIFE APPRECIATION AND ITS IMPORTANCE TO CHILDREN**

Being able to feel and show gratitude has been associated with happiness, optimism, and improved quality relationships, as well as physical and psychological health. In other words, when children put the time and make an effort to show appreciation and thankfulness, not only will other people see it, but they will have emotional strength. This will improve their quality of life, presently and in the future.

Some studies proved that lack of love and life appreciation can make children more stressed and develop the sense of not being enough now and throughout their life later. This is why it is essential that children show love and life appreciation at all cost. They are going to be healthier in the process of developing and maintaining a feeling of being enough. This is important and essential for having a fulfilled and happy life. In addition, they are going to grow up to become responsible adults with a sense of gratitude.

Also, it leads to a stronger family bonding. The expression of appreciation fills the relationships in strong families. Children who show love and life appreciation are more inclined to be more positive and fun to be with.

It is vital as a parent to teach your child/children always to have love and life appreciation as this will go a long way in showing them the value of life, relationships and living in harmony.

 **Habit** One

ENJOY ALL THE LITTLE THINGS.

WHY IS IT IMPORTANT?

A lot of people today are depressed about life simply because they are trying to live by the standards set by other people. There is a general lack of abundance and this translates to people not being too happy with their current situation. Oftentimes, we are constantly looking for meaning and validation in all the wrong places and we tend to ignore what we already have.

In the same vein, you find people who don't seem to have much in life but they lead a lot happier lives because they have learned to appreciate what they have. Your child needs to learn how to appreciate the little things in life and thread a better path to happiness.

Children are constantly learning as they grow and they might not appreciate the value of the things that they have at their very young ages, therefore, it becomes vital that you instil a sense of value in them and let them appreciate the gifts of life so as to help them to be happier people.

BENEFITS:

◆ INTELLECTUAL BENEFITS

• **More attention and Focus:** When children learn to appreciate the little things in life, they spend less time chasing after things that are out of their reach and consequently, this allows them to pay more attention to what is around them and focus more on the important things. This frees up valuable brain real estate which they can channel for a better use.

• **Higher reasoning:** With a deeper appreciation for life comes an increase in the level of reasoning. We tend to see beyond the superficial and focus more on the substance of things. This also applies to children and they must learn to achieve this state of higher reasoning.

💎 EMOTIONAL BENEFITS

Fulfilment: With gratitude and appreciation comes fulfilment. Fulfilment is being at peace with our accomplishments and belongings. Therefore, it is vital that children also experience this as it shapes their emotional makeup.

Happiness: With fulfilment and appreciation comes joy and happiness. When children learn to be appreciative of the little things in life, you'd be amazed at how much happiness they will show on a day to day basis. And as joy is very contagious, this becomes good for everybody.

Feeling enough: This still goes back to being content. When your child/children enjoy the little things, they feel content with what they have no matter how little, and thus they never feel inadequate about anything. This is very significant for their self-esteem.

💎 SOCIAL BENEFITS

Liberated interactions: Children can start to experience limitations in the way they interact with their friends if they feel like they don't have as much or are not deserving to be friends with children who are perhaps living a more privileged life. With an appreciation of what they already have, they will be able to see the bigger picture and will interact with people more freely without being held back by the seeming limitations of their own lives.

Empathy: Children also have a lot more empathy for those who do not have as much as they do when they appreciate life better. This is because they know how it felt when it was an issue for them to get all they craved for and they can extend their empathy in the way they deal with the people around them.

Role modelling: There is an aura of contentment that comes with enjoying the little things around you. When your children master this art, they will be looked up to by their peers because they will always appear so calm and collected by life and all of its issues. Everybody wants to be able to control how they feel about the things that happens to them and this is a very good way to have that control.

💎 COMMUNICATION BENEFITS

● **No inferiority complex:** It is very easy for children to fall into a spiral of inferiority complex, and this inhibits their ability to talk to people and make conversation. When they are happy and content with their status in life, they are more confident and they can be better at social communication and interactions.

💎 PHYSICAL BENEFITS

● **No anxiety:** A life of gratitude and appreciation is a life free of anxiety. This means that their body is free of stress hormones which can have a negative impact on their body.

CONCLUSION:

We are a cumulative of all the memories we have, and whether or not you have happy memories, it has less to do with how much you have in life but how much you appreciate what you have in life. Teaching your children to start to appreciate life at their young age will certainly help them be more emotionally balanced growing up. Kurt Vonnegut said, "Enjoy the little things in life because one day you'll look back and realize they were the big things."

PRACTICAL STEPS
CHILDREN CAN TAKE TO ENJOY LITTLE THINGS

In a bit to adapt to this fast-changing world, children often find it hard to live in the moment. Important events like birthdays and holidays are missed and much significance is not attached to them. This is not a healthy way for a child to grow up. In this section, we are going to explore various ways children can begin to enjoy little things.

1. GRATITUDE

Your children will begin to enjoy everyday moments if they start counting their blessings. The first step to enjoying little things for children is to start appreciating everything they have at their disposal. For the most part, life is made up of the regular, small and mundane things. They can begin by looking at all the clothes, books, family members and food that they have and be grateful. Even if there isn't much to look at, they can be grateful for the few in their possession.

In addition, they should thank people for all the things they do for them. By showing gratitude for all the little favours that people show to them, others will feel good, and they will feel good too. Also, they should also look for opportunities to be good to others. For instance, they can pick up litters or cheer someone up. The good that goes around always comes around.

2. FORGIVING PEOPLE FOR PAST MISTAKES

It can be hard to let go feelings of hurt. However, this is essential for a fulfilling and healthy life. However, by forgiving others of their wrongdoings, they are able to move on and have a positive mindset. The baggage of holding onto past hurts is overwhelming.

3. LOOKING ON THE BRIGHT SIDE

It takes a positive mindset to enjoy the little things of life. For children to have fun in all that they do, they must be able to see the silver linings in all situations. To do this, they can apply the following techniques:

- They can set aside 15 minutes daily for 4 weeks which they will use to list 5 things they enjoy about life (e.g. "getting a birthday gift" or "helping another child"). In addition, they should evaluate the time things didn't go well and describe the situation. Then, they can look for three ways they can look on the bright side of the ordeal.

- For example, if they fail the math test. Normally, they would be frustrated and want to take time off from studying arithmetic. But, taking time off to study arithmetic may be a good opportunity for your children to try other subjects like music and art. So they also have the time to try their hands on a new hobby. Finally, the frustration helps them to identify what might have gone wrong with the test.

Noticing the silver linings helps your children to see that there are often positive outcomes in negative situations.

 **Habit** Two

WORK ON FAMILY CULTURE

WHY IS IT IMPORTANT?

Family culture is very important and your child/children must grow in an environment where it is clear on what an acceptable behaviour is and isn't. There needs to be a clear distinction on how they should behave when they are at home. This behaviour will also extend to when they leave the house and are interacting with friends, classmates and teachers. This is basically what people refer to as home training.

Asides from things like good behaviour, culture also revolves around certain other issues like scheduling, manner in which you have fun together as a family, dinner time, chores etc. there are so many factors that contributes to the overall family culture and it is incumbent on you as the parent to create that specific culture and atmosphere that you want your child/children to grow up in. This goes a long way in shaping them to be the kind of children you really wish them to be.

BENEFITS:

💎 INTELLECTUAL BENEFITS

- **Study time:** When there is a clear schedule in place for your child/children, they will have time allotted for relaxing, watching TV and playing around the house. They will have time allotted for chores and they also will have time allotted to study and homework. When they stick to these schedules, they will do well academically as they are sure to get in a couple of minutes or hours of study time in their everyday routine.

- **Discipline:** Scheduling is a very important part of the family culture and this teaches your child/children discipline. This discipline is a skill that will serve them as they advance in age and transition into spaces where you don't necessarily have as much supervision rights as you used to when they were little.

💎 EMOTIONAL BENEFITS

Fun time: When you get together as a family every once in a while, to just have fun and you make the atmosphere at home light-hearted where your child/children can joke about things and be themselves, they are going to be happier and more at ease to be at home. This is very good for their emotional wellbeing and impacts positively on their growth.

Confidant: When your child/children are happy at home and they feel free to discuss issues that might be bothering them, they will surely confide in you when delicate matters that need your attention, your wisdom and your experience in life comes up. This is how you'd want your child/children to relate with you and it is up to you to create that family culture to back this up.

💎 SOCIAL BENEFITS

Home training: A family is a unit that mimics the general community and society. Whatever your child/children grow up doing at home, it will form the way in which they behave in public in some ways or the other. You need to help them to become better, jovial, optimistic and sociable people right from when they are at home before they begin interacting with people in the outside world. It comes more naturally to them to be amiable and respectful when you imbibe that culture in them right from home.

Bonding- connecting with family: There is no better way to create an atmosphere of bonding than to have family traditions, some fun others chores (which can be fun if they are happy to help). This way, every member of the family can bond and have deeper understandings of themselves and better connections.

💎 COMMUNICATION BENEFITS

Conversational skills: This also speaks to the social skill your child/children gain from being able to talk to you and their siblings about things that are on their mind or maybe things that often bother them. This skill is very useful when they are dealing with people in school or at their playgrounds or wherever.

💎 PHYSICAL BENEFITS

⦿ **Helping out at home:** There is a bunch of fun physical activity that you can infuse into family time and this eventually becomes a family culture where you all try to have as much fun as you can. Other things such as chores and general usefulness around the house too are imbibed in your child/children at this level.

CONCLUSION:

Family culture is ever so important because it informs how children behave in the society and determines whether or not they bring value to their immediate environment or not.

PRACTICAL STEPS TO DEVELOP A FAMILY CULTURE

Family culture is the summation of the traditions, practices, habits and values that defines a family. It is who you are as a family and what makes you different from other families in the world. Your family culture is your family true identity. Here are simple questions to know what your current family culture is:

- ⦿ **ARE YOU READERS?**
    › *Do you like to eat well?*
    › *Do you like sports?*
    › *How do you treat one another?*
    › *Do you watch a lot of movies with the children?*
    › *Are morning or bedtime devotions a normal part of your day?*
    › *Do you have any family sayings or mottos?*
    › *What do you do on the weekends?*
    › *Where are some regular places you go?*

The family culture questions will get you thinking about what your traditions, values, and practices are in your family. Having identified a bit, let's look at the following;

1. MAKING IT VISUAL

You can write out your family mottos, traditions or values hung on the wall. These writings must be bold and visible. When a child does anything that is consistent with the family's cultures and values, they should be pointed out immediately.

2. CREATING REGULAR TRADITIONS AND RITUALS

This may be morning routines, dinner time routines weekend traditions or bedtime routines. It should be part of your children's normal day. If you make occasional pancakes on Sundays and your children love it, you can make pancakes on most Saturdays. Apparently, children love doing something repetitively, and when they grow older, those moments become the events they will live to remember.

3. USING ELABORATION AND REPETITION

One of the best ways to reinforce family culture and traditions is to talk often about them. Not only will this reinforce the culture, it will also help them have a sense of security and belonging within the family unit. You can use statements like:
- Our family loves studying.
- Our family is patient with one another.
- In our family, rude people don't get rewards.
- Our family doesn't leave anyone out.
- Our family loves watching movies together.
- Our family loves the beach.

4. EMBRACING FAMILY CULTURE

The idea of a family culture isn't to have a bunch of To-Do lists. Instead, it is to have things that you believe in, enjoy doing and values you want your family to be defined by. There will be things that others do not agree with, so it is better to have a positive value like courage, kindness or love to define your family culture in order to build a positive atmosphere for peace and harmony.

Having a family culture is essential in building a positive and stable home. By following the steps above, not only are you going to be able to build a solid family culture, you are going to have a happy home.

 **Habit** Three

HOME IS THE BEST PLACE TO COME BACK

WHY IS IT IMPORTANT?

It is natural for children to want to spend time away from home; maybe at a friend's place or at a meetup point where they can just hang out and stay away from the routine of home life. They'd rather branch off to these places after school rather than come home straight. Sometimes, it's because they aren't too happy at home and sometimes, it's just because they are excited to be out with friends.

According to Marlow Hyrache, home is the safest place to be and it is sad to see that children don't want to be at home due to certain insecurities, loneliness and inadequate love that may occur at homes.

You must create a conducive, fun and loving atmosphere at home for your children to return to and teach them to value being at home over spending time outside of the house. This habit will follow them as they grow up into adults which will be very beneficial to them.

Sometime in the future, your children will become fathers and mothers and guardians. If they have a good sense of family and home, they will be better adults to guide their wards in the right directions.

BENEFITS:

💎 INTELLECTUAL BENEFITS

- **Spend more time studying at home:** When your child/children come back home after school, they have more time to spend at home and they can spend more time on their homework and ask for your help with school work if need be. This gives them an edge at school as they aren't wasting time fooling around

- **Learn wisdom from parents:** There are a lot your child/children will learn from you actively and passively when they spend time at home with you and with their siblings. This knowledge and wisdom will serve them a lot more in life than just hanging around friends aimlessly after school hours.

- **Learn and share good thing from siblings:** If your child/children have a sibling, home is the best place for your child to have intimacies in his/her small tribe. He/she could learn right from wrong, test the errors and again confidences. From this act, your child/children could receive unconditional love to build up support and company from their sibling and this is a bond that money cannot buy.

EMOTIONAL BENEFITS

- **Experience family love:** When your child/children spend time at home with you and their siblings, they experience a lot of love and they have a lot of love to spread too. This is very essential for their emotional wellbeing and they can't get this elsewhere. This is why it is so important that the home is a loving and fun place for them to be.

- **Be in an emotionally balanced environment:** When the home is as it ought to be, it should be an emotionally balanced environment where your child/children can learn to be stable individuals. They know what to expect and they are protected from the rollercoaster of hanging out with bad peer away from home.

SOCIAL BENEFITS

- **Stay away from negative influence:** More often than not, the friends your child/children will be hanging around with after school will be a negative influence on them. They are more likely going to be engaged in less than healthy or good activities. Spending time at home keeps them away from all of these negative influences.

- **Better relationship with parents:** Your child/children will develop a healthier and more beneficial relationship with you the more you are around them. They have a lot to learn and you are in a position in life where you can teach them so many things.

- **Better relationship with siblings:** Children need to be at home with their parents and more importantly, with their siblings. There is so much they can learn from each other and they can all act as support systems when any of them are in need of it.

COMMUNICATION BENEFITS

- **Better relations with parents and siblings:** When your child/children spend time with you and their siblings, they become better at talking to each other and in communicating their feelings. This will foster a stronger bond amongst them. This communication skill is adaptable when they are out in public also.

- **Self-expression:** Your child/children can share and express the feelings without fear of being condemned by anyone.

PHYSICAL BENEFITS

- **Staying safe:** At home, your child/children are under your supervision and are less likely to be engaged in otherwise harmful activity detrimental to their physical wellbeing and health. Home is supposed to be safe and it is definitely always safer than anywhere else.

- **Growth healthy:** When your child/children are at home, you have better control and supervision over what they do and what they eat. They grow up healthier this way.

CONCLUSION:

There are so many advantages to your child/children spending their time outside of school at home with you, and it is incumbent upon you to make the home a place they would want to be so you can always be there for them as well.

PRACTICAL STEPS CHILDREN CAN TAKE TO ENJOY HOME

There are many ways children can begin to have fun at home. In this section, we are going to explore various ways a home can become the best place children can always come back to.

1. STORYTELLING

No matter the age, children like stories. To have a good family time, telling good stories to each other is the right way to go about it. This basically keeps things rolling.

2. LOOKING AT PHOTO ALBUMS

Old pictures help children to remember beautiful moments in the past. For instance, pictures of birthday celebrations, vacations and other happy moments bring feelings of excitement and joy in the home.

3. PLAYING GAMES

Children like games and they will like to play games with the family members. Any game can work, and here are a few suggestions:

i. Video games: This can be for the whole family. The Wii, like Wii Play, Wii Sports, or anything can work, as they can have up to four players.
ii. Board games: Board games are great and are for several players, like Trouble, Sorry! Or anything else.
iii. Card games also work, like Yu-Gi-Oh! Or Pokémon card games.

4. SINGING KARAOKE

Singing karaoke is fun, and it is an excellent way to test the whole family's singing skills. There are no rules and mild fun may be poked at funny voices.

5. WATCHING MOVIES TOGETHER

Any movie can work. However, movies that are focused on controversial issues must be avoided. Movies should be chosen for fun or action. Family members can also use this time to watch old home videos and reminisce on good old times. This creates a serene atmosphere at home.

6. WATCHING YOUTUBE VIDEOS ON THE INTERNET

There are exciting and popular YouTube channels that the family can subscribe to. They can check for some music, videos, and comedies.

7. SPENDING NEW YEAR'S EVE TOGETHER

When children spend the New Year's Eve with at home with the family, they have an excellent opportunity have fun together, to bond, and bring in the New Year with their loved ones (family members). With all the possibilities for fun, drinks, food, games and activities, spending New Year's Eve at home can be a real treat and a joyous one.

By following the above steps, the home will again be a place to come back to; it will bring beautiful memories.

 **Habit** Four

RELAX LIVING ENVIRONMENT.

WHY IS IT IMPORTANT?

Stress is a part of our everyday lives and some people have understood how best to handle themselves when dealing with stress. Others haven't been so fortunate, which has caused stress to do a lot of damage to their mental health and wellbeing. This is because they do not cultivate the habit of living in a relaxing environment right from when they were growing up.

So it is very important to create a relaxing and stress-free environment for your children to have fun and be themselves. Children operate best when they feel refreshed everyday and are free from stress. They experience stress from the usual sources that we as adults experience too. You should protect, shield and isolate them from the seeming madness of the outside world and make the home a safe haven for their upbringing. A quiet and stress-free home allows your children to function at their best.

Try to avoid bringing with you the stress you gather from work to your home. Leave all the negativity outside and be a source of calmness and ease to your children at dinner and family time. This has a lot of long-term benefits for your child and they are better balanced emotionally and mentally.

BENEFITS:

INTELLECTUAL BENEFITS

- **Thinking straight:** It is a lot easier to think straight when children are in an environment where they can be comfortable and at ease. It gives them the perfect room for their creative juices to flow and they can express themselves a lot better in their homework, their art and their passions.

- **Quality study time:** In a conducive environment, children can better learn and study what they have been taught in school as they do not have to worry about stressful distractions, and they can fully devote their time and brain power to the academic activities at hand.

- **Sharp mind:** When children grow up in a relaxing environment, they are better poised to read more, study more, observe more and learn more. This helps them develop a sharper mind.

💎 EMOTIONAL BENEFITS

- **Connections:** Your child/children will also find it easier to talk to you and share their problems, insecurities and achievements when they are relaxed and feel safe in the house. This helps build their emotional intelligence and give them the necessary skills to reach out to people and to connect to your thoughts on a day to day basis.

- **Embrace the calmness:** In a relaxing environment, children can learn to be calmer and reduce their energy levels to match the mood at the time. They usually have a lot of energy to dissipate but they must learn to enjoy the calmness whenever they get it. And this calmness should be a symbol of the home.

💎 SOCIAL BENEFITS

- **Better expressions:** Children are more comfortable to express themselves when they are with you and their siblings if the stress has been reduced to a minimum level at home. They can interact better with their siblings, friends and neighbours and everyone will be happy.

- **Enjoying Solitude:** In a relaxing environment, children can learn to enjoy their own companies and be alone with their thoughts and reflections.

💎 COMMUNICATION BENEFITS

- **Improved communication:** Communication is at an easy pace in a stress-free and relaxing environment, and children are better equipped to represent themselves in a relaxing environment. They won't have the fear and limitations that come with a stress-filled set up and they can be outspoken without so many inhibitions.

💎 PHYSICAL BENEFITS

Reduction in stress hormones: It has been said so many times, but the effect of stress on children's body on a physical level cannot be overstated. The stress hormones can kick in to have a physical manifestation on their body and in the same light, you can imagine how much good it will do their bodies when they can relax and unwind in a stress-free environment.

Extracurricular activities: When children find themselves in a relaxing environment, they can engage in various extracurricular activities and games that are geared toward improving their social and mental skills. These activities are much more enjoyable when everything around them is in a relaxed state. They won't be able to have fun and be themselves when they find it hard to relax and they automatically become uncomfortable.

CONCLUSION:

Life can be stressful and there is usually so much going on in our lives, we need to ensure that our living spaces are as relaxing as possible. We need to protect our children's sanity and mental health by ensuring that they grow up in a relaxing environment.

PRACTICAL STEPS CHILDREN CAN TAKE TO RELAX IN LIVING ENVIRONMENTS

Everyone, including children, needs a day off once in a while. They need to relax and rejuvenate, and all they need to do is to make a few preparations ahead of time. There are a variety of options that children can choose from. From taking short naps to walking the dog.

1. PREPARING FOR THE DAY

To effectively relax, it must be scheduled. Certain activities have to be cancelled during relaxation moments. Activities like seeing the dentist or solving a mathematics problem. The day or period must be completely free for relaxation.

② SHUTTING DOWN THE SCREENS

If your children are watching the TV, they are not relaxing. All technology devices must be turned off. If they switched on the TV or go online, they may view things like the news, which may let stress intrude on your day.

③ CHOOSING A GOOD BACKGROUND MUSIC

Music had been scientifically proven to boost children's mood. A good classic or an upbeat song will work. It does not really matter what kind of music it is as long as it puts them in a good mood. The music should be played in the background as they carry on other activities.

④ CHOOSING THE MAIN FOCUS OF THE DAY

They should decide on how they want to spend the majority of the day. They can have a veg-out day, where they just watch their favourite movies and eat their favourite snacks. They should just pick what they most feel like doing and what will relax them the most.

⑤ GETTING A SMOOTHIE OR A FAVOURITE DRINK

If possible, they can make a strawberry-banana smoothie, provided they have access to the ingredients. All they need is 4 medium sized strawberries (frozen or fresh), 1 half of a banana (chopped into fourths), a cup of soy milk and 3-4 ice cubes. Then, they can add soy milk first then add the bananas, strawberries, and ice cubes then blend for about 20 seconds to enjoy a refreshing moment.

Relaxing is beautiful and healthy. It helps to relieve children from stress so they concentrate better. By following the few guidelines above, they will be able to relax better.

 **Habit** Five

ENJOY FREE THING AROUND: SUN, FLOWERS, PARKS, NATURE, AND WILD ANIMALS.

WHY IS IT IMPORTANT?

The best things in life are indeed free. Life is full of so many pleasures and so many things that bring joy into your child/children's lives. There is so much to explore in nature and when you build a habit of enjoying these free aspects of life with your child/children, they will surely appreciate the diversity in life a whole lot more. This is beneficial on a mental, spiritual and emotional level. Let your child/children go outside and experience the great outdoors. Let them enjoy the sun, the flowers, the animals and the sceneries. This is very exciting for them and you can clearly see how happy it makes them. This is a very good way to disconnect them from all of the technology around them.

When children engage in nature, it stimulates their sense of adventure and curiosity and they learn how to maneuver and adapt to various situations as they grow up and are tested with new challenges. Your child/children is always motivated to push himself to face new challenges and embark on new adventures. This is a skill that will be very beneficial to them as they grow up.

BENEFITS:

INTELLECTUAL BENEFITS

- **Learning about nature:** Your child/children will be eager to learn about nature and their curiosity is at a peak in their younger years. They are like a sponge and they absorb any new information they come across. As you all know, no knowledge is wasted and this new information they have about nature and the things around them will surely come in handy at some point in their lives.

⚜ **Enrich knowledge about life:** When your child/children learn to enjoy the seemingly basic things in life that are free, they will soon start to appreciate how important it is that they are privileged to have them and they will want to know more about life and all of the life that surrounds them. There is a lot of knowledge that sits right in front of us waiting to be tapped into and nature holds so many mysteries that a curious mind can really feed on.

⚜ **Increase observations:** A big part of appreciating nature and all of the free things around us is in being very observant. When your child/children starts to really observe nature, they begin to see patterns and a deeper sense of meaning and this helps them to better focus and observe some more in life.

⚜ **Stimulate wonderment and curiosity:** The more your child/children know this, the more they seek out knowledge. Nature can stimulate the mind and drive the curious ones into learning about any and everything.

💎 EMOTIONAL BENEFITS

⚜ **Relaxed learning environment:** Nature is calming and offers a relaxing environment where your child/children can ask deep questions and find beautiful answers as well. This is a stress-free environment of learning and they are not exposed to all the ills of the technologically driven world in media, smartphones and the internet.

⚜ **Soothing effect:** All of these things that are available in nature have a calming effect on us all. Your child/children can all sit back, relax and reflect on their lives and their goals when they are out in nature experiencing and appreciating the free gifts that they enjoy. This does a world of good for their emotional wellbeing and they go back home feeling more appreciative and feeling more gratitude for their lives and for the fact that your child/children could experience these things.

⚜ **Feeling free:** Nature can feel so liberating and if you embrace it, you can feel like you have no worries in the world. Children benefit immensely from this as they can easily disconnect from their day to day troubles and frustrations and focus on the relaxing time before them.

💎 SOCIAL BENEFITS

- **Enjoying the outdoors:** The great outdoors is a wide expanse of possibilities where one can interact, get together and relate with your child/children's friends, and loved ones. There are so many activities they can engage in that brings them all together like camping, picnicking and a host of other outdoor activities. This fosters a healthy pattern of relationship amongst all the members of the community and your child/children, and the other people will get to know each other in a relaxing and conducive environment.

- **Develop appreciation nature:** All of these things, your child/children can find when they spend time with nature. Sunlight, green vegetation, birds, butterflies and natural air. When they enjoy their time out, they get a better sense of appreciation for nature and they are more motivated to even do what they can to protect the environment.

💎 PHYSICAL BENEFITS

- **Exercise:** When your child/children explore nature, they will be doing a lot of walking, running and even climbing. This is a good exercise for their general wellbeing. It's a lot better than just laying around the house watching TV, playing with smartphones and eating junk food. We can all engage in healthier activity when we are out of the house and enjoying the gifts of nature.

- **Healthy growth of the body:** With nature comes a good amount of oxygen, a good amount of vitamin D with the early morning sun and a healthy habit of exercise. This engagement will help your child/children grow a lot healthier.

CONCLUSION:

There is so much to benefit from nature. The best things in life are free and we should take full advantage of all it has to offer. However, you must be careful to supervise your children when they are outdoors. There are also a lot of dangerous things out there that they must be protected from. Their curiosity levels are much heightened and they might throw caution to the wind in pursuit of thrills. So, keep this in mind.

PRACTICAL STEPS CHILDREN CAN TAKE TO ENJOY THE FREE THINGS AROUND: SUN, FLOWERS, PARKS, NATURE, AND WILD ANIMALS

Spending some time in nature can help your children experience reliefs after staring at a screen or being stuck inside all day. Nowadays, children spend a lot of time indoors watching movies and playing games that they often miss out on the free gifts of nature. There are a lot of things your children can enjoy absolutely for free: sun, nature, wild animals, flowers and parks. In this section, I am going to discuss how your children can enjoy these things and become better as a result.

❶ EXERCISING OUTSIDE

When your children exercise outside, they will notice a lot of small things. This is one of the simplest ways that children can enjoy nature. They do not have to go far to enjoy nature. They can go for a simple walk or run in the neighbourhood. The most important thing is that as they take their time in nature, they will notice the trees, animals and plants.

❷ RIDING THE BIKE

When going to the grocery store, they can ride the bike instead of running or walking. However, it is important that they wear protective gears and ride in a neighbourhood where they are familiar. Not only will they enjoy the weather as they ride, they will also be able to get some exercise.

❸ GOING FOR A HIKE

Many children have never been on the hill or seen a mountain. They will be amazed at the wonder of nature when they stand on one of the hilltops. Your children do not have to go to the Kilimanjaro in Africa before they can hike. There are a lot of places around where they can hike—parks, nature preserves, and trails. Hiking is an excellent opportunity for your children to experience different landscapes and see some animals as well. In addition, uphill climbing is a good exercise for children.

4 DOCUMENTING NATURE

They do not need to have the latest Canon camera to take pictures of the beautiful nature around. A simple smartphone will do the job. When your children begin to take pictures of the nature around them, they will begin to notice the unusual colours, shapes of the moon and the positioning of the sun. In addition, they will be able to find some unusual animals. One of the best places where they can find great plants and animals to snap is at a botanical garden. They can also visit a nature preserve to be able to appreciate nature even more.

Your children will find an enormous serenity in nature. Indeed, there are a lot of things to enjoy in nature. Nature gives them the immense opportunity to notice the positioning of the sun, of the moon and several other natural bodies.

 **Habit** Six

ENJOY THE GOOD MUSIC.

WHY IS IT IMPORTANT?

Studies have shown how much of an impact music can have on us and our physiology. It can inspire us to greater things. It also has a positive effect on our mental and emotional wellbeing in general. Music has a lot of good to offer and your child/children will gain a lot from listening to the right kind of music. Not all music is great so you have to carefully curate what they listen to. Although it is entirely subjective to the kind of music we love, you should try to keep your children away from senseless and meaningless music. Exposing your child at an early age to good music will give your child a natural antidote to most circumstances they may find themselves at different points in their life.

Music brings joy and it is an emotional boost. It lifts the mood and the spirits. Research has shown that music can trigger the brain to release small doses of dopamine which is the feel-good hormone. When your child listens to music she/he likes, they can overcome boredom, depression, sadness and you see them vibrant and happy all the time.

BENEFITS:

💎 INTELLECTUAL BENEFITS

● **Study music:** There is a genre of music that aids study. And studies have shown that certain people perform and study better when they have some kind of music playing in the background. This category of music will be soothing and have a calming effect on the body in general.

● **Expression of art:** Music comes with inspiration and your child/children will a lot of art inspired by music. Countless musicians owe their art to their love of a particular artist or instrument and they pass this love to give your child/children priceless art in various forms which goes on to inspire them to follow suit.

💎 EMOTIONAL BENEFITS

● **Dopamine:** As we have mentioned above, music can trigger the brain to release a neurotransmitter known as dopamine into the system. This hormone is known for its feel-good effect and it makes your child/children happy, excited and optimistic. This gives them emotional balance in times when they can easily be knocked off your rhythm.

● **Healing:** Music can also help your children in their healing. The right kind of music can transport your children to a different realm where it allows their heart and their mind recover from the effects of their loss. Music has been used in various forms of therapy and it has achieved great success toward healing.

💎 SOCIAL BENEFITS

● **Parties:** No party is good to go without good music. This is something children all know. Music brings life to the party. Children respond very well to music.

● **Concerts:** Music has a way of bringing children all together and uniting them. No matter what their fundamental differences are, when your children love the same music with the people around them, they can easily put aside those differences and get together to have fun and experience the music they love.

● **Having company:** Your children can get together to talk about the music and the musicians they love. They can exchange records and mp3 files and explore the internet for more of the same kind of music that has brought them together. This way, they get to spend time with each other enjoying something that they all have in common.

💎 PHYSICAL BENEFITS

● **Chores:** Music offers a means of distraction when you are engaged in chores. A lot of people like to listen to music during these times because it motivates them and puts them in the mood to stick with the routine of household chores, and sometimes even at work.

* **Releasing Serotonin, Dopamine, Endorphin:** Music will trigger the release of these hormones in your children's bodies and this will help them feel good about themselves. If for nothing else, at least you can be confident they are not being depressed and sad about life when they actively listen to fun music.

CONCLUSION:

The importance of good music can never be overstated. Music has an impact on every one of us to certain varying degrees. But it is very important you ensure that your child listens to good beneficial music. There is music out there that just encourages bad behaviour and violence, and children have to be careful not to expose themselves to this form of entertainment.

PRACTICAL STEPS CHILDREN CAN TAKE TO ENJOY GOOD MUSIC.

First, the concept of good music is subjective. Depending on culture, civilization and moral, the choice of a good music varies. In a world filled with all genres of music, finding a good music can be a bit challenging. Luckily, if the right approach is taken, it's fairly easy for children to find a good song to listen to when they are at home or outside the home. The first step will require narrowing down the search results. Then, they can focus their searches in strategic ways. Finally, they can also choose the best music site to look for good songs to listen too.

1. FOCUSING ON SEARCH RESULTS

There are several categories of music. Examples of music genres include rock 'n' roll, bluegrass, and rap. Children often have a wide range of musical tastes and finds it hard to find a specific genre that they love the most. This is especially true if they are growing up in a mixed-culture environment. There are simple ways that they can apply to narrow down their search results. The easiest way is for them to scroll through their iTunes library or any other musical library that they have. They can look for their favourite songs and check what genres they fall into. Ideally, they will want to choose about two to three genres.

2. SEARCHING FOR MUSIC WITH CERTAIN INSTRUMENTS

Some music has the feel-good effect because of their instrumentals. Many hip hop and rap songs rely heavily on their instrumentals. A good music often has a strong bass line (bass guitar), a guitar solo (electric/acoustic guitar), or maybe a trumpet playing in the background. Whatever it may be, they should write down some of the instruments they particularly like. They might even want to go through their entire music download library to see what instruments occur the most.

3. CHOOSING THEIR FAVOURITE ARTISTS

This is perhaps another easy way for children to identify a good music. Once they are able to find one good musician, chances are that the musician is going to produce more good songs. An easy way for them to identify their favourite musicians is to check their playlist and see how many times an artist appears. Then, they can check the search engine to look for the other songs that they have probably never heard before. The good thing about checking up these artists is that it gives the children the opportunity to see other artists that are similar.

In addition, they can choose subject matters that impresses them. For instance, fun, holiday and Christmas songs are good subject matters for children.

Songs are really beautiful. They make children fun to be with and also give them expression for their innermost emotions and experiences. Some songs help them to appreciate special holidays, and others help them to build beautiful memories of their childhood.

 **Habit** Seven

HAVING A GOOD DINNER WITH THE WHOLE FAMILY.

WHY IS IT IMPORTANT?

Family time is quality time and it is always priceless. There is really no point to existence if you don't have loved ones to share your time and accomplishments with. In today's world where everybody is working crazy hours to ensure that their family is comfortable with a roof over their head and food to eat, it is increasingly difficult to get everybody together to just have a good time.

Family dinners are an excellent way to get everybody together on the dining table and have a good meal with good conversations that will help you and your child/children get to know each other a little more. Dinner generally fits into everybody's schedule because parents will be at home from work, children will be back from school and you can all sit together and enjoy yourselves. This is a wonderful opportunity to ask questions about your child/children's lives and know what is going on with them. They can also talk to you about the things they are bothered about and ask you questions on issues that they need more clarification on. This fosters unity in the family and everybody will be happy.

BENEFITS:

💎 INTELLECTUAL BENEFITS

Tapping wisdom: There is a lot your child/children can learn from you and they won't really communicate with you if they don't get to spend adequate time with you. Family dinner is an excellent opportunity for them to ask you questions on any subject they need guidance on. You get to impart the knowledge and wisdom you have on them to help them solve and navigate the issues that they are dealing with.

💎 EMOTIONAL BENEFITS

Bonding: Having dinner together help child/children to bond better with the family. Family bonding is a powerful way to support each other in times of need, times of fortune and times of challenges. Children need all the emotional support they can get from their families. Family dinner gives children the opportunity to talk to other family members.

Feeling loved: Children learn love mostly by how much time you spend with them, and very little on how many gifts or how much money you spend on them. Family time is very precious and valuable to them as you are the only people in the world that they completely trust. They will always feel loved if you spend this dinner with them because they will be able to have access to your thoughts.

Feeling enough: When you spend time with your child/children and they feel loved, they learn to feel like they are enough and worthy. They do not have any self-esteem issues and doubts in their minds about how cherished they are to you, and so it is important that you continue to reinforce this belief in them.

💎 SOCIAL BENEFITS

Learn conversations: There are conversational skills that your child/children can learn from the dinner table that they can adapt to their interactions outside the house. They can also learn etiquettes that will help them become better in similar situations in public. This gives them the confidence to be in social gatherings and interact perfectly with people.

Learning good manners for table eating: There are so much table manners that your child/children can learn from you at the dinner table which they otherwise would have been ignorant of if you didn't have family dinners. They learn how best to present themselves when eating in the company of others and how to hold proper table conversations.

💎 COMMUNICATION BENEFITS

● **Interactions:** The above-named benefits under social benefits are also valuable communication benefits that will serve your child/children in a number of occasions. They are more comfortable on dates when growing up, picnic get together and lunch breaks at school. Your children will become better members of the community and they bring value to any gathering they find themselves.

● **Promote language development:** Your child/children will learn how best to relate with people, what terminology is appropriate and which ones are bad language. This skill will help them deal with people in the right manner when they are out in public.

💎 PHYSICAL BENEFITS

● **Great for digestive system:** When your child/children eat together as a family, you can better supervise how and what they consume, and this will be very beneficial for their digestion and nutrition. Moreover, there will be a great intimacy between you and your child/children that really counts.

CONCLUSION:

Family time is priceless and it cannot be overstated how important it is that you all spend some time together. Dinners are a great way to spend time together and are conversant with everything going on in each other's lives.

PRACTICAL STEPS CHILDREN CAN TAKE TO EAT A GOOD DINNER TOGETHER WITH THE WHOLE FAMILY

With today's busy schedules, many families eat separately. However, this is not good for your children. They need sufficient family time to bond so as to get to know more about the family's culture. Dinner time is a perfect time for your children to spend reconnecting with the family members. Dinnertime can be an incredibly beneficial family ritual for your children. Rituals are family routines that expresses your family's values - anything with a symbolic or expressive nature. Here are a few tips to help your children to eat a good dinner together with the whole family.

1. SETTING A TIME FOR THE FAMILY DINNER

A routine as special as family dinner must not be left to chance. It must be planned and worked toward. The setting of the family dinner must be in such a way that children are excited toward its build up like they would for any special holiday season like Christmas or Thanksgiving. When scheduling the time for the family dinner, all family members' schedule must be put into consideration. It must be set at a time when everyone will be available.

2. ASSIGNING EACH CHILD A TASK

Children are more likely to participate in an activity where they feel responsible for. By assigning a task to each child, they will be excited about its success. When a family works together preparing the meals, everyone is more willing to sit down and enjoy it together. It is important that tasks involving hot, sharp and fragile objects should not be out in the care of children. Instead, your younger children can take items to the table like salad dressing, ketchup, and bread/rolls. The older children can peel vegetables, and mix the beverages.

3 SAYING A BLESSING OR GIVING A TOAST

If your family is not religious, you can give a toast. The importance of saying the grace or giving a toast before dinner is to set a positive atmosphere for the family during dinner. For instance, grace is an expression of gratitude for the food. When appreciation is expressed at the beginning of the dinner, the children are excited, positive and optimistic for what the evening will bring.

4 THINKING ABOUT THE THINGS THAT CHILDREN CAN EXPRESS

Your children can find a whole lot of things that they can talk about. For instance, they can talk about their day, such as "This is delicious food"; "We all feel good"; "I had a great playdate today"; "Daddy gets to be home with us tonight"; "My cold is gone"; etc.

When children talk about their day, they will be able to talk about other things. The whole point is that they should get started talking. Otherwise, it is going to be a boring and forgettable evening.

Dinnertimes are excellent times for children to experience family bonding. If the family is experiencing challenges, dinnertimes are a great time where your children can learn about what is happening in the family and how they are expected to embrace the situation in other not to be emotionally drained. Indeed, if done properly, dinnertimes may be an essential part of your family.

 **Habit** Eight

WORK ON THE APPRECIATION OF NATURE.

WHY IS IT IMPORTANT?

As parents, we all want our child/children to be happy and healthy. With this in mind, we try to engage our children in beneficial activities that will add to their well-being physically and mentally. The aim is to help them develop lifelong skills that will help them at various points in their lives. It is not enough for your children to have healthy meals and engage in certain physical activities like exercise, dancing or martial arts. It is a good start but there is still something spectacular missing. You also need to teach them how to better appreciate life for what it is and one of the best ways to achieve this is to introduce them to nature. When your child/children is able to connect to nature and be in tune or in sync with it, he or she is on a path to a life of happiness, joy, appreciation and marvel.

By observing nature and actively engaging it, children can experience a dynamic free-flowing environment that will further stimulate all of their senses.

BENEFITS:

💎 INTELLECTUAL BENEFITS

- **Learn about nature:** Nature holds a lot of secrets and it can be quite fun learning about them. No knowledge is wasted and the knowledge your child/children acquire from interacting with nature will surely serve them at one point or the other.

- **Inspirational:** Nature can inspire all of us into a wide variety of things. Nature inspires art and it is nice for your child/children to realise how much power resides in nature at their young ages so they can continue to engage with it as they continue grow up.

● **Great imagination:** Nature holds a limitless potential for imagination and when your child/children learn to appreciate nature, they can begin to see a different world that surrounds them, and critically imagine all of the possibilities and potentials held by nature.

● **Promote writing:** Nature is inspiring and for your child/children that have the knack to write, there is so much inspiration that can be gotten from being out in nature. Asides from drawing inspiration, they also get to have a clear mind where they can better focus on their art.

💎 EMOTIONAL BENEFITS

● **Feel good factor:** : It is fun being outside with nature and your child/children are free to explore and play around nature with your supervision. This helps them build on their confidence and self-expression as they lose their inner inhibitions. Children love jumping and running around, and this might not be ideal inside the home. Going outside to be with nature allows them to enjoy themselves in this manner.

● **Soothing and Calming effect:** Research has shown that nature has a lot of calming effect on people and this is even more beneficial to children with attention-deficit/hyperactivity disorder. There is a sense of peace that nature offers you and this has an overall calming and soothing effect on the body.

💎 SOCIAL BENEFITS

● **Being with friends:** Depending on the event, your child/children can hang out in picnics, camps and other activities to experience nature and bond with each other. This is where they get to learn about each other and become supportive of each other. In nature, you find children working together to make up games with their own rules and they can just have fun being with each other.

● **Empathy and interactions:** When your child/children are playing around in nature, they tend to learn to slow down and be more cautious and gentler when dealing with their surroundings, and some of the animals they might encounter. They also learn to have empathy toward their fellow friends and other life forms as well.

- **Learn to appreciate the beauty of life:** You cannot appreciate the beauty that you have not been exposed to. When your child/children go out in nature, they observe and appreciate the beauty in all of the life that surrounds them and they start to better appreciate all of the patterns, flow, beauty and life around them. They will also be better committed to protecting the environment as they will see how beautiful it can be.

PHYSICAL BENEFITS

- **Healthy living:** It can be relaxing and also invigorating to spend some time with nature, and all of the physical activity that your child/children will engage in will typically be beneficial to them. They get to spend time under the sun and get vitamin D which contributes to their immune system. They also get to burn calories playing outside with nature as opposed to just sitting at home all day watching TV.

- **Oxygen intake:** When your child/children visit green spaces and parks, there is typically a lot more oxygen in those areas than you'd have in confined spaces at home or at busy public places. This is generally healthier and children need to be able to enjoy such atmosphere.

CONCLUSION:

Nature holds a lot of secrets and it is an open field for exploration by a curious mind. Children have it inherent in them to ask questions and seek answers, and nature offers them so much opportunity for discovery, creativity and interaction which exposes them to a lot of learning.

PRACTICAL STEPS TO GET YOUR CHILDREN TO APPRECIATE NATURE

Children no longer go to the park for a walk. They find comfort in the sitting room where they can watch the latest Disney films. As a parent who has understood the abovementioned benefits of appreciating nature, you may most likely want to help children that you know, such as foster children, nephews, grandchildren, nieces, as well as your own children on why they must love nature while outlining the benefits. If you'd like to know how your children can begin to appreciate nature, keep reading this section.

1. BE A GOOD ROLE MODEL.

Children learn more through association than through instructions. If you want your children to show appreciation for nature, you have to show love for nature yourself. If you are not a nature lover, you do not have to be overwhelmed by the thought of it. You can start with simple steps like reading a book about nature, going to a local museum or enrolling in an educational program. Your children will be inspired and would want to show appreciation for nature as well.

2. SPENDING TIME WITH NATURE.

By spending time with nature, your children will broaden their views. They can do this by walking under blossom trees and feel the pink blooms as they fall on their shoulders. They can pick one up and examine its texture in the process.

In addition, they can listen to birds singing in tune all together like a choir of animals. In so doing, it can drive their own curiosity by asking such questions as what they are singing about.

3. APPRECIATING ALL PLANTS

Some plants will naturally drive them bonkers, especially plants that have thorns. Your children need to understand that all plants are truly wonderful. On close examination, they will be intrigued about these weird structures with green stems that draw water and anchor it into the ground, an ovary, stigma and stamen for reproduction, pollen for other creatures, lovely colourful petals to attract insects - along with a filament, style and an ovule!

4. DEVELOPING INTEREST IN THINGS THEY WOULD NORMALLY BE DISGUSTED IN.

Children naturally have a preference for some animals and plants over others. For instance, some may find snails disgusting. Usually, they would just think "Ew!" and walk on by. However, on close examination, they would find out that their shells are fascinating. The gentle spirals and swirls on brown or green shells seem to appear like someone has painted them on a gentle animal.

Nature is filled with beauty and medicine. Medicine for the soul and for the body. When your children begin to spend more time in nature, they will be able to appreciate life even more.

 **Habit** Nine

START THE DAY WITH A HAPPY MOOD.

WHY IS IT IMPORTANT?

When I take a closer look at the children at my preschool, I observed that their mood at the beginning of the day has an overall effect on how they behave for the rest of the day. This applies to children the same way it applies to adults too. You have to start the day on the right foot.

The mood has a very direct relationship with performance and when children start the day with good moods, they tend to do better and behave better throughout that day. They learn faster, they are very interested and they engage in more. Generally, their spirits are just lifted. When they start the day off with a bad mood, they don't pay as much attention and learning is slow, and the overall quality of the day is affected by them.

BENEFITS:

INTELLECTUAL BENEFITS

Problem-solving: Mood has a direct effect on how your child/children operate mentally and consequently affects our problem-solving skills. It is not far-fetched to imagine someone in a bad mood finding it difficult to solve a particular problem because his/her thinking pattern has been completely affected. Research has proven that mood can impact your child/children's cognitive abilities and there are many theories as to why this is the case. But the parents can all agree that when your child/children are in a bad mood, they might find it hard to concentrate and focus on the task at hand.

● **Eager to learn new things:** Children and adults are eager to know more, and they tend to learn more when they feel well and happy. This will add more and more resources daily on the bank of knowledge for your child/children's life benefits in many ways.

💎 EMOTIONAL BENEFITS

● **Inner peace:** When your child/children start the day off with a good mood, there is an accompanying peace that keeps them calm, such that even when new challenges threaten to knock them off balance, they tend to hold their ground firmly and remain in a good mood.

● **No stress:** It is also important that your child/children start the day off in a good mood as this lessens the amount of stress they have to carry. Mood and stress are interlinked, and as such they must both be controlled as much as possible.

💎 SOCIAL BENEFITS

● **All round cheer:** When your child/children are happy, you are happy and the children around them are also happy too. There is enough cheer to go around and this cheer is contagious. When everybody is happy, they can all collaborate and work together to achieve great results during the course of the day.

● **Better interactions:** A happy child is a more relatable child. They relate better to their peers, with their teachers at school and with you at home.

💎 COMMUNICATION BENEFITS

● **Cheerful conversations:** Only people in good moods can communicate effectively and actually be interested in what is being said. When your child/children start their day off with a bad mood, it becomes a chore to talk to people, and those around them easily pick on these thing and tries to avoid them.

💎 PHYSICAL BENEFITS

Hormonal balance: Your child/children mood can be a reflection of the hormones in their system, and when they have a hormonal imbalance, they are very likely to be in a bad mood. Those in good moods will be at peace and will be free of all the stress hormones that can negatively impact their wellbeing.

CONCLUSION:

The manner in which your child/children start their day will affect how the day goes and how it ends. When your child/children starts off on the wrong foot, there is a very high chance that not so much will go their way that day and everything ends up deteriorating afterwards. The key to having a fulfilling and productive day is to start off on the right foot and in a happy mood. If your child/children can achieve that, then they can be unstoppable during the course of the day. A good mood at the beginning of the day can make all the difference to attain happiness.

PRACTICAL STEPS CHILDREN CAN TAKE TO START THE DAY WITH A HAPPY MOOD

For children, everyday can be a new, fresh beginning. By starting off with a happy mood, they can face the challenges of the day in the right frame of the mind. Here are a few tips that your children can follow to start the day with a happy mood.

1. ALLOWING AMPLE TIME TO START THE DAY

When children feel time-pressured, they are unable to stay focused, calm, and positive. To avoid this, they should wake up with enough time to feel relaxed. This may not be fun to do at first, but having even 10 more minutes to do what they need to do in the day can be a real improvement in their mood.

They can wake up slowly with a gentle alarm. Instead of a shocking, loud alarm, they should opt for a gentler wake-up and allow them some time to lay in bed before waking them up.

The alarm could be set at about 10 to 15 minutes before they actually need to get up so they will be no need to rush out of bed.

2 VISUALIZING A POSITIVE DAY

Your children should decide to approach the day with hope and optimism. They can do this by visualizing their day in a positive manner. They may envision themselves doing well on the math test, or doing well in the sport.

Optimism does not mean they will refuse to acknowledge things that do not always go as planned. If there are negative outcomes, they should counteract these thoughts by envisioning themselves overcoming these problems, getting over the disappointment, or simply trying again.

They should avoid beginning the day with "I can't," instead they should start the day off by saying, "I can."

They cannot fully control what happens in the day, but they can decide how they are going to approach the day's challenges. Starting the day off strongly with a positive mindset can help them deal with things in a healthy way.

3 ANTICIPATING THE DAY

Instead of dreading the day before the test or a major presentation, your children can do well by anticipating the day. They should find things to look forward to, even in seemingly ordinary days. This helps them to get off with a happy mood, instead of dragging their feet out of dreadfulness. The best way to do this is to prepare properly the night before. They should make a list of mental things they are looking forward to or intend to accomplish the next day, month or in life.

Starting the day with a happy mood is essential for children if they are going to stay healthy and grow up as responsible adults. There are sufficient things to worry about, but by embracing what the day brings, they are in an advantageous position to achieve greatness.

 **Habit** Ten

CELEBRATE GOOD BEHAVIOUR, AND ACHIEVEMENTS

WHY IS IT IMPORTANT?

Your child/children needs to be celebrated at all times. You must always stand by them during hard times when things aren't going smoothly in their lives as they'd like, and you must cheer them up when they are making strides and great achievements. This reminds your child that there are people in his corner that are rooting for him, which will spur him to do more in achieving greater heights. As parents, we must learn to celebrate our children's achievements no matter how small they might seem to us as this will make them understand the value of achievement and give them a sense of belonging in the family and in the society at large.

When children learn to acknowledge and celebrate their achievements, they are further motivated to do more and they keep their minds set on the goals. There are so many important things in life and things like learning, growing, loving and discovery is high on that list. Without celebration, all of these things will quickly lose meaning and relevance.

Your successes and lessons learned from your failures, your achievements and the celebrations provide you with the platform to move forward in life and attain happiness and fulfilment. So, take a time out to be grateful for where you are in life and celebrate.

BENEFITS:

💎 INTELLECTUAL BENEFITS

Identifying your strengths: When they take stock of what they do well and the achievements that follow, they can easily identify the things they are good at, and continue to build on them positively. This leads to continuous improvements and more achievements which continues to reinforce their winning mentality.

- **Get more study, and work done:** When they celebrate the milestones that they achieve from school and their academic work, they will be spurred to do more study and achieve a lot more at school. This is a healthy cycle of encouragement and achievement coupled with diligence.

- **Higher focus:** Your child/children will also learn to focus more on the better aspects of their behaviour, and try to avoid the things that do not get them any celebrations or encouragement. This way they will always be on their best behaviour and will try as much as possible to impress you against all odds.

EMOTIONAL BENEFITS

- **Timeouts:** Celebrations will allow your child/children to take a step back and appreciate the things that are going on well in their lives. It is a source of excitement outside of the routines and mundanity of life. Your child/children use these instances as an opportunity to be with friends and family that they love a lot and these are very good times to get rid of the stress he/she might be carrying and we can recalibrate and be re-energised.

Even if it doesn't feel like your child/children have achieved so much, just take some time out and reward them for all of the efforts they have put in so far in attaining their goals and push themselves to keep at it.

- **Feeling proud of self:** Celebration brings to your child/children a sense of achievement, recognition and identity. These lead to the feeling of being proud of themselves which is an important element of success later.

SOCIAL BENEFITS

- **Purpose driven life:** We need to constantly ask ourselves what really is most important to us as we move along in our life's journey. When we celebrate our achievements, we are poised to live life with purpose and set targets that we intend to fully pursue and celebrate. The same goes for your child/children. When we celebrate their achievements, they are motivated to live a goal-oriented life. When they live life with purpose, they will find meaning and ultimate happiness.

- **Greater commitment to self and others:** When you constantly encourage your child/children to be better human beings, they are better committed to making everybody around them happy and satisfied with their actions, and this inevitably also makes them happy about themselves. This teaches them commitment and accountability to the society.

- **Being happy:** Celebrations allow your child/children to relax and unwind possibilities in the midst of their everyday routine lives. These celebrations also strengthen the bonds they share with their friends of different backgrounds.

PHYSICAL BENEFITS

- **Release stress:** When children celebrate, they allow the stresses of life to fall behind them, and spend time doing things they love the most with the people they love. In the course of these celebrations, they engage in different physical activities which are fun and relaxing.

CONCLUSION:

In conclusion, wherever there is an effort, there is bound to be results and achievements and they must do their best to reward these achievements by celebrating them. This will fuel their continued dedication and commitment to living a purpose driven life.

PRACTICAL STEPS TO CELEBRATE GOOD BEHAVIOUR IN CHILDREN

When your child acts appropriately, or does something right, you may want to encourage them. If their actions are reinforced with a positive reaction from their parents, the children also reinforces their good habits and do well. To celebrate good behaviour, parents can use material rewards and social rewards. In addition, you can also use verbal praise to reinforce their behaviour and show your approval.

1 USING SOCIAL REWARDS

Children are social beings, and they respond well to feelings of affection such as arm or shoulder, a high five, a pat on the back, or a big smile. In addition, you can display other forms of affection, like kisses or hugs. One of the benefits of using affection to celebrate a good behaviour is that it is immediate and free. This implies that you can use it immediately to reward your children as soon as they do something good. By displaying affection for your children, it makes them comfortable to display affection in public and toward others.

In addition, you can display social affection for your children by spending extra time with them. This could be an additional five to ten minutes of reading time before bed, or extra time together after school doing an activity your child enjoys, such as playing a certain board game. Using quality time as a form of reward can also allow you to create stronger social bonds with your child.

2 GIVING OUT MATERIAL REWARDS

Children like material gifts. There are many ways you can materially reward your children. You can allow them to choose a special meal. To take it further, you can as well decide to enjoy this meal with them. There is a huge sense of responsibility that comes from having them choose their favourite meal. Although, you can use food to reward your children, but it is advised that you use it sparingly. This is to prevent your children from developing an unhealthy relationship with food. Often times, verbal praise and social rewards can be healthier and more effective for your children than material rewards, like food.

3 USING VERBAL PRAISE

Instead of using standard words of praise like "Good boy/good girl!" or "That's right!" you should try to get your child to evaluate themselves and their skills when you praise them.

For instance, you may say, "I'm happy you did that, you look pleased with yourself!" or "You look like you enjoyed that."

This will encourage your child to think about their own decisions and actions, rather than constantly seek your validation or approval. Also, it will help them to be empowered and see good behaviour as a positive way to act.

In addition, you can also ask your child series of questions as a form of praise. This also helps them to self-evaluate. For instance, you may ask, "Are you happy with how that piece fits into the game?"

The whole point is that you should try to encourage your child to reflect on their decisions and choices. This will greatly help to build your child's self-esteem, and also strengthen your relationship with them.

Habit Eleven
READ GOOD BOOKS.

WHY IS IT IMPORTANT?

The importance of reading can never be overstated. In today's society, children can't do without reading and it is important that you instil the culture of reading in your child/children as they are growing up. You have adults today who cannot even read the instructions on a prescription bottle, and this is heartbreaking. Outside of the direct importance of reading, there are also underlying benefits to reading.

When children take up the habit of reading, they transport themselves to different places depending on the nature, and genre of the book being read, and they get to learn new things, and live vicariously through the experiences of others. The value of this cannot be overemphasized. It is very important that both parents and their children engage in this activity of finding great books to read and actually seeing it through collectively.

BENEFITS:

INTELLECTUAL BENEFITS

- **Developing the mind:** The mind behaves like a muscle, and it can develop itself with continuous stimulation which your child/children can get from reading good books. See it as a sort of mental work out equivalent to what we get with body workouts. When young people learn to read and read good books, they get to develop their mind in various areas such as language, structure and disciplines.

- **Become better at listening:** Those with knowledge tend to listen more and speak less. A lot of people want to talk, but they have very little meaningful things to say. When your children read enough good books, they are hungry for more knowledge and information and this helps them become better listeners anywhere they find themselves.

● **Reading makes your child smatter:** Books are a wealth of information and knowledge, and your child/children will learn a lot from them especially when they read very good and inspirational ones. Books offer a cheaper alternative to actually taking a course on a subject, and you have the opportunity to take in a bunch of research delivered in a manner that you should understand in a relatively short period of time.

● **Improve spelling:** As students read more books, they automatically improve and close loopholes in their spelling and vocabulary. This is a given. They get to see all the different forms in which words can be used and all of the different contexts. They are no longer just new words, but words with meaning.

● **Built up concentration:** Reading books helps your child/children to improve their focus. The activity of reading is one that requires them to be entirely focused on the text at hand, and when this is a regular habit, they find this skill spilling into other areas and aspects of their lives.

● **Sharp mind:** Knowledge is power, and it will make you and your child/children a lot sharper. Reading is like the equivalent of a work out for the mind and with more and more information being processed by the mind through reading, the sharper and quicker it is.

● **Having great imagination:** In books, your child/children are able to live vicariously through the experiences and imaginations of others. Children especially, have a curious mind and an expansive imagination, and you can help stoke their fires of imagination by exposing them to a lot of inspiring and motivational books.

💎 EMOTIONAL BENEFITS

● **Improved self-esteem:** When your child/children read books and become aware of so many issues that ordinary people express in the writing. It helps to boost their self-esteem and they come to terms and accept themselves for what they are, now that they know they are not alone in their insecurities. People who don't read often do not know much about what people around them feel and experience, and so they estimate themselves based off of the façade that is on display on a day to day basis, and this can lead to low self-esteem on the long run.

◆ **Develop empathy:** We can learn about the lives of others through concise reading. And this is especially good for your child/children because they might not have necessarily met so many people in their lives or experienced so many things, but through utile information and ideas from books, they can better understand what people from all over the world are going through.

💎 SOCIAL BENEFITS

◆ **Be versed on topics:** Although, you don't automatically become better at expressing yourself after reading a bunch of books, you do become more versed on topics, and you can confidently contribute to more varieties of discussions. Children too can contribute to discussions at their peer level on different stories and subjects that may arise when they are well read and they are exposed to vast topics. This makes them better at making friends and more outspoken both at home and in public.

◆ **Connect with different people with different topics:** When your child/children read and gather useful information on various subjects, topics and stories, they can better relate and connect with people who have also read those same books. This fosters a sense of community and belonging when we all have something in common that we can sit and talk about.

💎 PHYSICAL BENEFITS

◆ **Activities:** When your child/children read a book, it stimulates their creative side and reasoning, and they often start thinking about the stories they have read, and go on to engage in series of activities, such as drawing scenes which they imagined from the book, discuss them with their friends and even acting them out in mini plays. Anything just to relive the stories they have read.

◆ **Stress reduction:** Studies from the University of Sussex have shown that reading reduces stress. From the study, you need to only read for a few minutes of up to 6 minutes, and signs of stress decline can be easily measured, such as a drop in heart rate, and ease of tension in the muscles. This is partly due to the transporting effect of reading where your child/children feel like they are in a different world.

CONCLUSION:

Reading is very important for both adults and children of all ages, and there are so many other benefits outside of the few that have been mentioned above. Your child/children always go right with a good book!

PRACTICAL STEPS CHILDREN CAN TAKE TO READ GOOD BOOKS

Thousands of books are being produced annually. There is so much that your children can read about. Out of this huge publication of books, few are worth reading. In this guide, I will show how your children can begin to start reading good books.

1. DECIDING WHAT MAKES A BOOK GOOD

There are fictions, non-fiction, adventures, horror, romance, biographies, or tinkering books such as craft or how-to manuals. Children who are in their tender age should abstain from reading books on romance. Apart from the moral implication, such books have no benefit for them as kids.

2. ASKING FRIENDS AND FAMILY MEMBERS FOR BOOKS AND BOOK SUGGESTIONS

This is a great way for your children to build their knowledge and expand their scope about interesting books. Oftentimes, the reasons given by a person who is explaining why a book matters to them will inspire them to want to read it too. Also, by getting book gifts from friends and family members, they are able to build a huge library in less time.

3) READING

This is an essential aspect of developing a reading habit. There is no point in gathering an amazing collection of books if they are not going to read them through. The best way for children to start a new book is to be fully concentrated into it. This implies that there are no distractions, no interruptions, and full attention is needed.

This is because, the beginning of a book is always the best part of the book. It introduces the reader to the characters and the content of the book, as well as the key storyline/plot of the book. This is the most vital information that children need to know about the story.

When reading, they should avoid having a long time in-between the complete reading of a book. Long-time periods may lead to a loss of interest. Therefore, the book should be read frequently.

4) FINISHING THE BOOK

This is an essential aspect of reading a book. Many children start a book, but do not finish them. This is not quite a good reading habit for a child to develop. Books are meant to be read and completed. Once they are completed, they can be returned to the library. It's very important that books borrowed from the library have to be returned in their due dates, otherwise, there may be a fine; even though, it is small.

5) WALKING WITH BOOKS

To make reading easier, your children should have a book handy always. This will help them to read often. In the subway and while waiting in the line, they can easily bring out their books and read. It is an excellent way to utilize and maximize their free time.

Reading good books will illuminate their minds, give them a broadened worldview and make them more exciting to be with.

 **Habit** Twelve

HAVING A MUSIC BACKGROUND FOR STUDYING AND WORKS.

WHY IS IT IMPORTANT?

Music has a lot of positive effects on both children and adults, and studies have shown that they can aid effective and more enjoyable study sessions. You have to consider the fact that there are various genres with different sounds. Therefore, this is entirely subjective depending on the type of student in question. Some kind of music or melody, however, has been found to make your child/children calmer and help them focus more in the course of studying. These kinds of music will help your child/children when they are trying to fully concentrate on a subject.

Music has been found to improve memory, focus attention on the task at hand, and keep your child/children active.

BENEFITS:

◆ INTELLECTUAL BENEFITS

- **Improved focus:** When there is music playing in the background, it will help to increase your child/children's focus and keep them active in the time they need to be. It can be a good source of motivation by lifting their mood and spirits. This applies to the young ones most especially. Music can also help your child/children stick to a prolonged task or a marathon study session, thus improving their endurance levels.

- **Improves creativity:** When studying subjects under art and even maths, music can put your child/children in a very creative mood where they just seem to flow with ideas inspired by their mood. It is perhaps a lot easier to study math with music playing in the background compared to other science subjects. Fortunately, creativity is a genuine skill that will also serve your child/children when they are trying to solve a math problem.

- **Help retain information easily:** Some studies have shown that music helps your child/children with long-term memory, and this is an advantage for them when they are studying a subject, and they want to memorize, or retain the information presented to them for a very long time.

- **Speed up the pace of work:** Music also has an effective way of putting your child/children's mind in the here and now without affecting their intellectual output, and if at the time they are totally focused on the work at hand, they tend to achieve their results a lot faster.

EMOTIONAL BENEFITS

- **Help control the mood:** Music mostly is created to put your child/children in a certain mood. That mood can be hyper, happy, sad, excited or whatever depending on the artist. So, when your child/children find the appropriate music to put them in that mood in favour of their study session, they can remain in that mood for the duration and even more.

- **Stress management:** Music that is soothing and relaxing will help your child/children as students to easily beat stress or anxiety while studying.

- **Getting thrive:** Young children thrive with music playing in the background. They will be happy and lively. Music also brings the calmness and good behaviours for them.

SOCIAL BENEFITS

- **Stress management:** Sometimes, our social life revolves around how well your child/children manage stress, and having to study under unconducive conditions can actually add to their stress on a daily basis. So, when they find ways to cope with otherwise stressful situations like studying, they find themselves being able to better manage their stress, and this ripples into the way they interact with friends and loved ones.

💎 PHYSICAL BENEFITS

⦿ Energy and Motivation: Music can have some subtle influence on your child/children systems, and it engages their autonomic nervous system which means that it has some control over their physiological functions. The right kind of music can have an effect on your child/children pulse, blood rate, breathing and all of this sums up to put them in the desired or intended mood for any activity. It also distracts your child/children from the boredom and fatigue that comes with prolonged study sessions.

⦿ Being more motivated: When your child/children also listen to their desired genre of music when they are engaged in a tasking physical activity, they tend to be more motivated and their body sets itself up to rise to the challenge. These effects can be heavily felt the moment the music your child/children are listening to resonates with them.

CONCLUSION:

Music is therapeutic, and it does wonders for the mind. It can help your child/children focus a lot better on whatever task they are doing at that particular time and this will yield better results.

PRACTICAL STEPS CHILDREN CAN TAKE TO USE MUSIC AS BACKGROUND WHEN STUDYING AND WORKING

Music has a way of making children get better at whatever they do. It permeates through every corner of their being, and fills up the environment with positive energy. It can also make them feel relaxed, feel alive and more intelligent. However, many children find it very hard to stay productive when there is a background music. In this section, I am going to show you how your children can profit from studying and working with a background music.

1. KNOWING WHEN TO USE BACKGROUND MUSIC

At this point, it must be emphasized that certain music worsen productivity. In fact, several studies have shown that popular music interferes with children's reading and comprehension. Based on those studies, it is important that your children choose the right kind of music when studying and working. Here are a few guidelines when choosing a type of background music:

- **Music without lyrics.**
  If your children have to shift back and forth while studying and reading, it is called multitasking. And multitasking is really counterproductive. Music with lyrics often affects concentration. This is because lyrics forces the children to focus on the message of the song, and interrupt their train of thought.

- **Songs with simple musical structure**
  "You're The Voice' by John Farnham is a classical Australian song.

- **Listening habits**
  If your children haven't been listening to music while engaging in a productive work, it may be counterproductive for them to start right now. However, through simple integration, they can be able to start enjoying their studies and works while listening to music.

- **Difficulty of task**
  Tasks that require a high level of concentration may not necessarily require a background music. For tasks like this, music can make it more difficult for children to work efficiently.

② CHOOSING A BACKGROUND MUSIC

There are several genres of music. Not all of them are ideal for studying and working. Your children will find these types of music more appealing and better for productive activities:

- **Nature music**

    Studies have clearly shown that when children listen to sounds of nature, they tend to experience an enhanced cognitive function and concentration. Nature sounds are soothing to the soul, and they include rustling leaves, flowing water and rainfall. Jarring nature sounds like animal noises and birdcalls should be avoided.

- **Classical music**

    Several research works have established the soothing effect of classical music. They increase concentration, and improve children's mood. Classical music composers include Vivaldi, Bach, and Handel. Your children can start with Vivaldi's quick-tempo "Four Seasons."

- **Epic music**

    When children listen to epic music, they feel like supermen. They feel like they are about to change the world. Epic music drives purpose and passion into children's activities. It brings aliveness to their tasks, and it gives them a boost of motivation.

- **Video game music**

    Your children are already used to video games. By playing video games in the background, they are able to have a virtual experience of overcoming various obstacles and accomplishing progress.

Having a background music will help them to have a better experience when working or studying.

Habit Thirteen
APPRECIATE AND LOOK UP TO GREAT PERSONS.

WHY IS IT IMPORTANT?

Mentorship is something that we all need in our lives. Some people are fortunate enough to be in close proximity of the people they would classify as their mentors, and some are even most fortunate to be receiving active mentorship from these people. All in all, it is very vital to have people who you look up to and people who inspire you to become a force to reckon with in life.

As parents, you have a two-fold task. One is being a wonderful parent to your child/children, and being there for them such that they look up to you as the first great person they know in their life. Another side of this task is to help them know a lot about wonderful personalities who will serve as a source of inspiration for them, and people to follow in their footsteps.

When children appreciate and look up to certain persons, they can easily strive to be like them, and do what is necessary to achieve some of the things they will be proud to show as an accomplishment to these people. You have to guide them in the right direction here.

BENEFITS:

INTELLECTUAL BENEFITS

Guidance: When your child/children have mentors, they get professional guidance on what they need to be doing in order to be better at whatever it is that they do. A mentor or a guide will show your child/children the right path which they must take to be successful at what they're doing, and show them everything that they must avoid. This helps them focus their minds and their brains and other resources toward the exact things they need to be focusing on.

⬢ **Having improvement in the thinking:** When children have people or a person that they look up to, they try as much as possible to emulate that person's lifestyle and this helps them to think better as even children because they are trying to behave, and act in alignment with their mentor.

💎 EMOTIONAL BENEFITS

⬢ **Emotional intelligence:** Our mentors can also mentor us in areas outside of the technicalities of our everyday jobs or responsibilities. A mentor can teach your child/children how best to handle life issues, and every other thing that it will throw at them. This guidance is necessary to help children navigate the maze of consistent unpredictability of life and this helps them to be in a healthy emotional state regardless of the challenge.

💎 SOCIAL BENEFITS

⬢ **Blending in:** With the right kind of guidance from the people your children appreciate and look up to, they can learn to be better people that will bring value and difference to any gatherings they might find themselves. They understand the intricacies of social interaction a lot better, and they are very comfortable in any crowd they find themselves regardless of the situation.

⬢ **Following in good footsteps:** Sometimes, your child/children will look up to athletes and sportsmen, and they become inspired to take up a sport or a physical activity that will benefit them physically. Even when they engage in other seemingly less physical intensive activity, but more mentally tasking, you can still see this as a physical activity that involves the mind and the brain. Help them discover people who are successful at great and beneficial things, and let them try their hands at various things that will help them achieve success in their strongholds.

💎 COMMUNICATION

⬢ **Improving communications:** Your child/children will speak more clearly, and demonstrate a command of language when they begin to have a mentor-mentee relationship with great persons. They will be able to master the vocabularies and language of industries and the learned society in.

CONCLUSION:

It is very important for your child/children as individuals to appreciate great people, and look up to them. It also inspires them to be great persons themselves, and be a source of inspiration to the people that will eventually look up to them in the future. This creates a cycle of continued excellence amongst generations.

PRACTICAL STEPS CHILDREN CAN TAKE TO APPRECIATE AND LOOK UP TO GREAT PERSONS

It may be hard for children to find the right persons that they can look up to. However, there are usually guidelines that they can follow in finding a great mentor that will help them in navigating the hurdles of life. A mentor is usually a voluntary teacher or counsellor who guides younger generations in school, or other areas of your life. Sometimes, mentorship is a formally organized relationship between the mentor and mentee, but most often it is informal. Children will often get into friendship with a role model. This section will offer the right guidance for children in finding potential mentors, and great persons they can appreciate and look up to.

1. CHOOSING THE RIGHT KIND OF MENTOR

Before children can rightly choose a mentor, they need to understand the role of a mentor. A good mentor will help your children learn to do certain things, but they will not do these things for them. A good mentor leads by example. For example, an academic mentor may offer efficiency tricks, advice, and examples to show them smart alternatives for success. However, an academic mentor will not copy edit their assignments in the waning moments before it is due. Apparently, this is the difference between a tutor and a mentor.

a. The ability to boost their ability to make decisions.

b. The ability to assess their strengths and weaknesses.

c. The ability to introduce new perspectives and correct any wrong thinking.

d. The ability to introduce them to important resources and useful references.

e. The ability to help them understand the structure and organization of the topic.

f. The ability to familiarize them with the tricks of the trade.

In addition, when children are considering mentorship, they should consider sports and recreational mentoring. They should think about people who excel at the sport that they are interested in developing. For this purpose, they can consider:

- Coaches and assistants
- Experienced players on your team or other teams
- Professional athletes or retired athletes
- Trainers

② FINDING A MENTOR

When picking the right mentor, they need to identify the specific roles where they'd like to have a mentor. To find mentors, they have to answer the following questions:

- What am I looking for from your mentor?
- What would I like to learn?
- How often would I like to meet? Where?
- How will the mentorship "look"?

Having answered these questions, they may make a list of potential mentors that fit those criteria. It is also important to note that when they are meeting potential mentors, they should not ask them to be their mentors straightaway. They should consider using statements like, "Can we meet for coffee and talk about physics sometimes?"

The world is full of many people who are toxic to your children. They may pollute their worldview, and affect their orientation toward life. However, by following the above mentioned steps, they will be able to identify the right people and learn a great deal.

Habit Fourteen
BE KIND

WHY IS IT IMPORTANT?

It is very important to encourage your child/children to be kind toward the people they deal with, as this makes them grow up to become compassionate adults. Your child/children will benefit so much from learning how to adapt and adjust their demands with respect to the needs of others. Kindness can come in any form and any size.

Studies have shown that a child who is always showing gratitude and appreciation is more likely to exhibit compassionate behaviours such as being fair, kind and tolerant of others. They are thus more rounded individuals as they grow up. When your child/children do a good deed to others, they are invariably being kind to themselves as they feel good about what they have done, and they want to do more especially when they see how much of an impact they have made in the lives of others.

BENEFITS:

INTELLECTUAL BENEFITS

Positive mindset: Children all like to think of themselves as being kind, and every act of kindness that they exhibit helps them to demonstrate the positivity that resides within them, and this makes them feel proud about themselves. When your child/children are kind to people, they are also kind to themselves and they therefore feel more grateful about their situation in life, and they are optimistic about the future.

Finding a better solution for self and other: Being kind will sometimes entail helping others to look for solutions to their problems. When your child/children learn to be kind and help others in their time of difficulty, they are inadvertently learning to solve problems in their own lives and in other people's lives as well.

💎 EMOTIONAL BENEFITS

● **Feel Good Factor:** Even children in their very early years recognise how much better they feel about themselves when they are kind to others. They feel better as individuals, they feel complete, and this makes them happy. This effect is magnified when the act of kindness aligns with inner aspects of our personality. For example, when an animal lover can show kindness to an injured animal by rescuing it. Life has a lot more meaning.

💎 SOCIAL BENEFITS

● **Helping the community:** Small gestures of kindness might seem insignificant, but it will have a compounding effect on the way your child sees himself/herself, and the way they see those around them and treat them. It is never too late to learn kindness, and it is never too late to teach your children to be kind also. In order to do this, they must live by certain codes, and form the habit of being helpful to others and impacting people's lives positively.

● **Kindness and bonding:** When children are kind to people, they open themselves up to connections and social bonding with the people around them. Those that received the kind gesture will be comfortable to open up to your child/children, and he/she will be willing to listen to them and be there for them in their time of need. This helps your child/children to have a better understanding that everyone becomes stronger as a community of people when everybody is willing to help a friend out in his time of need.

● **Gaining respects and gratitude:** When children are kind to those around them, they gain the love, respect and adoration of those they come in contact with. This helps them feel a lot better about themselves, and put them in good spirits to do even more.

● **Ripple effect:** Teaching children to be kind is an important step in making the community we live in a much safer, and friendly environment. This has a ripple effect on generations after you as they also learn to teach their own children the same kindness that they have learnt.

💎 PHYSICAL BENEFITS

● **Having good physical wellbeing and positive mindset:** Being kind makes your child/children feel very good on the inside and this is in part due to the fact that they are happy to see that they have helped to make something easier for someone, and help put things right. This effect is more prominent when children help who they are close to, and it also extends to humanitarian acts where they extend their help and services to a multitude of people in need. Getting involved with things like this will lift your child/children spirits, and keep them in a good physical wellbeing and positive mindset.

CONCLUSION:

Being kind will make your children genuinely happy, and this is good for all of us. A happy child is a cooperative child, and this makes for less stress on your part as the parent. There is no negative result to be kind, if you are being kind without ulterior motives. If we all learn to be kind to each other, the world would be a much better place today.

PRACTICAL STEPS CHILDREN CAN TAKE TO BE KIND

Kindness is an important way by which children can bring meaning to their own lives. It also brings joy to the lives of others around them. From the above benefits of kindness, it is apparent that being kind allows the children to communicate better, be more compassionate, and also to be a positive force in people's lives.

However, being kind isn't always easy. The ancient Greek philosopher, Plato, enthused, "Be kind, for everyone you meet is fighting a hard battle." This is even truer for children. Sometimes, it may require some real effort to be able to treat others with the kindness they would hope to receive. However, through practice, they can alter their perception and start seeing kindness as more worth the effort.

1. DEVELOPING THE ATTITUDE OF KINDNESS

Research has shown that when children act with good intention, they are able to improve their mindset. In addition, this helps them to be able to enjoy their acts of kindness. Also, being aware of their kind acts help others to be able to find meaning in their kind acts. Hence, it is important that children decide to do something nice for someone before they actually do it. This is because acting with intent will help them to enjoy the kindness better. By enjoying being of service to others help them to reinforce this habit, which makes them do it more often.

2. DEVELOPING KIND QUALITIES

Kindness is not this large and gigantic value that a child either has or not. As a matter of fact, it is composed of several different qualities like being compassionate, being nice and being empathetic. For instance, children need to know that others may be fighting a secret battle that they do not know of. It is quite easy for children to assume that people are perfect, and would live up to an ideal image in their mind. However, they have to know that other people may be experiencing uncertainty, pain, hardship, sadness, disappointment, and loss.

Another quality of being kind is to be a very good listener. Children need to learn to truly listen to others. This involves making eye contact, avoiding all distractions, and giving the other person the time of day. This is genuinely one of the greatest acts of kindness. By taking the time to truly absorb what the other person is saying before responding with a pre-made answer or interrupting, they will appear kinder and lovelier.

3. TAKING AN INTEREST IN PEOPLE

Your children can begin to develop an interest in other people by genuinely caring about their welfare and what they do. Here are a few questions that children can ask to take an interest in people:

- How are you doing?
- What are your favourite hobbies?
- How did you spend last Christmas?
- How was the test?

While asking these questions, your children should avoid all forms of distractions and genuinely mean what they say.

To be more kind, they can work on developing an interest in other people, and show them that they care by asking questions, being attentive, and paying attention to them.

 **Habit** Fifteen

HAVING COMPASSION

WHY IS IT IMPORTANT?

"Love and compassion are necessities, not luxuries. Without them, humanity cannot survive." Dalai Lama. We thrive in a community where we can experience a connection to our fellow man, our neighbours and our loved ones. It is true that in the act of giving we receive. With compassion comes meaning, and purpose in our daily lives, and this is a great stride toward happiness. Compassion fills various holes in our hearts, and it heals us of so many things that we may not even be aware of, thus putting us in great physical, mental and emotional health.

The world would be a fair and beautiful place to live in if we could all be compassionate toward one another. Compassion is an emotion deeper than empathy, because it involves imagining the pain and suffering of others on a much deeper level. With compassion, you can teach your child/children to be loving and benevolent toward themselves and others around them.

BENEFITS:

INTELLECTUAL BENEFITS

Empathy: Studies have been carried out that examined the brain, and it was evident that the regions in the brain that's responsible for the processing of emotions and general brain activity, was lit up in times of compassionate behaviour as compared to when at rest. The areas associated with empathy and understanding people were also most active.

New perspectives: By acknowledging the areas where people need help and assistance, your child/children gains more perspective on how best to solve their own problems, and this helps them to navigate their own feelings and mindsets rather than complicate things. There is a direct correlation with people with high emotional quotients and leadership, and this is because they can understand people on a much deeper level.

💎 EMOTIONAL BENEFITS

● **Increased emotional quotient:** As compassionate people, your child/children are more emotionally balanced, and this boosts their emotional quotients. With a high EQ comes a higher probability of seeing this through with people, and helping them out in their times of need. They are also able to get the best out of people.

● **Empathy:** You can't understand people's pain, and act accordingly if you do not have any compassion in you. Teach your child/children to have this compassion for the people around them, and help them to better understand and appreciate their own privileges so that they may be better people, and add value to the society they find themselves in.

💎 SOCIAL BENEFITS

● **Action:** Compassion motivates children into acting on issues that they are deeply concerned about. It is a highly motivating force, and it can spur children into tackling various social problems and finding ways in which they can right the wrongs that they feel they have the power to. With compassion, children better understand how the people around them are feeling, and they can listen to them better and work toward creating a fair, equitable and just environment for everyone to comfortably thrive in.

● **Be part of making the world a better place:** The world is fast becoming a self-centered place. It takes compassion to think globally and act locally. It takes compassion to be interested in issues like global warming and environmental preservation. Children who are compassionate are more interested in improving and changing the world around them.

💎 PHYSICAL BENEFITS

● **Live happier and healthier:** Compassion will have a direct benefit on your children's physical and psychological health. Children feel better when they are able to contribute in ways to improve the conditions around them. Children's health, wellbeing and relationships are at a much better condition when they become more compassionate.

⬤ **Health:** Research has also found that compassion leads to a reduced risk of heart disease, and it has a positive effect on the Valgus nerve which is responsible for human's heart rate. Compassion makes your child/children a lot more resilient toward stress and consequently, their immune system gets the better side of it.

CONCLUSION:

Teach your child/children compassion and let them experience the world of benefit it brings. They will grow to become fine young men and women that you will be proud of at every point in time. The world needs us all to be compassionate and help each other out when we can.

PRACTICAL STEPS CHILDREN CAN TAKE TO BE MORE COMPASSIONATE

Many children like to see themselves as a good person—someone who is considerate, caring, and kind. In other words, children want to see themselves as compassionate. For such children, there are ways they can follow to be more compassionate. For those who feel they haven't been as compassionate as much as they would want to be, but want ideas on how to show compassion to themselves and others; there are also ways they can be more compassionate. To develop true passion, children must be able to show themselves and others more compassion. In addition, they must be able to expand their perspective on the world.

❶ DEVELOPING SELF-COMPASSION

It is a common saying that you cannot give what you do not have. Your child/children need to be able to develop self-compassion before they can be compassionate toward others. To develop self-compassion, there are lined up ways in which they can go about it:

- Practicing mindfulness.

   Some research studies have suggested that mindfulness can help a child develop self-compassion. This is truer when you realize that mindfulness helps a child to focus on the task at hand. Mindfulness is a practice of awareness and acceptance of one's feelings and emotions. When your child/children are able to accept their own feelings, they are less likely to judge others, and are going to be kinder to them. To develop mindfulness, your children should learn to focus on only one thing at a time. Multitasking is very bad for attention. In addition, they should think about what they are doing while they are doing it. To do this, they can narrate their actions to themselves. For instance, while they are exercising, they can say to themselves, "I am swinging and jumping up."

2. PRACTICING GRATITUDE

Some studies have indicated that gratitude helps in the reduction of stress. Apparently, the less stressed a child is, the kinder they become. To practice gratitude, your child/children can start being more grateful for the good things they have in their life, and show more compassion for those that do not have these things. Also, they can keep a gratitude journal where they record all the things that they are most grateful for. This can include little things like their favourite candy to big things like their family members. In addition, they should write down the things that they are grateful for every single day before they sleep at night. They should purposefully look for these things.

3. FORGIVENESS

Forgiveness is in two parts—forgiveness of oneself and forgiveness of others. Your child/children need to know that everyone has done something that they are not really proud of. These things often bring feelings of regrets and shame upon them. One way to increase self-compassion is by forgiving oneself first. It sets children on the path to spread compassion across the entire world.

The pinnacles that hold the world together are rested on compassion. It is the major reason why people do not turn on each other. When your child/children follow the above steps, they will become more compassionate and kinder to others.

 **Habit** Sixteen

WORK ON SHARING AND CARING

WHY IS IT IMPORTANT?

The world is a much better place when we all learn to care about the people around us, and we are willing to share what we have with those who do not have as much or at all. Teach your child/children from a very early age to share and teach them the love in sharing with others. Make them understand that it is not enough to have it all, but you must do what you can to ensure that those you care about, those you love, and those around you can benefit from whatever you have been blessed with.

If we all could have this mentality and mindset, we would be better off as citizens of this world. We would be able to look past all of our differences, and just be better human beings overall. A lot of what our children eventually become usually starts from the home, they pick up on little cues, and you have to be careful to show them the better way of doing things. You have to caution them when it seems like they want it all. You have to imbibe selflessness in them as they are growing up. This is the only way that they are going to be useful members of the society.

BENEFITS:

♦ INTELLECTUAL BENEFITS

Build themselves: Sharing can also be in the form of information and knowledge. When your child/children have knowledge about a certain subject, encourage them to pass on this knowledge to other people around them who needs that same knowledge. When we teach, we tend to know more and see more knowledge. So sharing of knowledge will eventually add to your own knowledge in the long run, thereby broadening your horizon.

💎 EMOTIONAL BENEFITS

Love others, love thyself: Children will indeed feel better about themselves when they extend care toward the people they love, and in turn and they will receive back what they give out. When children are there for the people they love, they are doing themselves a favour by setting this straight and making room for others around them to be happy and feel loved. When children are the ones in need of a listening ear or a helping hand, these people will surely come to their aid.

💎 SOCIAL BENEFITS

Amiable: A huge part of friendships and relationships is built around caring and sharing. Your children could be sharing their time with them, their belongings or their ideas. Whatever it is, children get along with people when they share what they have with others. This enables an atmosphere of trust where children can all be open to each other without fear of being mistreated.

Helping out: When children care about people and are willing to share what they have with others, they are invariably putting themselves in a position to help out when they can.

Being part of a community, country and world – Children can create a better world and role modelling for others to follow.

💎 COMMUNICATION

Building the positive internal dialogs: Children need to get all the positivity they can while growing up, and sharing and caring is a major way to make them express this positivity, and reap the rewards in how they feel about doing a good deed no matter how small it may be. With a good bank of good deeds, they can reinforce the conversations in their mind about the positivity they bring to others.

CONCLUSION:

Just imagine how positive the world would be if we all care about each other, and we weren't hesitating to offer help, assistance or information that will improve the lives of our fellow human being. This will be like a utopia of sorts and no challenge will be too great for us to surmount as a specie. This is why it is so important that your child/children start to learn this at their tender age.

PRACTICAL STEPS CHILDREN CAN TAKE TO WORK ON SHARING AND CARING

Being caring allows your children to display more empathy, show more affection, and love the people around them. Caring helps children to avoid the emptiness of selfishness, and focus on goals and desires that are positive for others too. If your children want to know how to be more caring, kindly read further:

1. DEVELOPING AN EMPATHETIC PERSPECTIVE

For children to be able to share and care, they have to be sensitive to the feelings of others. If they want to have a more caring perspective, then they have to spend more time thinking about how other people are feeling. They have to be on the lookout for people's reaction to situations. The children who are caring are more attuned to the moods of others, and can tell when someone is feeling down or upset, and take measures to do something about it. The next time they are around other people, whether they are in class or hanging out with friends, they should pay serious attention to know how others are feeling in a given situation.

The children who are self-absorbed or who only care about themselves tend not to care when other people around them are upset, even if they caused it. Your children should ensure that they are not like this person.

② DEVELOPING CARING QUALITIES

Children often see politeness as a product of kindness. However, by being polite, your children will be more intent on sharing and caring. They will be determined to treat the people around them with love and respect. Being polite means having good manners, not being overly vulgar or rude in front of people, holding doors for people and asking people about their day.

For children, it can also mean smiling at people, not getting in another person's way, and having common courtesy when its need arises.

③ HELPING OTHERS IN NEED

One of the major aspects of caring and giving is the ability to help others who are in dire need of assistance. A child cannot be caring if he or she is selfish. They must be able to help both their friends and family members who need help in their lives, and also helping out the less fortunate people in your community, or even people you may not know that well who need assistance.

Your children should be on the lookout for people who need help and find a productive way to get involved if they want to be more caring. In addition, your children need to know that their friends and family members may not always admit it when they need their help. However, it's up to them to notice when they are just being polite, and really need some extra help.

They should get involved in a literacy centre, soup kitchen, teen help program, local library, or another program in their area that allows them to make other people's lives more fulfilling.

 **Habit** Seventeen

MAKE PHYSICAL CONTACT WITH TRUSTWORTHY AND LOVED ONES

WHY IS IT IMPORTANT?

Nowadays, there are people who are very untrustworthy. Without trust, the world is largely a non-empathic place. People become narcissistic and selfish. This is not good for the world, and it explains why there are wars and strives between nations and people.

Research studies have clearly shown that children who do not make physical contact with people have bullying issues. They get bullied or bully others. Easily, it leads to mental illness such as anxiety, depression, anger and fear in children.

Children are going to have to engage in social interactions with their loved ones, and trustworthy people. Most importantly, these have to be people who they know very well, as they have to be careful in trusting strangers too quickly. There are so many benefits of engaging in physical contact with trustworthy and loved ones.

By having physical contact like hugging, they are able to be friendlier, build trust and show affection. In this section, you are going to explore the various benefits that your child/children can obtain from making physical contact with trustworthy and loved ones.

BENEFITS:

💎 INTELLECTUAL BENEFITS

Enhanced clarity and confidence: Research has shown that children who hug family members and friends have more clarity. According to scientists, the benefits of hugging goes beyond that warm feeling you get when you hold someone in your arms; children who hug others have benefited intellectually as they feel worthy and enough. These benefits include enhanced clarity and enhanced confidence.

💎 EMOTIONAL BENEFITS

● **Hugs make children happier:** Oxytocin is a chemical in children's bodies that scientists sometimes call the "cuddle hormone." This is because its level rises when they hug, touch, or sit close to someone else. Oxytocin is associated with happiness and less stress. Here are a few other emotional benefits that children have when they engage in physical contact.

a. It reduces stress

b. It makes children happier

c. It alleviates their fears

💎 COMMUNICATION BENEFITS

● **Enhance two ways communication and expression:** By making physical contact with others, children are able to create innovative ways of communicating and relating with others.

● **Asking for help when needed:** Also, it helps them to be able to seek for help whenever they feel they need to.

💎 PHYSICAL BENEFITS

● **Improving health:** Apparently, physical contacts should be able to produce physical benefits.

Hugs, holding of hands, or sitting close to trusted loved ones, can help your child/children to have an improved health as they have a sense of belonging and being loved.

CONCLUSION:

In a study of over 400 people, researchers found out that hugging may reduce an individual's chances of getting sick. The participants with a greater support system were less likely to get sick, and those with the greater support system who did get sick had less severe symptoms than those with little or no support system. Helping your child/children to get comfortable with their loved ones with healthy physical contact is the gift to them for both mental and physical benefits.

HOW CHILDREN CAN MAKE PHYSICAL CONTACT WITH TRUSTWORTHY AND LOVED ONES

There are a few approaches on how your children can begin to have more physical contacts with trustworthy and loved ones. In this section, we will discuss the salient approaches:

1 **BEING APPROACHABLE**

To be more approachable, your children need to smile more often. They do not have to smile at everyone though. Instead, they can make it a goal to smile a little more each day. They can also make it a goal of smiling more during the course of a conversation.

They can practice smiling every day, even when they are by themselves. The act of smiling—even when they are making themselves smile instead of doing it naturally—causes their brain to release feel-good chemicals and lifts their mood.

In addition, they have to possess an open body language. If they want people to feel like they are approachable and open to talking to them, then they have to master the act of open body language. Here are the things that they can do to make people want to talk to them more:

- Keeping legs together instead of crossed
- Having good posture instead of slouching
- Keeping arms at the sides instead of crossing them
- Leaning forward toward other people

2 **DELIBERATELY HAVING MORE HUGS**

In the words of Psychotherapist Virginia Satir, "We need 4 hugs a day for survival. We need 8 hugs a day for maintenance. We need 12 hugs a day for growth." Since children are developing and growing every day, they need to be hugging at least 12 times a day.

 **Habit** Eighteen

SELF-ENTERTAINMENT

WHY IS IT IMPORTANT?

We all need to know how to enjoy our own company, and your child/children must have this too in them. It is very important to be able to entertain yourself, so you don't go out looking for bad influence to help you get excitement. This is where children get to mix with bad company, and learn very dangerous habits. They must be capable of being by themselves, and enjoying themselves preferably at home.

There are so many things that they can learn to do to keep themselves company, and you can nudge them in various healthy distractions and hobbies that they can engage in. children naturally have a curious mind and they are always ready to explore, so all you have to do is spark this curiosity, and encourage the exploration in them in healthy directions.

BENEFITS:

INTELLECTUAL BENEFITS

• **Reading:** One of the things your child/children can do on their own time when they are alone is to read books. This will help them in so many ways. They are exposed to so many different stories that expand their horizons and their thinking. They get to improve their vocabulary and their spelling, and they also get to learn a lot of new things afterwards. This will do them a lot of good, and it is a much better way for them to spend their time compared to many other ways.

• **Art:** Your child/children can also engage in various hobbies around the house that allows them to be more self-expressive. There are a number of areas that they can spend their time on, and you will be amazed at how much good stuff comes out of their play time.

◉ **Discover new ideas:** When children learn to keep themselves entertained, they are in a creative space where they can discover new ideas on their own, and pursue their interest. All you have to do as the parent is to observe them, and make sure they aren't indulging in any harmful activity that can affect their intellect.

◉ **Problem solving:** Your child/children are also better equipped to solve their own problems, and overcome challenges if they can be by themselves and forge ahead without the need for other parties input.

💎 EMOTIONAL BENEFITS

◉ **Self-sufficient:** Your child/children should learn to be self-sufficient and they should as well know where to get validation from. The most important source of validation is of self and your child/children won't really value themselves if they do not know how to spend time alone and entertain themselves. When they constantly seek others to have fun, it has a negative effect on their self-esteem, and they aren't as confident in themselves as they ought to be.

◉ **Find personal interests:** It follows naturally that when your child/children entertain themselves, they quickly find things that are of interest to them, and that they can be passionate about. They have the full freedom to pursue their interests, and find new hobbies which can even grow into something bigger in the future.

💎 SOCIAL BENEFITS

◉ **Self-love:** How can you love anyone if you don't love yourself? This saying can be adapted for self-entertainment. How can you entertain anybody if you don't know how to entertain yourself? How can you spend time with people if you don't know how to spend time with yourself? When your child/children are comfortable in their own company and they can entertain themselves, it becomes a lot easier and more natural for them to be around friends and loved ones and they have a lot of cheer to spread.

♦ COMMUNICATION

● **Self-reflection:** Alone time is the time your child/children can use for self-reflection, when they fully understand themselves more. They find it easier to express themselves to other people and freely communicate exactly what they have in mind. There is lesser inhibitions in your child/children's mind when they get comfortable with themselves, and knows themselves a lot more.

♦ PHYSICAL BENEFITS

● When your child/children know how to entertain themselves, they can engage in many fine activities without involving you and other people who might want to do something else at the same time. They can be by themselves and not bother anybody, and this is such a relief for you as the parents and perhaps their older siblings too.

CONCLUSION:

Self-entertainment is a very crucial skill to be learned right from when your child/children are growing up, and they must all know how to entertain themselves otherwise they run the risk of being bored all the time because they can't always have the people you love around them. This also brings a great benefit for a healthy mental health along with the time your child/children are growing up to a maturate adult.

PRACTICAL STEPS CHILDREN CAN TAKE TO ENGAGE IN SELF-ENTERTAINMENT

Children are creative beings, and sometimes they have a lot of time to themselves. There are plenty of ways in which they can take advantage of this plenty time to entertain themselves without giving into some unabashed self-indulgence. Here are a few ways that children can begin to engage in self-entertainment.

1. ENJOYING THE FREEDOM OF ALONE TIME

To fully entertain themselves, children have to begin to embrace the abundance of time that they have at their disposal. They should learn the benefits of being alone, and resolve to make positive things out of it. Also, they should embrace free time to say, think, do or act the way they want to. When they are by themselves, they do not have to worry about the thoughts or judgments of others. They can be utterly and unabashedly themselves, and never think twice about what someone else might think or say. The children should love the independence that comes with having time to themselves. They do not have to succumb to anyone else's tastes, preferences, or desires when making their decisions.

2. LOVING ALL THE QUIRKS

For children to entertain themselves, they have to be able to love themselves and enjoy all their quirks. Self-entertainment affords them the time to be actually true to themselves, and appreciate their own company. They can talk to themselves and to the chairs. They can engage in weird dance while brushing their teeth with the other hand. They can take the time to truly appreciate their unique awesomeness. To fully entertain themselves, children need to start defining their own unique qualities rather than by the opinions of others.

③ APPRECIATING SMALL THINGS

One of the most neglected ways that children can entertain themselves is by appreciating every little things that comes their way. They need to start noticing the little things that happen around them. By staying away from media and other forms of distractions, they will be able to pay attention to these little details. They can be observant, and pay attention to small shifts in their mood, thoughts, feelings, and perceptions. Also, they should try to pinpoint what led to that shift, and how it affected them physically and emotionally. As they get more tuned into themselves and what makes them tick, they will start to gain amazing insights into what they may have never realized before.

③ MAKING A PAINTING OR A DRAWING

They can use the pencils and papers around the house to make their own special drawings. Also, they can go to a Craft store and get a few supplies for more art work. If they are not artistically savvy, they can get a paint-by-number set which are fun and easy to complete. Once they are done, they can hide their beautiful creations on the wall.

Your children will have to learn to entertain themselves if they are going to keep up with their self-esteem. The steps itemized above will help them in entertaining themselves without engaging in any form of self-indulgence.

 **Habit** Nineteen
FINDING PASSION

WHY IS IT IMPORTANT?

When children find passion, children find the drive, and this propels them through life's challenges. Children find meaning and purpose. With passion, your child/children can experience abundance, and keep a positive mindset at all times. Children are unique in their own ways and as parents, you must identify what these things are that make them stand out, and help them nurture those skills and abilities. It is a tragedy when a talent goes wasted especially now that people make comfortable living from these talents that they possess. Whatever your child/children have a passion for will present itself as a hobby, and you need to watch them closely and help them develop those hobbies.

BENEFITS:

💎 INTELLECTUAL BENEFITS

- **Success:** Help your child/children to understand that a lot of people who find true high levels of success attribute this success to the fact that they love what they are doing, and they are very passionate about it. This passion is the fuel that pushes them to overcome several challenges and obstacles.

- **Tenacity:** When your child/children is/are passionate, they work harder and are determined to succeed no matter what. It is the passion that lifts them out of bed in the morning, and motivates them to get on with the task that will enable them to achieve our goals. With passion your child/children work harder, longer and setbacks do not knock you over.

- **Growth:** Passion will help your child/children come up with innovative, and ingenious ideas on how best to move forward on a project. It increases their level of assimilation of new concepts, and helps them to effectively dissect information faster and your child/children become a lot more disciplined, and they start to value their time a lot more. Having belief in something and getting it done helps to build confidence, and this is in the right step toward your child/children growth.

💎 EMOTIONAL BENEFITS

● **Feels Good:** Letting your child/children do what they love will definitely feel good to them. They will enjoy the whole process thoroughly, and the fruits of their labour will be that much sweeter. This is a very sharp contrast when you compare it to those who are just doing the things they do just because they have to. With passion your child/children sleep better, they are more enthusiastic and optimistic about the future, and this shines through their disposition on a daily basis.

● **They will get more fulfilment when they finally make it:** There is only a handful of things that your child/children feel better about, than finally achieving a goal that they set out for by themselves. It feels so good to cross out things from their bucket list, or to do list and when they finally reach that peak of success, it is much more pleasurable. The reward seems to be in tenfold.

💎 SOCIAL BENEFITS

● **Unlocking True Potential:** When children are able to identify what they are really good at and passionate about, they are already on their way to unlocking their full potential because they will put in their absolute best in any endeavour that they are truly passionate about.

● **No obstacle will stop them from achieving success:** When your child/children find their true passion, nothing can stand in their way and they see the goal very clearly, and stick with what needs to be done to achieve that goal. They feel unstoppable, and the confidence they have in themselves shoots through the roof into space. Even when others around them don't have as much faith as they should, it doesn't deter them in any way.

CONCLUSION:

When your child/children live their life with a purpose and with their passion, they are happier and more confident in themselves. This reduces stresses of their daily life activities in their body systems, and improves their mental and physical health in so many ways.

PRACTICAL STEPS CHILDREN CAN TAKE TO FIND PASSION

For children, being passionate requires hard work, dedication, focus, and the willingness to fail over and over again. However, if they are ready to put in the work, then being a passionate person who knows what he or she wants can bring joy, excitement, and a sense of true purpose to their life. If your children want to be passionate, then they have to know what they want, and be willing to work hard to go after it, even if it means making more than a few sacrifices along the way.

Passion is the major reason children wake up in the morning, and just the thought of it can keep them up late with excitement. It can also be a quieter feeling of satisfaction, knowing that they are living life on their terms. However, not every child knows exactly what his or her passion is right away. There are a number of things your children can actually do to find their passion.

1. EXAMINING THE CURRENT POSITION

Before your children can identify their passion, they have to know what truly motivates their decisions. Too much often, they listen to their "social selves," which is the part of their personality that wants to follow the societal norms and fit in. While it is good for children to be part of a larger community, they should be careful that they do not lose their true identity and unique passions.

"Passion" comes from authenticity, it is a feeling that makes children feel like they are honouring themselves in their own decisions rather than trying to be or satisfy someone else. This is highly personal, and no one else can tell them what feels "authentic" to them; only your children can actually decide that.

2. ASKING SELF-REFLECTIVE QUESTIONS

Children are hyperactive. This makes it difficult for them to sit down, and figure out what their values are. They should take some time, and ask themselves these self-reflective questions.

- Are there topics that excite me?
- When am I most fulfilled?

- What are my goals?
- What do I do most of the time?
- What activity makes me feel completely in my element?
- What am I doing when I feel "right" or "beautiful" or "connected"?
- What would I do, even if I didn't get paid to do it?
- What makes me feel like nothing else exists?
- What do I keep on trying to do?
- What draws me?
- If I could do one thing for the rest of my life, what would it be?
- What do I love to do?
- What activities satisfy me?
- If I could change something about my family and neighbourhood, what would it be?

② LOOKING FOR PATTERNS

Once your children have answered the above questions, they should think about their answers and find the common pattern to them all. For example, perhaps they remember feeling proud of themselves when they had accomplished something on their own. This suggests possible values like self-reliance, independence, and ambition. If they feel most satisfied when they are able to express themselves through artwork, this implies exploration, creativity and vision.

Life is all about compromise. Children will not have all the energy they need to do every possible thing they desire of themselves. However, by focusing on things that are more rewarding, they are able to get a good benefit for their time and energy.

2. RESILIENCE

▶ **RESILIENCE AND ITS IMPORTANCE TO CHILDREN**

When we mention resilience, we're talking about a child's capability to cope with ups and downs and come back from the challenges they experience during childhood strongly – for example changing home, changing schools, preparing for an exam or going through the death of a loved one and so on.

Building resilience enables children not only to cope with present challenges that are a part of everyday life but also to develop the necessary skills and habits that will help them deal with challenges later in their future, during adolescence and adulthood.

Resilience is determined partly by the individual features we are born with (our genes, emotions, and personality) and partially by the environment, we grow up in – our family, community and the larger society. While there are some things we can't alter, such as our biological composition, there are a lot of things we can change.

Resilience is essential for children's mental health. Children with exceptional resilience are better able to cope with stress, which is a common response to difficult events. Stress is a risk factor for mental health conditions like anxiety and depression if the degree of stress is severe or continuous.

As parent/parents, you can help to nurture essential skills, habits, and attitudes for building resilience at home by helping your child to build good rapport with others including adults and age-mates, to build their independence and courage. Besides, they need to learn to identify, express and manage their emotions consistently, to build their confidence by providing them with personal challenges to work on,

None of the human is immune from the challenging and difficulties of life. Therefore, resilience is a must attribute that needs to be equipped to your child/children's life as early as possible.

Habit Twenty

TURNING PROBLEMS INTO OPPORTUNITIES.

WHY IS IT IMPORTANT?

Problems can present themselves in various ways. Obstacles can be frustrating and quite often, even adults tend to give up when the going gets tough. This can be particularly tricky for your child/children, as they have a shorter attention span and will naturally move to something else if they can.

You need to teach your child/children. Let them understand that there is no gain without pain. Help them better embrace adversity, inconvenience, and challenges. This is the only way they can grow. When we overcome obstacles, we can innovate and create new opportunities. This holds true for everybody regardless of age, status or experience. Your child/children need to be taught to stick with peculiar problems that they face and better yet deal with it themselves.

There are so many benefits to turning problems into opportunities. There are several success stories of people who have overcome one disability or challenge to become inspirations to us all. Jackie Chan is a world-renowned actor and martial artist. He is who he is today because he was able to turn a problem into an opportunity in his childhood. He used to be bullied as a child growing up, and this led to him into enrolling for martial art classes to defend himself.

BENEFITS:

💎 INTELLECTUAL BENEFITS

- **Promote learning at school:** When your child/children learn to persevere and stick to problems, they develop their mental capacity and endurance to deal with technical subjects in school such as math and science.

- **Better student:** When your child/children know how to solve problems, these help them become better students at the end of the day. They can also adapt these skills to their daily activities and approach to problem-solving.

- **Promise future:** When your child/children know how to turn problems into opportunities, they can see things from two different angles. These children often grow to become successful engineers, doctors, lawyers, etc., or hold important positions in the future.

- **Memories:** Your child/children will have fond memories of different pastimes when they have been able to find ingenious ways to overcome their problems.

💎 EMOTIONAL BENEFITS

- **Empathy:** Collaborating with people to solve problems will expose your child/children to different people of different means and privileges. Their interactions will help them better understand other people's shortcomings and predicaments.

- **Appreciate life:** Naturally, with empathy comes a better appreciation for the life that your child/children have. They begin to appreciate the things that they are privileged to have or have access to. This makes them more grateful and happier.

💎 SOCIAL BENEFITS

- **Building tolerance:** In dealing with problems, your child/children will have to work with other people at some point in time or the other. They will learn how to best handle people of different personalities, and how to tolerate them when they don't approach issues the way they would themselves.

- **Respect:** Asides from tolerating people, your child/children also learn to respect people when doing things together. No successful relationship is devoid of respect.

- **Role modelling:** Your child/children gather leadership skills and in the course of their adventures, they get to interact with people who can mentor them; and they too, in turn, mentor others.

💎 COMMUNICATION

● Improved communication skills: In the course of overcoming the obstacles they face on a day to day basis, children learn better ways of communicating their frustrations and ideas on how they intend to move ahead. This is a very important life skill as a problem shared is already half solved.

● Inspire others: Also, people who successfully navigate adversity and overcome different kinds of problems, tend to be better motivational speakers and can have a very strong influence in the minds of people. Your child/children can be the one who changes people's lives!

💎 PHYSICAL BENEFITS

● Tenacity: Sometimes, children experience challenges in problems that are physical and require them to physically endure certain tasks or scenarios. Continuous exposure to similar physical problems can help develop them into more enduring versions of themselves.

CONCLUSION:

Turning problems into opportunities makes them more creative, exciting, and fun to be with. Children are highly creative and as such, they give full expression to their beings when they turn problems into opportunities.

PRACTICAL STEPS CHILDREN CAN TAKE TO TURN PROBLEMS INTO OPPORTUNITIES

Challenges bring out the best in human beings; and, children are no exceptions. Children face challenges in their own little ways, but those who are ultimately successful in life are often the ones who find ways to create opportunities out of their problems. From adapting to new environments to picking up new hobbies, children must be able to know how to turn problems into opportunities. No matter how difficult the situation may seem, they can overcome it. The problems they face today can be their source of strength tomorrow.

1. EMBRACING CHALLENGES

To effectively convert problems into opportunities, children must be able to come to terms with the reality of the situation. Depending on the situation, it may be difficult for children to accept it as part of their lives, and that it may change how they define themselves. The first step for children to turn a problem into an opportunity is by appreciating their new limitations and accepting themselves as they are.

Also, they should not try to evaluate things in terms of what's "fair." While their situations may feel as though it isn't fair, they are not going to move forward by brooding on such thoughts.

In addition, they should embrace the perspective that their situation provides. No matter the condition, they must be able to come to terms with adversity. Whether they are struggling with depression, have been severely injured, or are dealing with any other kind of adversity, their experiences will change how they see the world around them.

To take advantage of this new perspective, they must find something productive that they can do with the new knowledge of themselves.

For example, they may start a support group for other people that have had similar experiences. Also, the new perspective will give them a better understanding of the struggles experienced by others as a result of their own. They should use that understanding to alter how they interact with people and encourage others to do the same.

2. FINDING A NEW DIRECTION IN LIFE

When your children feel helpless, this is the point where they need an external help. Whether looking for new friends or struggling to accept a new way of life due to family relocation, it's perfectly normal to feel overwhelmed and not be sure what to do next. When this happens, they can ask friends or family for their input.

They need to know that their friends and family care about them. These can help them in seeing the positive side to their experiences, and where they can go from there.

Once your children are able to identify and apply these ways of turning problems into opportunities, they will be able to have a positive outlook towards life.

 **Habit** Twenty One
LETTING GO OF THE PAST

WHY IS IT IMPORTANT?

Memories cut both ways. As you have good memories, so you have negative ones, and sometimes it is important to let go of the past depending on what effects it has on you today. As a parent, you need to teach your child/children to let go of negative and painful memories. They can hold on to all the good memories they have for as long as they want, as long as it serves them positively. Living in the past is no good for anyone, so it is important to find ways in which you can forget or ignore at the very least, some of your past.

Teach your child/children to channel the emotions from memories of their past into creating a better present and future. We all have regrets and have all been hurt in the past, but, what is most important is how we move on from the hurt, and how we channel that pain to fighting for a better today. As an adult, you must have found ways to deal with this problem and you need to help your child/children out in this regard too. Let them understand that life is a continuous learning process and teach them to confront and deal with their pasts properly. This is the only way they can truly let go.

There are so many benefits to letting go of your child/children's past and a few of the most prominent ones will be highlighted below.

BENEFITS:

💎 INTELLECTUAL BENEFITS

- **Continually pushing themselves through challenges:** There are two ways your children can benefit from letting go of the past intellectually. First of all, when they don't dwell too much on their successes in the past, they can focus on continually pushing themselves to achieve more, be it in class or in sports and other extracurricular activities.

- **Overcome failures:** Also, when they do not allow the failures of the past get to them, your child/children can keep on trying and giving their best efforts, to endeavour that all works out as well as they'd hoped for in the present.

💎 EMOTIONAL BENEFITS

- **Facing Fears:** Before your child/children can let go of the pain or regrets they might have had in the past, they must know how to properly confront the issues. And this will require them to face their fears head-on. For instance, if they have resentment towards someone or something in their lives, they will have to come face to face with the source of this resentment in order to finally let it go.

- **Not blaming others:** Your child/children will learn to take responsibility for some of the things that haven't quite gone as well as they hoped for in their past. You need to help them understand that nobody is responsible for their happiness and if they get this mentality, they will have a very powerful tool for survival in the years to come.

💎 SOCIAL BENEFITS

- **Focusing on the present:** When your child/children learn how to let go of the negatives in their past, they can fully focus on the present and enjoy the things before them now. They can appreciate life more, like the weight of the past is no longer on their shoulders. This does wonders for their social life as they blend in more and interact more positively on a day to day basis.

💎 COMMUNICATION

- **Expressing Pain:** If your child/children do not know how to acknowledge the pain they may feel in their past, there is no way they can let go of it. Thus, when you teach them to express their pain either directly towards the person causing it or the issue, they can get these things off their chest and out of their systems. There are various ways they can express this pain ranging from journals, letters, talking to people, etc.

💎 PHYSICAL BENEFITS

● **Being at peace:** This refers mainly to a kind of pain that others may have been responsible for or caused. Teach your children to forgive those that might have caused them pain in the past, no matter how little, as this will help them have a free and clear mind. The burden of resentment might not be tangible, but it weighs heavy on the heart.

CONCLUSION:

Letting go of the past is essential if your child/children are going to live a healthier and happier life. It puts their mind at peace and helps them to become more responsible. The importance of having a child/children with sound minds cannot be overemphasized. It makes them more brilliant, self-aware, and healthier.

PRACTICAL STEPS CHILDREN CAN TAKE TO LET GO OF THE PAST

When children experience bullying, trauma, a strong pain or embarrassment, they find it difficult to let go of the past. However, letting go of the past is healthy for them. Letting go of the past is crucial if they want to get the most out of their life, and for children to truly move forward, they have to discover the right attitude and, depending on the situation, accept themselves and/or forgive others.

① DEVELOPING A POSITIVE ATTITUDE

For children to be able to let go of the past, they must be able to face it and think about it from an objective perspective. They should reflect on their past, and try to narrow down exactly on what is holding them back. They should identify the common detractors:

i. Lack of motivation or energy
ii. Restlessness/agitation
iii. Doubt

iv. Ill will (wishing harm or trouble upon others)
v. Aversion (pain from the past causes them to avoid a person or opportunity, for example)
vi. Sensual (obsession with or shame about sexual matters or material things, for instance)

Your children need to know that deeply-held mistaken beliefs, often affect their actions and thoughts in ways beyond their control. A conscious or subconscious belief may affect their ability to let go of the past. For instance, they might have held the belief that they need a birthday gift to be happy. However, situations may cause the non-provision of such gifts. Instead, they can challenge such a belief by genuinely enjoying their hobbies and spending some time with their family members.

② SELF-ACCEPTANCE

The first step towards self-acceptance is self-forgiveness. Your children must desist from hiding a painful past, which leads to false pretence. Towards self-forgiveness, they must allow time to heal.

In addition, they have to allow time to heal. Instead of having this kind of self-talk, "My heart will never heal," they should choose, "All pains dull, but I had learned good lessons from them. They will pass with time."

They may never completely get over some things, such as the loss of a loved one, but as long as they accept the idea that they are allowed to move on, some level of healing can still occur.

③ FORGIVING OTHERS

This is an essential step to letting go of the past. Children are keen beings, and they often forgive others. However, if they are holding onto any form of anger due to hurt in the past, they have to change. There are enormous psychological benefits associated with forgiving others.

In addition, it is important that they do not place blame on others. While others may be at fault, putting the blame on them doesn't work. Instead, they should acknowledge the issue and focus on moving on. They must be keen on letting go of grudges. If anyone has hurt them in the past, retaliating is not worth the effort.

By following these steps, not only are your children going to be able to let go of the past, they are going to be more responsible and positive.

 **Habit** Twenty-two

ABILITY TO RESPOND TO STRESS.

WHY IS IT IMPORTANT?

Today, people do not have the right response to stress. Stress is a feeling we all go through at different points in our lives. It comes with all of the challenges you will face, and whether it's as basic as cramming for a test or worrying about a project that must be delivered at work, we will experience some form of stress. It is crucial that you acknowledge stress and find ways in which you can respond to it.

The same thing goes for your child/children, and although they might be stressed about little things such as, not getting the toy they want or preparing for a test, and things like that, the effect is the same on them if not greater. So they must also learn how to respond to stress.

Stress is more than just a physical emotion. It comes with a physical response that affects your child/children's entire body. Stress is not necessarily their enemy as it can be beneficial in short and periodic doses. When it becomes prolonged, then your child/children have an issue with their bodies. It affects their hormonal balance and the effects of this will be felt physically. These changes can be detrimental.

Therefore, your child/children must be taught to channel stress into productivity, and they must be able to respond to stress, so it isn't prolonged and becomes chronic. There are a lot of benefits to this and some of them will be highlighted below.

BENEFITS:

INTELLECTUAL BENEFITS

- **Finding solutions for the problem:** Stress in adequate doses can make your child/children uncomfortable, nervous, and spur them into finding solutions to problems, much faster than if they were relaxed and comfortable. If for nothing else, the motivation to make that uneasy feeling go away will push your child/children into finding solutions to problems.

⦿ **Achieve higher outcomes for studying or any kind of work:** When your child/children learn how best to respond to stress, they are invariably regulating the number of stress hormones, like cortisol, in our systems. This regulation will help them achieve greater heights academically because there is a better focus.

⦿ **Building metal strength for adult's life with work:** Your child/children consistently grow and build their tolerance for challenges and inevitably, stress. This is like a mental workout that helps make them stronger, in preparation for bigger challenges that they might have to face in the future. Being able to manage stress and respond properly will set your child/children up for the roles they will have to play later on in life.

💎 EMOTIONAL BENEFITS

⦿ **Built up confidence:** When your child/children recognise stress in all its forms and they know exactly how to handle it, it builds their confidence, and they can dive into any situation knowing what to expect, and how to deal with it. This confidence translates into believing in themselves and this gives your child/children the extra push they need to approach life with a fearless attitude.

⦿ **Good self-image and self-esteem:** Those who can better manage their stress feel better about themselves and are generally more confident. This energy comes with lesser stress levels.

💎 SOCIAL BENEFITS

⦿ **Attract friends or people in all age with confidence:** Stress sometimes can be worn physically and mentally such that, it manifests in the way your child/children deal with people around them. This puts people off and they end up being alone and frustrated. When your child/children learn how to respond to stress, they are able to be better friends and have better relationships.

- **Role modelling among peer:** When your child/children successfully master the art of managing stress and they have all the tools to respond in the best way possible, your child/children can become role models to those who are still finding it difficult to navigate the obstacles in their day to day life. This will help your child/children gain respect amongst their peers and build their confidence, as they continue to be sources of inspiration to them.

COMMUNICATION BENEFITS

- **Handle the communication with calmness:** A lot of people allow stress in different other aspects of their lives overflow into how they communicate with people, and you often find people transferring aggression in this state. Being able to respond to stress helps your child/children communicate with calmness even in the face of daunting challenges. When they can express themselves smoothly, they will be able to accomplish more and get the support of those around them.

PHYSICAL BENEFITS

- **Cope with fight and flight well:** Part of managing and responding to stress is being able to do the best thing in every stressful situation. The ability to respond to stress will make your child/children make better decisions in times when they are torn between fight and flight.

CONCLUSION:

In conclusion, stress can be your child/children's ally if they manage it properly and respond in constructive ways. It quickly becomes your child/children's enemy when it is prolonged and they don't know what to do to stop it from affecting other aspects of their lives. It can also manifest itself physically, and change the chemistry of your child/children's brain and body. So it is very important to know how to teach your child/children the best ways to respond to stressful situations, and stress in general.

PRACTICAL STEPS CHILDREN CAN TAKE TO DEVELOP THE ABILITY TO RESPOND TO STRESS

Your children are going to be doing a lot of new things because they are young and are children. The stress response causes their bodies to secrete stress hormones (cortisol, adrenaline, norepinephrine, and others) into their bloodstreams, where they travel to targeted spots in the body to bring about specific psychological, physiological, and emotional changes that enhance their body's ability to deal with the threat.

There are actually many physical changes that happen in a child's body when there is stress. When stress response is triggered in a child, the following physical changes occur in their body:

a. A burst of adrenaline

b. A quickening of your pulse

c. Redirection of blood away from extremities and instead to major organs

d. The release of cortisol and other hormones, which bring other short- and long-term changes

So largely, stress kick-starts a process in a child's body that is almost reflex. However, by knowing the foods that trigger a stress response in children, they will be able to know what to avoid. Here are the top 4 stress-causing foods that children should avoid if they are experiencing stress.

1 SUGAR

If your children want to reduce stress, they must reduce sugar. This is one of the first ingredients that they must cut out of their diet. Too much of sugar is not good for children as it may lead to being hyperactive. It also leads to stress and can cause diabetes.

2 ARTIFICIAL SWEETENERS

Sugar is bad enough on its own, adding artificial sweeteners like saccharine makes it worse. Many foods and snacks sold in stores contain artificial sweeteners. As parents, you must train your children to be able to check if a food item contains artificial sweeteners. Artificial sweeteners contain chemicals that may not be healthy for children.

3. PROCESSED CARBOHYDRATES

This is another common food type that your children should avoid. Processed carbohydrates are many at the food store. They contain too many refined sugars and have little to no nutritional benefits.

4. EXCESS CAFFEINE

Caffeine is present in many of their drinks—from coke to coffee. Caffeine must be reduced in your children's food intake, as too much of it can lead to restlessness in them.

The following approaches can be taken by your children in responding to stress:

1. Habits

They need to build habits that will help them build resilience towards stress. These habits take more effort and time to build. Example of stress-relieving habits include:

  e. Exercises

  f. Clean diets

  g. Gratitude

  h. Enough amount of sleep and rest

Once these habits become a regular feature in the lifestyle of your children, they are more likely to respond well to stress.

2. Shifting the perspective

A healthy perspective towards stress is important in relieving stress. Your children need to be able to look at stressors in their lives as impulses to check if there are risks involved in a situation and how real these risks are.

Stress happens to everyone. They happen when children are exposed to unique situations. However, by approaching a stressful situation with a positive mindset, they will be able to stay healthy.

 **Habit** Twenty-three

ABILITY TO FIND A SOLUTION FOR CHALLENGES.

WHY IS IT IMPORTANT?

If you want to lead a successful and fulfilling life, you must fight back against certain forces that might be against you. These forces can come in the form of fear, challenges, problems and boredom. This message should be preached every day to your child/children as they grow up. When your child/children learn to find solutions to their problems and challenges, they are overcoming these issues and becoming their strongest self. They should accept these challenges as part of their lives and learn to find proactive solutions to them.

Having problem-solving skills is something that will be beneficial to your child/children throughout their lives. We all run into obstacles and we need to know how to understand these problems and how best to tackle them with a calm and logical frame of mind.

BENEFITS:

INTELLECTUAL BENEFITS

Mental Growth: When children are committed to solving their problems and finding solutions to challenges, they are forced to pick up new skills and find new and innovative ways of approaching everyday issues. This translates to growth and they are more comfortable venturing outside of their comfort zone. This helps them develop crucial mental skills that will help them succeed.

Analytical Mindset: When children constantly find solutions to challenges, they develop problem-solving skills and approach a lot of things with a more analytical mindset. Tackling problems require planning and logical thinking through all of the issues that may surround the problem.

💎 EMOTIONAL BENEFITS

Overcoming fear: Negative emotions such as fear, doubt and uncertainty, feed on children's reluctance to face the challenges in their lives and work to address them. When they start to face their challenges squarely, they start to wield all the power.

Self-confidence: Your child/children need to believe in themselves and learn to be independent. This they will achieve by constantly trying to solve as many of their own problems as they can. This allows them to have faith and trust in themselves as capable individuals.

💎 SOCIAL BENEFITS

Relevance: your children become relevant to society when they have an input that is useful to people. When they are able to solve problems, they can add value to any gathering they might find themselves. They become invaluable, as the world needs problem solvers.

Assist others in need: A lot of times, children are not necessarily solving their own problems but helping those dear to them solve theirs. When your children are well equipped to solve problems, they quickly become useful and contributing members of society.

Role modelling: Your child/children's friends and peers will quickly begin to look up to them if they prove themselves capable of solving their problems no matter how small. This gives your child/children a bigger sense of responsibility and this is good for their development.

💎 COMMUNICATION

Avoiding Isolation: A big part of overcoming challenges is asking for help and collaborating with people of various and diverse skill sets. Your children's challenges will help them reach out to people, ask for help when needed, and connect with professionals and experienced people in their network. This will help them get insight into their ideas and tap from their experiences. This way, they are never alone and feel supported.

- **Improved communication skills:** A big part of solving problems is asking the right questions. When your child/children learn how to engage a problem and talk to people who might have directions for them, they invariably build their communication skills.

💎 PHYSICAL BENEFITS

- **Fighting boredom:** What is life without challenges? Probably a very dull and uninspiring one. Your children's challenges pull them out of their natural relaxed state, and engage them in various activities if they do decide to overcome them. Their brain also becomes active.

- **Balance fight and flight hormones:** When faced with stress or stuck with something, the body produces fight and flight hormones. If your child/children could find the solutions for the challenges, fight and flight hormones will be reduced in the body which prevents damage to the nervous system, muscle system, etc., and this also reduces the tiredness and tightening of the body.

CONCLUSION:

Success and fulfilment come with overcoming challenges and your children should expect to deal with them on a day to day basis. The path to success and mastery in life is a consistent commitment to solve problems and overcome challenges. They must have a certain level of control over their lives and constantly fight for results, direction, and order.

PRACTICAL STEPS CHILDREN CAN TAKE TO FIND THE SOLUTION FOR CHALLENGES

> Everyone faces challenges in life.
> It's a matter of how you learn to overcome them and use them to your advantage.
>
> **Celestine Chua**

A t an early age, children must be taught how to generate solutions to their challenges. In problem-solving, there are six basic steps.

1 STEP ONE: DEFINE THE PROBLEM: "WHAT IS THE PROBLEM?"

Without identifying the problem, it will be a bit hard to solve the problem. This is because there are several solutions, and it is important to match the right solution to the right problem.

2 STEP TWO: IDENTIFY THE CAUSES OF THE PROBLEM: "WHY IS THIS HAPPENING?"

Often, what causes most of the challenges children face are not obvious; it has to be rooted up. For possible solutions to be produced, your children have to identify the causes of their problems.

3 STEP THREE: BRAINSTORM POSSIBLE SOLUTIONS.

A challenge often has many solutions. Before picking a solution, your children need to brainstorm several possible solutions. A time should be scheduled for this, and all possible solutions should be gathered, not minding the solutions that appear silly.

4 STEP FOUR: SELECT THE BEST SOLUTIONS.

Once the possible solutions have been gathered, they can now choose the best possible solutions.

5 STEP FIVE: IMPLEMENT THE PLAN.

Once the best possible solution has been identified, they have to implement it by drawing a plan. Without a plan, a solution is simply a theory. A plan must be drawn and executed.

⬤6 STEP SIX: FOLLOW-UP, EVALUATE, AND MONITOR PROGRESS.

Once the plan is executed, they have to monitor their progress. This is important, so they can decide whether they have picked the right solution and how effective it is.

The above six-steps to problem-solving are very effective and have been in use for decades. Your children are going to find immense solutions to their challenges by following the steps. Here are other techniques that children can follow in finding a solution to their challenges:

i. Be on time.
ii. Be consistent.
iii. Do what you say you will do.
iv. Be fair, even in an argument.
v. Don't lie -- not even little white lies to your partner or to others.
vi. Be sensitive to the other's feelings.

In addition, if your child/children are below the age of four, the following activities promote cognitive development in them:

g. Asking questions
h. Visiting interesting places
i. Practising counting
j. Identifying noises
k. Sing-a-longs
l. Practising shapes and colours

Children are creative and can solve a lot of problems. By helping them improve their abilities to find solutions for their challenges, they will be able to move ahead in life.

Habit Twenty-four
RECOVERING FROM A STRESSFUL TIME.

WHY IS IT IMPORTANT?

We all have to deal with stress in our lives on an ongoing basis, and at any given day, you might experience an unexpected and sudden stress in your life. It can come in form of a loss, defiantness, failure, deficiency, a new challenge or a move; something you have to deal with. It is crucial to know how to deal with stress in your life and the skills and resources necessary to cope and eventually recover from it. Your child/children often go through the same forms. They will experience various forms of stress in their lives and they need to quickly learn how best to recover. This will help them get through hard times and struggles and make them more resilient. There are various ways in which your child/children can recover from stress, but we will be focusing on the benefits of doing so.

BENEFITS:

INTELLECTUAL BENEFITS

- **Protecting the brain:** Chronic stress and high levels of cortisol, have been discovered to have long-lasting negative effects on the structure and connectivity of children's brain. Children who are exposed to long-term high levels of stress early in their life are more susceptible to mental issues such as anxiety and mood swings. When children are able to recover from stress at various points in their life, they are basically protecting their brains from these negative changes.

- **Building up mental strength:** When children and even adults learn to fall back to default settings after a stressful time, they are building up their mental strength, resolve and resilience. You can think of it as a mental workout of sorts when we continually recover from stressful situations. This ultimately helps us, children and adults alike, to think sharper.

💎 EMOTIONAL BENEFITS

● **Positive thinking:** It is vital to find ways to recover from stress in order to avoid burnout. When children allow stress to take over, they run the risk of slipping into a negative spiral of thinking which is detrimental to their wellbeing. When your children successfully recover from stress, they have put themselves in a situation where they can begin to see more positives instead of negatives. Positive thinking leads to a positive outcome on life and this translates to impacting the lives of the people around them positively.

● **Self-esteem:** There is a feel-good factor that children experience when they are in control of themselves, and being in control entails being able to revert to default settings when the body experiences something different like stress. This feeling continually builds self-esteem.

💎 SOCIAL BENEFITS

● **More cheer, less aggression:** Sometimes, when stress piles up in children's lives, they start to transfer aggression without even realising it. The people around them start to avoid them and the negativity that surrounds them. It's almost like an air around them that people pick up on. When children recover from stress, they suddenly become a lot more cheerful and positive and this is felt by those that come in contact with them. Every interaction is now pleasurable and your children get along with others a lot more easily.

● **Role modelling:** As expected amongst any age group, the person who has got his/her affairs in order tends to be a role model that others look up to. This exactly is the case amongst children.

💎 COMMUNICATION BENEFITS

● **Pleasurable interactions:** When the mood is relaxed, tensions are non-existent and there is all round positivity. Children tend to communicate a lot better and without fear of judgement or rebuke.

● **Better communication flow:** Interactions and communications free of the stress around children tend to flow better and smoothly and there is little room for misunderstanding.

💎 PHYSICAL BENEFITS

● **Get the rest you need:** Your body needs rest. The kind you get from sleep and naps keeps you going on a day to day basis. But stress tends to be cumulative on the body and mind, so you need to disconnect from all that is responsible for your stress levels. When you successfully do this, you allow your mind and your body to recover a lot more intensely from the travails of day to day existence. This kind of rest is more deep-seated and it propels you to be a lot more productive going forward.

● **Maintain healthy immune system:** Cortisol and other stress hormones ultimately have a negative effect on the immune system, and being able to keep them in check mean children are keeping their immune system as strong as can be at every given time.

CONCLUSION:

It is very important for children to be able to revert the body and its systems back to a default or more sustainable state in the event of stress; and this skill is crucial for children growing up as they do not quite understand why exactly they can't focus or get anything done, when they are stressed out about something.

PRACTICAL STEPS CHILDREN CAN TAKE TO RECOVER FROM A STRESSFUL TIME

Children are hyperactive, but they also experience stress. Unlike adults, children may not recognize that they are stressed. However, parents are able to notice quickly when they suspect new or worsening symptoms. Physical symptoms of stress in children can include, decreased appetite and other changes in eating habits. Here are stress warning signs to be mindful of in children:

- Apathy, lack of energy.
- Difficulty making decisions.
- Difficulty "keeping track" of things.

- Feeling on edge.
- A change in eating habits.
- Sleeping more than usual or difficulty getting to sleep.
- Being more emotional.

If a child is experiencing stress, there are proven ways that they can follow to recover from it:

1. SLOWING THINGS DOWN.

Even though the human brain is sophisticated even at the child-level, the human brain is designed to face acute stressors and then have a period of recovery to relax, eat, or sleep, before facing the next one. Hence, when children are stressed, they need to slow down. If they are having trouble with their arithmetic, they need to slow down. If they are having trouble with the house chores, they need to slow down.

2. EXERCISING

Exercises cannot be overemphasized. Exercises release the positive hormones in the children's brains. Exercises are also the best way for children to relieve stress.

3. GETTING IN THE GREEN.

When children are stressed up, they need to spend more time in nature. They need to go for a walk, swim or visit the zoo. They will be relieved of stress quickly by going green.

4. SMILING

The "feel good" neurotransmitters endorphins, dopamine, and serotonin are all released when children smile, which helps relieve stress and control heart rate. Smiling not only relaxes their body, but it can lower their heart rate and blood pressure. Indeed, the benefits of smiling are immense in children. Smiling can trick your children's brain into happiness — and boost their health. A smile spurs a powerful chemical reaction in the brain that can make your children feel happier. Science has shown that the mere act of smiling can lift your children's mood, lower stress, and boost your children's immune system.

5 **TRYING TO SEE YOUR STRESS AS A CHALLENGE.**
This is perhaps the modern approach to solving stress. Modern psychologists and neurologists have examined the brain when under stress and when excited, and they found an interesting fact. The same neurons in the human brain are fired under both situations. Hence, if your children are able to see stress as a challenge instead of a bad thing, they will be able to handle stress much better. For example, if they are nervous about public speaking, they can begin to rephrase public speaking as a conversation, and as an opportunity.

It is important that children recover in time from a stressful time. This helps them to be able to enjoy their youthful years and have more fun. In addition, they will be able to stay focused and concentrate on their academics and hobbies—which are essential for their physical, emotional and intellectual wellbeing.

 **Habit** Twenty-five

RECOVER EMOTIONAL BALANCE AFTER CHALLENGES.

WHY IS IT IMPORTANT?

Balance is maintaining equilibrium in the face of many other variables. This definition can be extended for emotional balance and we can see it as the ability of the mind and body to maintain a desired level of equilibrium, even after recovering from a stressful situation. These flexibilities and resilience are necessary for emotional health and well-being.

We cannot afford to stay in any given emotional state perpetually, be it a good emotion or a bad one. Children are most especially affected by this as their emotions can be very fleeting. They can be super excited this minute and take a complete U-turn the next minute. There needs to be restored, a more balanced neutral position. When facing a challenge, certain emotions spring up such as fear, anxiety, doubt, expectation, hope, etc., and your words might not understand how best to deal with these changes. So, it is crucial to be able to return to a more balanced state after the challenge has been overcome. It is essential to develop the resilience of your child/children's mind at an early age, and they will benefit a lot for their lives later.

BENEFITS:

INTELLECTUAL BENEFITS

- **Declutter the mind:** Returning to a state of emotional balance will help your children clear their mind and get rid of things that might be lingering at different recesses of it. Children will be able to learn better and faster if they can make this sort of recovery.

- **Refocus on work:** As you know and are aware, the attention span of the average child is very limited. As soon as they lose interest in something due to an emotional unbalance, it is very unlikely they will go back to it. So it is important to teach them how to recover and refocus on what they were doing before then.

- **Think quicker and wiser:** A quick recovery to an emotionally balanced state will allow you or your child/children to make quicker decisions and act faster.

EMOTIONAL BENEFITS

- **Be calmer:** When children cultivate the habit of emotional balance, they are in control of their thoughts. They become better at enjoying the subtleties of life; they rest better, and attain a certain level of inner peace that can be priceless.

- **Gaining resilience:** A continuous back and forth between emotional balance and unbalance eventually builds the mind to be more resilient and this will be useful to your child/children as they grow up and face bigger challenges.

SOCIAL BENEFITS

- **Better interactions with people:** Your children won't relate with people as they would on a very good day if they are carrying residuals of the emotional state of fighting or trying to overcome a certain challenge. There is a constant need to return to a balanced state so as to interact with the people around them as they would at any given day. They have to put their best self forward in order to make new friends and get along well with the ones they already have, and a big part of that is being in an emotionally balanced state.

- **Role modelling:** Even though they are not old enough to be role models in the sense that we understand it, they can still serve as models to their peers; and as such, children must learn how to recover to a balanced emotional state so as to teach their friends the better way to be.

- **Good leadership:** This points back to the above point on role modelling. It is never too young to start learning leadership traits, and one of them is being able to recoil from a stressful emotional event to a balanced state.

PHYSICAL BENEFITS

- **Hormonal balance:** A lot of the emotions children feel are as a result of the hormones that the body secretes in order to prepare their body to face a certain challenge. It can range from adrenaline resulting from fear to cortisol. These hormones aren't meant to linger for too long in their systems, as they can have a negative impact on their physical wellbeing. Returning to an emotionally balanced state after a challenge is mostly centred on allowing the body get rid of these hormones when the task is done.

CONCLUSION:

When children master this return to equilibrium, they don't get derailed as they would normally by circumstances and challenges. They start to feel more in control as they now have the tools to separate the different components of their being. This amounts to a generally healthier state of mind, a better outlook to life, and better interactions with those around them.

PRACTICAL STEPS CHILDREN CAN TAKE TO RECOVER EMOTIONAL BALANCE AFTER CHALLENGES

When bad things happen in the family or the outside world, children are often immature enough to handle them. They may be unable to respond well to challenges like changing neighbourhoods or cases of divorce. This is why the subject of emotional intelligence has to be taught properly at home and at school. It is better to teach your children these techniques earlier in life so that they will be well equipped to handle the challenges of life. The following are tips that your children can follow to recover from an emotionally challenging situation:

1 **KEEPING A JOURNAL OF FEELINGS.**
Research has proven the therapeutic effects of journaling. They help children to put their feelings into perspective. Your children need to understand that their feelings aren't going to go away because they opt not to deal with them. By being brave and intent on penning down their thoughts and emotions during an emotionally challenging situation, they will be able to recover quickly and wholly.

2 **SEEKING OUT A LIKE-MINDED COMMUNITY.**
The family should be the first point of contact for children if they are going through an emotionally challenging time. However, when the family is the problem, there are communities that are built to cater for the children.

3 **CREATING SPACE**
When things go wrong, sometimes, the children just need to create space for themselves. They need to get out of the problem and focus on what is positive, good, and right. They can walk in the park, relocate to another environment or spend more time with positive people.

4 **PUTTING DOWN THE SNACK FOOD.**
One of the natural responses for children going through a setback is to eat a lot. Impulsive eating is not healthy for children. It makes them fat, lazy and unhealthy, and these also create more emotional imbalance. They need to learn to put down fatty foods and focus on eating healthy and drinking lots of clean water.

5 **START EXERCISING.**
Exercise is a great way for children to take their mind away from bad happenings. They can do yoga or join a jitsu class. They will find many positive children there who they can mingle with and develop new interests. In addition, they can take up new and exciting hobbies like swimming and running. A healthy body will lead to happiness and a healthy mind.

6. CONFIDING IN OTHERS

When challenges come in the way of children, they are more likely to be moody, and this is not a healthy emotional reaction. They need to know that there are people who deeply care about them in the world, and who can help them get through their life challenges.

Life for children should be fun and exciting. However, there are times when they may find themselves in situations that are not satisfactory. When these things happen, it is going to take emotional intelligence for them not to get stuck in the trauma. Traumas in childhood often become cognitive flaws in adulthood. Hence, it is important that children are properly taught how to handle challenges, and most importantly, how to recover the emotional balance.

 **Habit** Twenty-six

ASK FOR HELP WHEN NEEDED

WHY IS IT IMPORTANT?

A lot of times, we feel stuck, stressed out and overwhelmed, and we really need help from the people around us to help us see things through. But sometimes, it can be daunting to ask for help, and we often find it difficult to put ourselves in positions of vulnerability. Its one thing to ask for support, and it's a whole different thing to feel comfortable with receiving it, so most people fight their own battles alone. Naturally, your child/children will be comfortable asking you for help, but they also need to be comfortable asking their peers and classmates for help with stuff you might not be around to help them with, or be in a position to do anything.

To a child, the parents are always the world. However, there are some situations where the parents may not be available, and the child will be in need. An example of such instance may be in an emotional state, as it is a known fact that children are always emotional. A child should be taught from when he or she is young that it is okay to seek help in times of trepidation, fears and loneliness. They should be taught that they may be vulnerable and need a shoulder to cry on. We have seen some situations whereby people die from depression. Sometimes, help is always available, but because such a person is not used to asking for help, he may end up going another way.

BENEFITS:

INTELLECTUAL BENEFITS

- **Refocusing:** When children ask people to help them with things, they might be having difficulty with it in terms of the challenges involved, allowing them to focus on other things that may be more pressing and require their personal attention. This basically frees up their mental space to focus on more critical things.

⬤ **Finding the right solution for the problem:** You can't do everything on your own and neither can your children. They need to learn how to ask for help from their peers and from adults around them in order to find the best solutions to certain problems.

⬤ **Be able to see things clearer:** Naturally, with help from others, children can begin to form a better picture of problems that will have otherwise been unapproachable by them. They get to see a better glimpse of the bigger picture.

⬤ **Add on the new knowledge and wisdom for life:** When your child/ children learn to ask for help, they will get the help that they need, and in the process, they learn a few things which will be useful to them in later years.

💎 EMOTIONAL BENEFITS

⬤ **Emotional Support:** When children support each other, they all share in the joy and happiness of giving and receiving. During this act, their bodies actually release hormones like oxytocin which is a powerful bonding hormone. This emotional support is invaluable as they get more comfortable and bolder to face all the challenges ahead of them.

⬤ **Being vulnerability:** It takes a lot of vulnerability and putting yourself out there to admit that you need help to solve a problem. Children need to learn that vulnerability is not weakness and it is ok to ask for help.

⬤ **Being humble:** With vulnerability comes humility and these two can be learnt. Teach your child/ children that it is okay to ask those around them for help even if they feel like they are ahead of them; be it in age, grade or whatever.

💎 SOCIAL BENEFITS

⬤ **Being relatable:** Asking for help makes children more relatable and approachable amongst their peers, as they identify with the idea of helping out and needing help. By asking for help, they are invariably showing the people around them that they aren't perfect and therefore they can be free to also ask them for help.

- **Fostering Trust:** When children ask those around them for help, they are showing they have faith in their capabilities and that they trust them. This strengthens the bond of trust between all parties involved.

- **Understanding the meaning-giving help to others:** When we interact with a group of committed and loyal friends, help is something that is received and is given. When children learn how to ask for help, they also learn the importance of offering help when they can. It is a two-way thing.

- **Sting sense of community:** This sense of community also goes back to the last point just made. Helping each other out in times of need fosters a deep sense of community amongst people. Children aren't exempt from this feeling.

COMMUNICATION BENEFITS

- **Team Player:** It is not always the best thing to approach issues and solve problems from only one point of view. When children ask for help, they are demonstrating their ability to work as a team and communicate well with others. More often than not, the results are often quite surprising. With this approach, children continue to hone the communication skills that help them work smoothly with different people.

PHYSICAL BENEFITS

- **Rest:** No child is an island and nothing is really achieved alone. Sometimes, children need to take some burden off their shoulders and seek the help that they need so that they can get some of the rest that they deserve. This will go a long way in helping their body recover from the challenges of any given day.

- **Reduce stress hormones:** Trying to solve a problem on their own and failing at it can lead to increased levels of stress hormones in their systems. It is therefore natural to see these stress levels fall when children have someone who can help out.

CONCLUSION:

There are so many benefits that come with asking for help when children actually need it. It is not so easy to trust people and be vulnerable enough around them to ask for help, but it is important that children find people who they can rely on. They shouldn't face the world alone. Also, it is their responsibility to follow up on whatever help is offered to them by those around.

PRACTICAL STEPS CHILDREN CAN TAKE TO ASK FOR HELP WHEN NEEDED

Maybe they are new to a school and are overwhelmed with adjusting to the environment. Or maybe they are students struggling with a tough homework assignment. Children often get in a situation where they could use some help. Unfortunately, it can feel tough to ask for it. Maybe they feel embarrassed or scared that they will be turned down.

These simple tips will help your children on how they can ask for help when needed.

1. KNOWING WHAT IS NEEDED

The first step that children can take in obtaining help when needed is to make a list of what they need. It is normal for children to feel overwhelmed in general and just want some help. However, they will be better prepared to ask for help if they can clearly articulate their needs.

2. KNOWING THE PEOPLE THEY NEED

While it might seem daunting for children to ask for help, they need to remember that there are likely plenty of people in their life who will be more than happy to help them. They can start with family and close friends and then think about other parts of their connection. Their list might include:

- Siblings
- Best friends
- Neighbours
- Mentors

3 MATCHING PEOPLE WITH SPECIFIC NEEDS

In addition to identifying their needs, they need to match their needs with the right persons. If their best friend is good at grammars, they could learn sentence structures and pronunciation techniques from the friend. Also, they could ask the neighbour if they would mind picking up a few things at the grocery store the next time they make a run. By choosing people based on their abilities and their relationship with them, they are effectively delegating tasks. This can help them reduce stress, especially in times when they need extra help.

4 CONSIDERING THE TIMING OF THE REQUEST

When asking for help, it is important that your children consider the timing, so they do not ask for help at the wrong time. A neighbour who is busy with his business will find it difficult to handle grocery shopping for your children. Hence, timing is important. If they are not sure whether or not it is a good time, they should just ask. They can say, "I'd love to ask for your help with something. Is there a time that's good for you to talk?"

5 SPECIFICITY

They should not be vague in their requests. It is important that they are specific as much as possible. Also, they have to know that people do not read minds. Instead of just saying, "I need help," they should state precisely what it is that they need on. For example, instead of saying to their teacher, "I'm confused. Can you help me?" they should say, "I don't understand how to solve the equation for X. Can you please show me a sample problem?

Asking for help can be scary for children. However, by following the above steps, they will be able to confidently approach others for help. In addition, they will be able to leverage their connections to get things done faster.

 **Habit** Twenty-seven

ACCEPT MISTAKES AS A CHANCE TO BE BETTER.

WHY IS IT IMPORTANT?

It's difficult to talk about failure as no one wants to embrace it as part of their lives and of their growth. A lot of people won't even admit to them. Ironically, it is one of the most relatable topics as everyone has tried and failed at something at a specific time in their life. From little things like exams and drivers tests to bigger failures like losing your family, job or business, failure is woven into the fabric of all of our social experiences.

Failure has a negative influence on children if they are not taught what it means and how to manage it. Some children have sharp brains to decipher information beyond them, but a kid will always be a kid. As a parent or as parents, it is essential to always educate a child on how they should perceive failure. Nobody loves to fail, but whenever it happens to them, ensure you let them know it is not the end of life and in fact, if the lessons of failure are learnt, it will lead to better things. This is a big matter to work with your child/children as early as possible, as they will face this issue a lot in different aspects of their lives and at different ages.

Children will make mistakes and experience failures at their very young ages, and it is up to you as a parent to guide them on how they can accept these mistakes, live with them, and become better for it.

People rarely talk about their failures until after they have become successful. But you must constantly engage failure at every point in your life and see it as an opportunity to evaluate where you are at that point, and how much better you can be. Your children must understand this.

As parents, we need to accept that failure is a part of our general growth. There are lots of potentials that can be tapped from it if used judiciously. In the long run, every failure is a golden opportunity for you to be better, and this can be a good way always to use yourself as a reference to teach your child/children, how they can handle failure in the future.

BENEFITS:

💎 INTELLECTUAL BENEFITS

Become wiser: Thomas Edison is famous for his 1000 failed experiments on the light bulb, and we have all come to be acquainted with his view on his failed experiments as 1000 ways not to build a light bulb. He did eventually succeed. Every failure makes you wiser. Let your children learn how to accept their failures as only momentary blips in their journey. Teach them to have a positive mindset to failure and try to improve and become the wiser for it.

Make better decisions: It goes without saying that once beaten, twice shy. When children try to do something a certain way and fail at it, they know not to go that route again. This knowledge will help them in future endeavours.

Avoid long-term mistakes: When your child/children learn to make better decisions and they acknowledge the mistakes they have made, the chances of repeating these mistakes in the future are very slim. Also, some mistakes will have a compounding effect if not properly acknowledged, so this needs to be taken seriously.

💎 EMOTIONAL BENEFITS

Freedom: When children accept their failures and adopt the positive mindset of being better and learning from them, a huge burden is lifted off their hearts and it can be quite liberating. They do not need to dwell in regret and keep holding themselves back. They need to quickly bounce back from defeat and try again with an improved strategy.

Apology: Sometimes, your children's mistakes can be in the form of wronging to someone else, and when they accept these mistakes, they find it easier to own up and apologise to any aggrieved parties. This also takes away a lot of burden from their emotional self.

Healthy emotions: It is unhealthy for children to avoid taking the blame for their own mistakes. Some children are so used to throwing blames at every other person but themselves, and this is a very unhealthy habit.

SOCIAL BENEFITS

Being relatable: When children own up to their failures and are open about them, people can relate better with them and they can let their guards down during interaction. This makes for an open and safe space for bonding among colleagues, friends and family. When children are open about their imperfections and are constantly working to get better, they can be a source of inspiration to those around them.

Being respected for humbleness: It takes courage to admit to mistakes and when children do this, people around them will respect them for it. Shying away from their mistakes will only make things worse and deteriorate the relationships they have.

COMMUNICATION BENEFITS

Embracing story: When your children accept their failures, it is much easier to talk to people about these failures and possibly seek help or advice in getting better. Without the fear of the stigma associated with failure, your children can better relate with the people around them when things aren't going particularly well.

PHYSICAL BENEFITS

Reduce the risk of physical harm: Sometimes, your children's mistakes can hurt them physically. Seeing how they could have done things differently or safer in these instances helps them make better decisions in moving forward. This reduces the risk of the same physical harm befalling them.

CONCLUSION:

Mistakes are inevitable in life and they are a vital part of growth and experience. Teach your children to embrace them, learn from them, and become better versions of themselves as they grow up. This will help them to see mistakes as growth experiences instead of evils.

No one is perfect and no one knows everything, we can only achieve more through synergy. Teach your children the importance of teamwork from a young age as this will prepare them for future challenges and help them maintain productive relationships.

PRACTICAL STEPS CHILDREN CAN TAKE TO ACCEPT MISTAKES AS A CHANCE TO BE BETTER

The most important life lessons that children will ever learn will be from the bad decisions they make. It is often said that "good judgement comes from experience, and experience comes from mistakes; therefore, good judgement comes from mistakes." Children need to learn from their mistakes so that they do not run the risk of repeating them. Better still, they need to know how to convert their mistakes into opportunities to be better. Your child/children must develop the wisdom and sense to make good decisions and choices. In so doing, they will be able to develop good judgment which will help them in life. Here are how your child/children can accept mistakes as a chance to be better:

1. RECOGNIZING THE MISTAKE.

This is the first step, and it is a crucial step. The act of recognizing their mistakes is the first step to creating a chance of getting better.

2. PINPOINT THE CAUSE OF THE MISTAKE.

Identifying the mistake isn't enough. Your child/children must be able to pinpoint exactly what the cause of the mistake is. When children make mistakes, they often associate the mistake with the feeling. However, the feelings and the source are often not the same. For instance, they may feel embarrassed because they said something wrong. The embarrassment isn't the mistake; it is only the result of the mistake.

3. DISSECTING THE RATIONALE AND FINDING THE FLAW IN THE THINKING

In the above example, they shouldn't conclude that saying something wrong is the main cause of the mistake. Instead, they should ask themselves questions like:

i. Why did I say what I said?

ii. Was it a reaction to what he/ she said?

The best approach to identifying the underlying rationale behind their mistakes is by asking the 5 WHYs—which is simply asking why 5 times. For example:

c. Why did I say something wrong? Because I was not happy

d. Why was I not happy? Because I didn't eat in the morning

e. Why didn't I eat in the morning? Because I woke up late

f. Why did I wake up late? Because I did my school assignment at 10:00 pm

g. Why did I do my school assignment at 10:00 pm? Because I watched the TV late into the night

The 5 WHYs is a powerful method that will also help your children's critical thinking.

4. TAKING RESPONSIBILITY.

This is important. If your child/children are pushing the blame on others, they may not be able to see mistakes as an opportunity to get better. They have to admit that they were wrong and committed to being better.

⑤ APPLYING THE LESSONS.

The beauty of the mistakes is in the lessons. If all your child/children did were to learn the lessons and not apply them, they have not learned anything. They have to apply the lessons, so they can easily move forward. For instance, in the example used in this section, they will be able to move forward and be better if they learn to reduce the TV time, especially in the evening.

Mistakes hold powerful lessons that children can convert into rich treasures. If they are able to see mistakes in the right light and are able to follow the above steps, they will become better.

3. SELF-DISCIPLINE

▶ **SELF-DISCIPLINE AND ITS IMPORTANCE TO CHILDREN**

Children who have self-discipline can healthily deal with awkward emotions. They've learned anger management skills and are able to regulate impulsive behavior. They can react respectfully when adults correct them, and they always take responsibility for their behavior.

They've also learned to make informed decisions for themselves based on considering the merits and demerits of their choices. Instead of saying, "I have to do this because my parents want me to," they know the importance of making healthy choices. They can make good decisions in relation to chores, assignment, money, peer pressure and self-care.

When children don't have self-discipline, parents always end up taking more responsibility for the child's behavior. For example, forcing a child to do his homework or making continuous threats to try and propel a child to do tasks, always means a parent puts in a lot of effort than the child does, to get the work done.

Teaching your child/children self-discipline skills while they are still growing can help them throughout their lifetime. People who never learn self-discipline skills seem to struggle to keep healthy habits, and it often follows them into adulthood.

Managing schoolwork, employment, money and household responsibilities, all need a good grasp of self-discipline. Adults who don't have self-discipline may struggle with problems like time management and money management skills, which may affect them in many other aspects such as relationship, work, health, etc.

It is advisable for parents to start early in fostering the habits of self-discipline on their child/ children to make it easier as they grow up.

 **Habit** Twenty-eight

OBTAIN ABILITIES TO TELL RIGHT FROM WRONG.

WHY IS IT IMPORTANT?

Today, there are rumours of war and political instabilities in nations across the world. When people are unable to differentiate right from wrong, they find themselves in messy situations that can affect those around them. Therefore, children must learn not to involve in the wrong things. Bad habits learned early in life are very hard to stop in children.

Research has proven that the ability to tell right from wrong makes children more inclined to do the right thing. Children who are able to tell their rights from their wrongs are able to consciously choose what is right. And, when they do wrong, they are able to correct themselves and move forward.

Good things come from your children when they know better, but bad things come from them when they don't know any better. If children knew better, they would not do bad things. Every child has a right to know better. The right to tell right from wrong.

Your children should not be good just because they fear punishment. That doesn't work because when children are not at home, they may choose to do the wrong things they are warned against. If they know the benefits of telling right from wrong; choosing right over wrong; and doing right as against doing wrong, they are more likely to choose right over wrong.

BENEFITS:

INTELLECTUAL BENEFITS

- **Strong sense critical thinking:** How children think, reflects who they are. To cultivate the kind of intellectual independence implied in the concept of telling right from wrong--children must recognize the need to foster intellectual (epistemological) humility, integrity, courage, empathy, perseverance, and fair-mindedness.

⬤ **To be independent adults:** When children are able to choose what's right, they show the world that they have solid critical thinking skills and can grow up to be independent adults.

⬤ **Free from pressure:** In a world where social pressure is forcing people to claim identities that are not biological or cultural, obtaining the ability to tell right from wrong will be of immense benefits to your children.

💎 EMOTIONAL BENEFITS

⬤ **Have positive emotions:** Moral Knowledge helps your children to have positive emotions like:

a. Satisfaction
b. Innocence
c. Honour
d. Glory
e. Dignity
f. Confidence
g. Joy
h. Success
i. Happiness

These are just a few of the emotional benefits of obtaining the abilities to tell right from wrong. Imagine how beneficial these awesome benefits will be to your children. Moral knowledge helps to guide your child so that they can make good decisions.

⬤ **Independence:** Being able to tell right from wrong feels great. Your child can be left alone to make personal decisions like the choice of food, cloth or exercise.

💎 SOCIAL BENEFITS

⬤ **Fit right in the social structure:** Social rule systems include institutions such as norms, customs, laws, regulations, taboos, and a variety of related concepts and are important in the social sciences and humanities. When children are able to tell right from wrong, they are able to fit right in the social structure without losing their unique identity.

⬤ **Respect by peers:** When your children are able to tell right from wrong, they earn the respect of their peers. This invariably boosts their self-esteem.

- **Right direction for life:** Life can feel confusing for a child that is just growing up. The world feels large and many options force themselves on a child. However, when your child is able to tell right from wrong, they are able to get the right direction for life.

- **Group representative for a speech:** A child who is able to tell right from wrong is going to be picked to represent a group.

- **Having a voice for own right:** It takes the unique ability to tell right from wrong to be able to have the dignity of voice. Your child builds up a voice for his own right when he or she is able to tell right from wrong.

COMMUNICATION BENEFITS

- **Virtues and moral excellence:** The communications of a child who has the knowledge of what is right and is ready to do what is justifiable, are pure and sweet to the ears. These children would be principled and well behaved. Trust, honesty, and honour will be their watchword, and they will be adored by their peers. Other communication benefits of knowing how to tell right from wrong are:

a. Patience

b. Politeness

c. Tolerance

d. Understanding

e. Propriety

f. Humility

g. Generosity

h. Fidelity

i. Liberality

j. Courtesy

k. Respect

CONCLUSION:

The benefits of knowing what is right are an important ability that cannot be overemphasised. It births virtues and moral excellence in children. It also brings to the fore their creative ability to think and understand complex situations. Parents should pay utmost attention to this part as it will help develop their children's decision-making skills.

PRACTICAL STEPS TO OBTAIN ABILITIES TO TELL RIGHT FROM WRONG

Teaching children how to tell right from wrong can be very frustrating. We live in an age where the government, the society, and the media are constantly telling us what is right and wrong. What we call morals is fast becoming an after effect of civilization. Hence, the need to ensure that children can be able to tell right from wrong is very important.

The process of enabling your children with the ability to tell right from wrong does not have to be frustrating. Instead, if you live the values every day, your child/children will watch and be able to pick up this remarkable and important ability. Here are four ways you can teach your children how to tell the right from wrong:

1. DEMONSTRATE YOUR MANNERS AND VALUES

The most impactful way children learn is by watching their parents. Children learn more by observation than by rote memorization. Hence, when you are around your child/children, make it noticeable that you have a choice to choose between right and wrong; and, you are choosing the right option. Make them know that in every situation, there is always the wrong thing and the right thing to do. When you keep choosing the right opinions even though it is uncomfortable, you are subconsciously putting this ability in your children.

2. TELL THEM EVERYDAY STORIES OF RIGHT AND WRONG CHOICES

In the news, and at the office, there are always stories of men or women who made the right choices and ended up being a success. Also, there are people who choose wrongly and end up being failures and disasters to their community. Try to tell these stories over dinner or before saying the goodnight.

3 INTRODUCE THEM TO SITUATIONS

Deliberately put your children in situations where they are forced between going with what is right or choosing the wrong option. When they choose what is right, make sure you reward them. However, if they choose the wrong thing, try to make them realize the consequence of such action. Teach them that following the wrong path, no matter how appealing it is, leads to paths of regrets, disappointment, and harm.

4 CELEBRATE GOOD CHOICES

There are times when your children will make mistakes and choose the wrong choice over what is right. It is good to look out for these wrong choices; however, we should never let good choices go unnoticed and unrewarded. Rewarding children do not have to drain the family's pocket. A simple "you did well." Or "excellent choice" could be all you need to celebrate your child's choices.

Ensuring that your children are able to discern between what is right or wrong, is one of the most crucial skills you can teach them. The world is getting to a point where children who are not properly brought up in the proper discernment of right and wrong would find it hard to fit in. As parents, it is our responsibility to ensure that our children do not only know what is right and wrong; also, they must be able to choose what is right over what is wrong.

 **Habit** Twenty-nine

FOLLOW A REGULAR BEDTIME ROUTINE.

WHY IS IT IMPORTANT?

Nowadays, children do not have a regular bedtime routine. They sleep where they watch TV. Children need regular rest. This is because physical and mental weakness leads to frustration, low self-esteem and being bullied at school. And if care is not taken, they may find themselves facing long-term illnesses. Hence, having a regular bedtime must be taken as a habit of utmost importance in children.

Research has shown that a good and regular bedtime routine is important for your physical and emotional wellbeing. Whether it is reading a book before bed, meditating, or listening to calm music, you probably have a bedtime routine that helps you sleep. Your children are no different. Parents should develop a bedtime routine for their children that will help them unwind and get to sleep. Little or poor quality of sleep can lead to fatigue the following day. This may affect their academic and athletic performances. A poor bedtime routine can also lead to increased feelings of fatigue. Obviously, these are not desirable qualities you want to see in your children. The following points will show you the benefits of following a regular bedtime routine for your children.

BENEFITS:

INTELLECTUAL BENEFITS

Having a better sleep outcome: Research has shown that, consistent bedtime routines for your children, are just as important for their developing brains, as the number of hours of sleep they get. Children who have consistent bedtime routines have better sleep outcomes. These benefits include:

- Increased sleep duration
- Earlier bedtimes
- Less night waking

- Decreased sleep problems
- Less amount of time in bed before falling asleep

💎 EMOTIONAL BENEFITS

Nurturing relationship: Having a bedtime routine is one of the ways to nurture your relationship with your child/children. You can include such activities like bedtime reading or short prayers in your child's bedtime routine. These activities ensure that you bind properly with your children. They improve your relationship with your children as they feel loved and valued.

Giving undivided attention: Although often a struggle, bedtime is the best time to give your child/children your undivided attention. It is this moment that they are going to remember when they become adults. You can snuggle, read a book, and talk. Your child/children will often save their most sensitive questions for this time.

💎 PHYSICAL BENEFITS

Feeling safe and secure: The familiarity routine sets expectations and boundaries. It has been scientifically proven that a regular bedtime routine helps your child/children feel safe and secure. Randomness brings confusion, purposelessness, and frustration. However, when there is order, your children are more likely to feel safe and secure. It is in this kind of environment that they are able to ask their most sensitive questions. Therefore, ensure that you create a positive and comfortable sleep environment. Your child/children need this type of structure to feel safe and secure and to know what to expect next.

CONCLUSION:

The importance of maintaining a healthy bedtime routine cannot be overemphasised, as it is very important. It can spell the difference between having a healthy child and taking your children to sick bays. Your child/children are naturally active, and you do not want to inhibit their growth. Instead, you can control how they grow, so that they are able to grow healthier, better and stronger. It's never too early to start a bedtime routine. Once a few weeks old, your infant will look forward to this calm time before sleep and, soon enough, will begin to make the connection between his/her bedtime routine, and time to blissfully nod off to dreamland.

PRACTICAL STEPS TO FOLLOW A REGULAR BEDTIME ROUTINE

A good and regular bedtime routine is important for your physical and emotional wellbeing. Little or poor quality of sleep can lead to fatigue the following day. This may affect their academic and athletic performances. A poor bedtime routine can also lead to increased feelings of fatigue. Obviously, these are not desirable qualities you want to see in your children. The following tips will ensure that your children follow a regular bedtime routine.

1. DEVELOP A WRITTEN SLEEP SCHEDULE

It is easier for your children to follow a routine when it is written and posted in a place where they can easily see it. You cannot always trust their memories to ensure that they follow some random bedtime routine. When developing your routine, it is important to bear these points in mind:

a. Ensure that the bedtime schedule is consistent. You shouldn't set 10:00 PM on Monday and 12:00 PM on Tuesday. You want to keep it uniform. This will avoid such questions as, "Hey mum, I slept 10 yesterday. Why 12 tonight?"

b. Ensure that every activity within the bedtime routine is written. The activities may include revision of academic activities, bedtime stories, short prayers, etc.

c. Paste the bedtime routine where the children can easily see it

d. Make changes slowly. Do not feed your children with new rules forcefully. If your children have been sleeping really late, you can incrementally reduce the late sleeping hours by adjusting the time they go to bed by a factor of 15 to 30 minutes.

2. FEED THEM LIGHTLY BEFORE BED

The food you feed your children will determine how active they will be at night. If you do not feed them, they will not be able to sleep because of hunger. If they take heavy foods for dinner, it may keep them too active. Instead, you want to ensure that they only take healthy light foods. If you are considering the kind of food to feed your children, here are healthy suggestions:

a. Vegetables

b. A fruit smoothie with spinach, frozen cherries, and fruit juice without added sugar

c. Foods high in healthy carbohydrates and protein

d. Avoid processed foods

3. USE LIGHTING TO YOUR ADVANTAGE

The human body reacts to light. To ensure that your children go to bed in time, dim the lights. Lighting can help your children wake up or fall asleep. If you want your children to maintain a regular night-time routine, you have to control the lighting. In getting this right, make sure that about 30 minutes to bedtime, children are not allowed to watch the TV or use the computer. Also, ensure that the light is dimmed.

The importance of maintaining a healthy bedtime routine cannot be overemphasised. It is very important. It can spell the difference between having a healthy child and taking your children to sick bays. Children are naturally active, and you do not want to inhibit their growth. Instead, you can control how they grow, so that they are able to grow healthier, better and stronger.

 **Habit** Thirty

ENGAGE IN PHYSICAL ACTIVITY

WHY IS IT IMPORTANT?

Today, there are several health movements—from yoga to gym. This is because many people are falling sick because of the lack of physical activity.

It has been proven that children who engage in physical activity are fitter and healthier than those who do not follow a fitness plan.

Keeping in shape can help your children throughout their lives. With so many electronic gadgets taking up children's time, it is important that you take the physical activity of your children seriously.

Physical activity has been proven to help children improve mentally, socially and physically. Children who do not engage in any physical activity are often docile and inactive. This makes them shy and less active among their peers. As a result, it leads to low self-esteem. Children must take physical activity seriously if they want to maintain top physical fitness and shape.

It is essential that physical activity takes an important role in a child's life if they are going to maintain their creativity as they grow up in life.

BENEFITS:

INTELLECTUAL BENEFITS

- **Sharp mind:** Exercise helps the brain to have sufficient blood and oxygen supply— which are necessary for a sharp and sound mind.

- **Alertness:** Physical activities help children to be able to act quickly. It improves their reflexes.

- **Long study:** With sound mind obtained from engaging in a physical activity, your children will be able to stay longer in their study sessions as the fresh body connects to the clear mind.

- **Accurate end results for studying:** Children are able to stay productive when they read. And, at the end of their studying sessions, they are able to retain more from their studies.

💎 EMOTIONAL BENEFITS

- **Happiness:** A physically healthy child is a happy child. Your children will easily find pleasure in the playground.

- **Thriving:** It takes a sound mind to thrive. When your children are physically fit and mentally sound, they are able to thrive in all conditions.

💎 SOCIAL BENEFITS

- **Boosts the physiology:** Physical activity boosts the physiology of your child/children. It makes them active and positive, and is indeed a good habit to imbibe in your children. When you encourage physical activity in your children, you will begin to see your child/children gaining many social benefits.

- **Improved social skills:** Child/children who engage in one physical activity or the other will be cheerful and more positive towards relationship building. This is because many physical activities are best enjoyed when there is more than a child involved.

- **Improved self-esteem:** Self-esteem is developed through one's competence and interest. When your child finds a physical activity that he or she likes, he develops self-esteem naturally. This is good for both the child and the family. This ensures that the child does not grow up to be narcissistic.

- **Improved confidence:** If you want to boost the confidence of your child, the easiest way to do that is by engaging him or her in a physical activity. By getting them to engage in a physical activity for three hours spread throughout the day, you will be giving the self-confidence of your child a significant boost.

💎 COMMUNICATION BENEFITS

● **Love to express:** When your child/children engage in physical activities, they are excited to express themselves. Definitely, they would love to talk about the events that took place on the playground, and about the people they met.

💎 PHYSICAL BENEFITS

● Physical activity in children is important for a wide variety of health reasons. It helps in the reduction of obesity and overweight. It also helps in increasing strength in bones and muscles. Exercise is a vital component of any child's development—laying the foundations for a healthy life. Other benefits include:

a. It strengthens the heart. The heart is a muscle and should be regularly exercised. When children engage in a physical activity, the heart is strengthened.

b. It helps keep arteries and veins clear.

c. It strengthens the lungs.

d. It reduces blood sugar levels.

e. It controls weight.

f. It strengthens bones.

g. It regulates blood pressure.

CONCLUSION:

Physical activity helps in improving your children's psychology. It has been proven that physical movement enhances the mood of the children and help put the body back to default. It is essential to imbibe the spirit of working out to the children during their early years so it will be easier for them when they grow up.

PRACTICAL STEPS TO ENGAGE IN PHYSICAL ACTIVITY

With so many electronic gadgets taking up the time of your children's time, it is important that you take the physical activity of your child/children seriously. According to health experts, it is important that children have at least 60 minutes of physical activity every day. With the overwhelming academic obligations, TV and video games, it can get really difficult getting your child/children to see the essence of being physically fit. As a result, it takes a massive amount of effort to get your child/children to keep a keep physically fit all year long. However, if you follow the following tips, you will be able to engage your child/children in physical activities.

1. THROW A FAMILY DANCE PARTY

The easiest way to introduce a new routine is by making it as fun as possible. Pop on some music and start dancing. To make your family dance party more fun and rewarding, ensure that you bear these points in mind:

a. Curate a playlist of favourite songs

b. Move furniture to create space

c. Wear fun costumes

d. Use fabric, ribbon and scarf props

e. Learn new dance moves together

2. ENCOURAGE YOUR CHILD/CHILDREN TO PLAY WITH THE PETS

Children would want to play with toys and the computer. Instead, you can encourage your children to throw the ball for your dog, or play with the cat.

3 TAKE THEM TO PARKS AND PLAYGROUNDS

Taking your child/children with you to playgrounds and parks will allow them to make new friends based on the common interest of play. With these new friends, your children will be willing to play more and explore new physical activities.

4 ALLOW YOUR CHILD/CHILDREN TO CHOOSE THEIR SPORT

Even though there are certain sports you would want your child/children to engage in, the easiest way to encourage them to engage in physical activity is by allowing them to choose what feels right to them. If your boy or girl chooses what activity to do, they are going to be more excited to pursue such activity. To get them to choose their own physical activity, you can follow this method:

a. Ask them about their favourite physical activity. You can also get to know what could be their favourite physical activity by allowing them to try different activities and notice their enthusiasm as they engage in them.

b. Ask if they would like to go to sport camps. At sport camps, they will be exposed to a variety of physical activities. From there they will be able to pick which would hold their sustained interest.

c. Sign them up for whatever sport that excites them.

d. Enrol them in physical education classes after school hours.

e. Perform unstructured exercise programs that include:
   i. Riding bicycles
   ii. Throwing a Frisbee
   iii. Routine walking of the family dog
   iv. Playing a game of table tennis with another family member
   v. Flying a kite at the beach
   vi. Regular swimming at a local pool
   vii. Jumping on a trampoline
   viii. Dancing to a favourite music

By now, you know that regular physical is good for everyone, and most importantly for your children. The first five years of your children's lives are the most crucial. This is the developmental stage where lifelong routines and habits are developed. By finding a way of incorporating at least a physical activity in your child's life, you would be able to set them up for a life of success.

 **Habit Thirty-one**

TALK OPENLY AND CALMLY EVEN WHEN YOU'RE UPSET

WHY IS IT IMPORTANT?

The community, family, work problems, when people don't know how to express themselves when upset, are myriad. Many nations have gone to war because of misunderstanding.

When people do not talk openly and calmly when they are upset, they breed conflicts that otherwise would have been avoided.

Several research reports have emphasized on the importance of soothing words in upsetting times. Talking openly and calmly when upset helps children to be able to handle tensed moments. Thus, they are able to avert several problems that may arise.

Speaking calmly and openly may not come naturally to children. However, they must understand that this is a learnable skill. The ability to speak calmly and openly when hurt will help them to get out of many self-destructive habits like jealousy, envy and anger.

What do your child/children do when they are angry? Do they curse, kick at things, and scream obscenities while scaring away all of the people in their orbit? These are not healthy ways for your children to express themselves when they are upset. You cannot stop people or things from upsetting your children. However, you can help them see the benefits of talking openly and calmly even when they are upset.

BENEFITS:

💎 INTELLECTUAL BENEFITS

- **Intelligence:** Nothing tells the intelligence level of children more than the words that come out of their mouths. By talking calmly when upset, they are able to display a peak level of intelligence.

● **Positivity:** By pausing, empathizing and rephrasing their thoughts in a positive manner, your child/children will be able to show their intellectual civilisation. It is not civil to use cursive words when angry. Your children should know that instead of raising their voices when angry, they should be able to raise the quality of their words.

● **Focus:** By talking openly and calmly, children can stay focused and productive. Strife and anger destroy productivity.

● **Being able to control the right choice:** It also helps them to control their choices.

💎 EMOTIONAL BENEFITS

● **Assertiveness:** Feeling guilty after expressing their concerns when angry, is not good for a child. There is always a healthy way for your child to give expression to his or her thoughts.

● **Confidence:** You need to let them know that they can feel more assertive, confident and positive if they can calmly and openly express themselves even when they are upset.

● **Relaxation:** When they talk openly and calmly even when upset, they will be able to minimize stress and feel more relaxed.

💎 COMMUNICATION BENEFITS

● **Diplomacy:** No one wants to associate with a troublesome and lousy child. When your child/children use the powerful "I- statements," they are able to express their feelings without attacking others. It also allows them to take responsibility for themselves.

● **Conflict resolution:** Your children will be able to realize that yelling is not good, and extend goodwill to the other person. The ability to communicate positively in emotionally tensed situations will help in building your children's conflict resolution skill set.

💎 PHYSICAL BENEFITS

Prevention of injuries: When your child/children use the right words during a heated conversation, they are able to protect themselves from physical injuries.

Increased in perceived physical strength: Words like "Alright" and "Ok," help to make others feel comfortable. Your child/children will be able to avert many fights if they are able to openly and calmly express themselves even when they are upset. A gentle word will soothe both themselves and diffuse the situation.

CONCLUSION:

When your child/children choose to be assertive and openly express themselves, they operate from a position of equality and respect. They respect their own values and convictions while respecting others' values and convictions. It may take time for your child/children to learn not to yell when they are upset, but do not give up on them. Tell them to make it a goal that they are going to express themselves calmly and respectably whenever they are upset; and, it even gets easier if they are able to know the benefits of talking openly and calmly. Children that are able to express themselves without insulting others grow up to be respectable adults in the society.

PRACTICAL STEPS TO TALK OPENLY AND CALMLY EVEN WHEN YOU'RE UPSET

- As parents, it is your responsibility to teach your child/children how they can stay calm in situations that have to do with anger.
- How do you respond to angry situations? How do you control your anger? Children learn most of the habits they exhibit from their parents, and this is a core area that you shouldn't let them down.
- Shouting, destroying things or sulking, are not good ways to show anger and you need to let your children know this. You can't keep other children away from annoying them, but you can always train them on how to manage the situation calmly when the need arises.

1. TEACH THEM TO CALM DOWN

This is easier said than done. Calming down when they could literally see their blood boiling over an issue isn't always easy. To ensure that your child/children know how to calm down in the heat of situations, they can do any of the following:

   a. Tell them to go for a walk. Getting outdoors and focusing on nature can help them focus more and make the right decisions.

   b. Encourage your child/children to meditate. Meditation can help regulate emotions. Meditation does not have to be something sophisticated. Instead, they can follow these simple steps:

      i. They should take slow, deep breaths.

      ii. They should visualize a peaceful scene like a calm sea. In visualizing a peaceful scene, they should focus on every little detail. They should pick a place that makes them instantly feel calmer and at peace, and they will quickly find their breath returning to normal.

      iii. They should make meditation a habit. They should meditate even when they are not angry. This will help them to stay calm when they are angry.

2. TEACH THEM TO THINK BEFORE THEY SPEAK

If your children tend to shout when they are upset, they are emotional communicators. This means that they act based on how they feel rather than reasoning things out. By taking a few minutes out to evaluate their reactions, they will be able to communicate more effectively.

3. TEACH THEM TO APOLOGIZE FOR YELLING

Make them realize that yelling is not good, and show them how to extend goodwill to the other person. For them to genuinely apologise for their yelling, teach them the following steps:

   i. Teach them to start with calming words. Words like "Alright" and "Ok," help to make others feel comfortable.

   ii. Make sure that whenever they are trying to apologise for yelling, they are honest and genuine.

   iii. They should remove cursive words and other words that can spark conflict and arguments from their language.

iv. Let them know that the "I- statements" are powerful. These statements allow them to express their feelings without attacking others. It also allows them to take responsibility upon themselves.

It may take time for your child/children to learn not to yell when they are upset, but do not give up on them. Tell them to make it a goal that they are going to express themselves calmly and respectably whenever they are upset; and, it even gets easier if they are able to follow the above tips. Children that are able to express themselves without insulting others grow up to be respectable adults.

Habit Thirty-two

POSSESS A GOOD STUDY ROUTINE

WHY IS IT IMPORTANT?

When children do not have a good study routine, they are unable to develop a strong work ethic which is needed to survive in this world.

The rewards of possessing a good study routine include delayed gratification, hard work, and enhanced expertise.

Research has shown that children who develop a good study routine early in life are able to go on to have a healthy work-life balance. A healthy work-life balance helps people to be able to handle stress while paying attention to basic needs.

Learning about life and the world we live in is very important for successful living. By encouraging your child/children to embrace a lifelong habit of studying, you are setting them up for success. This is probably one of the best things parents can do for their children. Even though this habit is often laid out to teachers, it is important that parents focus, improve and stabilize the study routines of their children.

BENEFITS:

INTELLECTUAL BENEFITS

Goal setting: If you want to produce intellectually healthy children, help them to develop a good study routine. A good study routine doubles as goals.

Time management: Your children's life cannot always be about their academics, but if they have a major examination coming up, you are going to need a study schedule to ensure adequate time is allotted to tasks that will help them in achieving long-term academic goals.

- **Productivity:** There's nothing that improves children's productivity as well as a good study routine. This is because children are able to inculcate the discipline of execution.

EMOTIONAL BENEFITS

- **Confidence:** It helps them to be able to be confident about their academics because they have done their arithmetic right several times in their study period. This is a much better approach to raising your child/children than having them live without a structure.

- **Fulfilment:** In the end, they would have been able to accomplish a lot of things, and also relax without guilt.

- **Positive mindset:** Having a study routine has many benefits, but one important benefit for children is that a routine helps boost their mood. It is amazing to think that such things as a study routine would help children physically. Study routines help them stay focused and have peace of mind.

- **Minimization of anxiety:** Regular study sessions help reduce anxiety, which they may feel because of an unregulated lifestyle. For many children, studying is a difficult endeavour which is plagued by interruptions, procrastination, and lack of free time. Establishing a study routine is a time management practice that can reduce your children's level of stress, by teaching them how to set aside the necessary amount of time for studying, and also how to use that time wisely.

SOCIAL BENEFITS

- **More friends:** The numbers of hours in a day are not infinite. Helping your child/children to develop a good study routine will help them to be able to focus on study, and have time to socialize.

- **More playtime:** When children procrastinate on doing important work, they will not be able to enjoy their free time as they would be worrying about what they should be doing.

💎 PHYSICAL BENEFITS

● **Physical strength development:** Study routine could also be improved with exercise. For instance, your children could do some chair squats at their desks. To do this, they will stand up from their chairs, then squat down without sitting down. Hovering just above the chair for about 10 seconds, they can repeat this practice 20 times. This is an excellent way for your child/ children to obtain maximum physical benefits from their study routine, especially if they do not have sufficient free time.

CONCLUSION:

Teaching your child/children how to maintain their study schedule is the best way to ensure that they stay sane in a world going wild with compromised information and fake news. It is in the study hours that they develop important critical thinking skills.

PRACTICAL STEPS TO POSSESS A GOOD STUDY ROUTINE

Learning about life and the world we live in is very important for successful living. By encouraging your child/children to embrace a lifelong habit of studying, you are setting them up for success. This is probably one of the best things a parent can do for their children. Even though this habit is often laid out to teachers, it is important that parents focus, improve and stabilize the study routines of their children.

 CREATE A PERFECT STUDY PLACE FOR YOUR CHILDREN

Find a place where there are no distractions. Pick a spot away from the television and any other kind of screens. Ensure that the TV is switched off whenever it is study time. If the TV or the computer is loud and colourful, it may be hard for the children to focus.

2. PUT ALL PHONES ON SILENCE

When it is study time, set a rule that everyone put their phone on silence. When a phone rings, it breaks the attention of the children. Make this a rule that is consistently followed. When the children see the respectful effort that you are putting into their study routine, they are going to be more inclined to put in their effort to stay true to the routine.

3. HAVE A WELL-LIT SPACE

If you want your child/children to stay awake during the whole study session, ensure that the area you have allocated for their studying session is well lit. The abundant light will keep them focused, awake and prevent them from straining their eyes.

4. TEACH THEM BY EXAMPLE BY WORKING ALONGSIDE THEM

If you are watching Netflix while your children are studying, you are not setting a good example. That way, you are going to make them jealous and distracted. Instead, you should be doing some productive work in their space that will keep them from feeling alone. Sit down next to your child/children and work on something while they study. This could be writing a grocery list, finishing your work, or paying bills in their study space while they're working.

5. TEACH YOUR CHILD/CHILDREN HOW TO USE PLANNERS AND CALENDARS

You should buy your child/children a planner and teach them how to use it, in addition to their list of assignments and syllabi. Fill in all the big due dates for assignments, tests, school breaks, and extracurricular events. Make sure that the calendar is exciting by including the school play as well as winter break. This will make the children have something to look forward to.

Show your child/children how to use the planner to remember important daily and weekly chores. Teach them to get excited about checking things off their to-do list. You can give them stickers and markers to make writing in their planner more fun and personal.

Teaching your child/children how to maintain their study schedule is the best way to ensure that they stay sane in a world going wild with compromised information and fake news. It is in the study hours that they develop important critical thinking skills.

 **Habit** Thirty-three

USE ACTIVE LISTENING SKILLS

WHY IS IT IMPORTANT?

Back in the day, children were not allowed to speak until they could prove that they had listened. Listening is important in children. Active listening helps children to be able to learn about the world around them. It also helps them to know what to say or do. Communication is not a one-way process. It requires that both parties involved in the communication are actively involved. As a result, listening is almost as important as speaking. This is why it is important to imbibe active listening skills in your child/children when they are still young.

Without active listening skills, children will find themselves in positions where they may be unable to express themselves because they do not understand the conversation going on around them.

In addition, active listening helps children to be aware of their environment. They are able to learn about what is happening in their environment and devise a means of action. Listening is the most fundamental component of interpersonal communication skills. It involves giving full undivided attention to the speaker.

BENEFITS:

💎 INTELLECTUAL BENEFITS

- **Active listening has five components:**
    - Testing understanding by restating or rephrasing the facts that have been said.
    - Questioning to clarify what has been said.
    - Building on the speaker's proposal.
    - Feedback to the speaker about the impact of the message.
    - Summarizing to reinforce the speaker's message.

These components require a high level of intelligence. When your children are focused on building their active listening skill, they are able to reap intellectual benefits like:

⦿ **Critical thinking:** It takes an enhanced level of critical thinking to be able to follow through the process of active listening. The child must be able to ask the right question at the right time. This helps develop their ability to think critically before making any decision.

⦿ **Vocabulary Development:** To build rapport with people, children must be able to have access to an abundant storehouse of vocabulary resources. Active learning helps your child/children to build their vocabulary and metaphors.

💎 EMOTIONAL BENEFITS

⦿ **Love:** When your child leans towards others to hear them clearly, they are building rapport. This helps them to build healthy emotions like love and peace.

⦿ **Empathy:** The emotional benefits of leaning into someone's else world, absorbing their intention and actively filtering what's right, good, and useful, is what empathy is all about.

💎 SOCIAL BENEFITS

⦿ **Rapport building:** The ability to listen and to comprehend what people say allows children to build a strong rapport with colleagues, parents, and others. Teachers and peers have confidence in children that can listen to instructions and then do what is expected with minimal follow-up. It takes active listening to be able to listen to instructions and follow them actively.

⦿ **Conflict resolution:** Good listeners also have a better track record resolving problems with others. This is really an incredible skill to have. In life, there will be challenges and conflicting moments. However, a child who is highly skilled in active listening will be able to navigate his or her way out of conflicts.

- **Ability to work in a group setting:** When your children are able to demonstrate active listening, they will be able to work better in a group. Team members are usually assigned a portion of the work. Later, their completed tasks will need to fit in with other team members' results. Those who were able to listen well and perform accordingly will find their work results fit better than those who misunderstood.

- **Gaining the respects from the others:** Children who are able to demonstrate active listening skill are able to garner the respect of their peers.

COMMUNICATION BENEFITS

- **Two ways communication:** Listening helps children to be able to develop their communication. When they listen actively, they are able to develop the appropriate response. This makes them courteous and eloquent.

- **Allow the other to express:** By listening to others, they are able to allow others to express themselves. This makes others to respect them more.

- **Showing attention to others:** Other children will appreciate them more because they feel honoured. Active listening skill cannot be overemphasized in children.

- **Receptive skills:** It also helps them develop receptive skills. They become more attuned to the happenings in the society. They are able to perceive others feelings.

CONCLUSION:

When your child/children are able to demonstrate active listening skills, they will be set apart from their peers. They are able to build rapport with their peers, resolve conflicts and function effectively in a group setting.

As parents, it is imperative for us to ensure that our children follow a study routine designed to enable them focus on matters of importance anytime. This will also give them a sense of direction and purpose as it will take their minds off frivolities.

PRACTICAL STEPS TO USE ACTIVE LISTENING SKILLS

If you are wondering why your child/children are not paying attention and retaining vital information, teaching them how to use active listening skills could help them out. As a parent, empower your child/children by listening to them, giving them instructions, and fostering discussion and debate.

1. PRACTICE ACTIVE LISTENING AT HOME

When your children are telling you about the events that happened at the school playground, pay attention to them, listen to them, and reciprocate their enthusiasm. Ask questions and be genuinely interested in whatever they are saying. Do not let your attention to be drifted. Drop whatever it is that you are doing, and give them your full focus. In short, be their number one fan at that moment. This will definitely impress them, and they will pick up active listening skills subconsciously.

2. MAKE THEM ASK QUESTIONS

If you want your children to develop active listening skills, make them ask questions. Questions show that they are genuinely interested in what the other party is doing. Also, make sure that they ask the right questions. They should focus on asking positive, open-ended, and curious questions.

3. MAKE THEM PARTICIPATE IN DISCUSSIONS

Teach them to answer questions, and also ask questions when they have a thought or got confused. Make your home democratic by ensuring that it is discussion based. When active discussion is encouraged at home, children will tend to be active participants. In your home, encourage all views no matter how absurd they may sound. Children are generally known to approach subjects from strange angles, so do not kill their curiosity, instead, encourage it. However, gradually make them see the reality of things by making them engage in active listening and questioning.

4. TEACH THEM TO TAKE NOTES

When they take notes, even outside the school environment, they are forced to engage in active listening. Whenever they are in family meetings, religious gatherings, or any social event where it is not too awkward to take notes, equip them with pen and writing pads. Tell them to take note when words or phrases are being repeated; and, underline or circle in their notes any words that seem to be significant.

Note taking can significantly increase active listening as well as comprehension. However, caution must be exercised that they do not take too many notes. Taking too many notes will not translate into active listening as they would be copying verbatim whatever is being said.

5. ASK THEM TO EXPLAIN THINGS TO YOU

Deliberately ask them to tell you how their day went. Ask them to explain how they would cook a certain food. Ask them to explain in their own words what the speaker said. Whenever you give them instructions, ask them to repeat whatever you said. Deliberately engage them in the question and answer method so as to improve their active listening. Whenever they show positive signs of active listening, praise them for paying attention. When you praise them, they are going to be proud of their active listening superpowers.

 **Habit Thirty-four**

ALLOW THE RIGHT AMOUNT OF TV

WHY IS IT IMPORTANT?

The world's problem with too much TV watching is that we do not produce adults who are able to build a new future.

Research studies have shown that children who watch more than 20 hours of TV weekly are less likely to be creative. This is because they have filled their alone time with TV time. It was during these alone-times that children like Mozart were able to develop their genius skills.

Watching TV is a common pastime in many homes. Many homes have more than one TV units. While TV can be entertaining for children, it can easily take over their lives—making them lazy. Children who watch TV a lot binge eat. Hence, they become fatter and less physically active.

The TV can take most of the productive hours and energy of the lives of these children. This can take a toll on their health. For example, they can become obese, depressed, and less creative.

However, you can help your child/children break bad habits, spend the right amount of time in front of the TV, and become more useful at home. When children spend less time watching TV, they are able to have time to engage in more productive activities like studying their books, engaging in a physical activity, or learning a new skill.

BENEFITS:

♦ INTELLECTUAL BENEFITS

More study time: A moderate TV time helps the children to have more time to study. When the time spent watching the TV is regulated, your children will be able to have sufficient time to study.

* **Increased awareness of the world:** Studying allows children to gain insight into incredible new worlds, new perspectives, and new things that can help them become better family members, students, and friends.

* **Improved vocabulary:** By limiting TV time, children can up their reading statistics by 5 to 6 books in a year. This is an incredible statistic if you consider the immense intellectual value that is in a book.

EMOTIONAL BENEFITS

* **Controlled exposure to fake news:** Television is a wonderful technological invention. It allows children to stay informed about the happenings in the country and all over the world. However, too much TV time can expose children to the consequences of biased news. The news is overly negative—showing natural disasters, mass shootings, and crime movies.

* **Optimism:** These are not healthy contents for your children to feed on. This information is too big for the mind of small children to handle and they can corrupt their worldview. However, by regulating the TV time, children are able to spend equally important time on important things like their academics, hobbies and physical activities.

* **Decreasing fears:** News and TV programs are filled with fearful stories of things happening around the world. When children stay away from TV, they are able to avoid unnecessary fears.

SOCIAL BENEFITS

* **More social connections:** The social benefit of allowing the right TV time cannot be overemphasized. It helps children to be able to connect more with others. When there is less time to spend watching TV, children are forced to be more creative.

* **Rapport building:** Hence, they start sharing their experiences throughout the day. This helps them to bond better with you as well as with others. It helps in creating a unique family experience.

⬥ **Not being manipulate by the advertising:** When children are not overly exposed to TV, they are able to avoid the deceptions and manipulations that are shown on it.

💎 PHYSICAL BENEFITS

⬥ **Improved body shape:** After a long day at school, coming home and plopping down in front of the TV/computer to watch their favourite show is bad for your child/children's health. To control the stress hormone, cortisol, children need to move or exercise. When the body is put in a moving position, especially after a stressful day at school, it helps elevate the mood and cognitive functions.

⬥ **Optimal body weight:** Also, by helping your child/children reduce TV time, they will be consuming fewer calories that may contribute to body weight.

CONCLUSION:

Studies have shown that children who eat while watching TV, are more likely to consume more at the time than later in the day.

You should help your children in their academic pursuits, by regulating the hours they spend in front of a TV and reading alongside with them, so as to give them a sense of belonging that they are not being punished by it.

PRACTICAL STEPS TO ALLOW THE RIGHT AMOUNT OF TV

Watching TV is a common pastime in many homes. Many homes have more than one TV units. While TV can be entertaining for children, it can easily take over their lives—making them lazy. Watching TV can take most of the productive hours and energy of the lives of these children, taking an ineluctable toll on their health. However, you can help your child/children break bad habits, spend the right amount of time in front of the TV, and become more useful at home.

1. DON'T PUT A TV IN EVERY ROOM

At a time in history, it was the norm to put TVs in every available room in the house. This no longer seems to be a good idea. By limiting TV viewing to one room, you reduce the temptation to watch more channels.

2. CANCEL ALL CABLE SUBSCRIPTIONS

By cancelling all your cable subscriptions, this eliminates mindless flipping of channels and leads to less time in front of the TV. When the remote is with the children, it is natural to want to switch from one channel to another seeking what would catch their fantasy. This is why they spend more time in front of the TV in the first place. If the channel they are viewing is boring and they have no other chance of looking up another channel, they would stay away from the TV except when their favourite program is being aired.

3. UNPLUG YOUR TV WHEN NOT IN USE

When your TV is not in use, unplug it from the main socket. This will make it difficult for anyone to watch TV, and gives a greater opportunity to exercise their willpower. Keeping your TV plugged in actually wastes quite a bit of energy, so pulling the plug is also a great choice for your pocketbook and the earth.

④ UNPLUG YOUR TV WHEN NOT IN USE

These are excellent ways of ensuring that your children spend less time in front of the TV, but, there are other few things that you can do to ensure that they spend the right amount of time in front of it:

a. Track their TV time: Give your children a daily and weekly amount of TV time and have a way of measuring it. What gets measured gets controlled.

b. Use TV as a reward: This is probably the best way to minimize TV time. Make the children see TV as a reward for being diligent and responsible rather than as an object of pleasure. To gamify it, you may want to create a list that details the number of TV minutes certain tasks are worth. Also, do not forget to enforce a daily limit.

c. Do not encourage eating in front of the TV: Binge eating in front of the TV has many negative consequences and should not be encouraged.

d. Replace TV time with other productive activities: These activities can include exercising and studying.

The TV can be a good technology as it helps inform your children about the world they live in. However, if the TV time is not properly regulated, children may have a hard time focusing on important life subjects like academics, capacity building, and exercise. Ensure that you help your children to understand the physical, emotional and intellectual benefits of regulating TV time.

 **Habit** Thirty-five

EAT HEALTHY FOOD

WHY IS IT IMPORTANT?

Unhealthy foods are the major cause of infant mortality, diseases in children, and stunted growths. Today, fast foods and snacks are taken as breakfasts and lunch. This is inappropriate; that's why children fall sick.

Research has shown that children who eat unhealthy food end up being plagued with diseases later in life.

It is natural for children to want to eat snacks, fatty hamburger, and soda. However, if a child is constantly eating this kind of meal, it can cause a health concern. There are incredible amounts of sugar and fats in processed food, and when they are too much in the body, they can be harmful.

A healthy diet can benefit your child/children's mental, emotional, physical and social well-being in powerful ways. Children who eat healthily are more likely to stay physically fit. Also, they will look good and appear more confident in public. Nutritious whole foods, such as fruits, vegetables, whole grains, nuts, and fish, provide the body with the right amount of calories. Calories provide children the needed energy to stay active.

BENEFITS:

INTELLECTUAL BENEFITS

- **Clarity in thinking:** Eating rightly and healthily helps in clearing foggy moods, and promotes clear thinking. Children who show symptoms of Autism Spectrum Disorder are often asked to examine their diets. According to a research by Wellness Centre, "A healthy diet creates a solid base for learning new techniques in education and improved social and interactive behaviour."

● **Success:** Eating nutritious meals regularly gives your child/children the energy they need to live and complete the daily tasks necessary for a happy, balanced life. Without enough energy, they may not be able to achieve what they ought to do, which can negatively impact their mental health.

💎 EMOTIONAL BENEFITS

● **Reduced fatigue:** Certain nutrients like thiamine, Iron, and folic acid, are important nutrients that have strong links to children's moods. For example, iron helps in stabilizing the energy levels of children. When their energy levels are stable, feelings of fatigue, and moodiness are largely reduced. Foods like broccoli, egg yolk and meat are highly rich in iron.

● **Positive outlook:** For your child/children to maintain a positive outlook, it is important that they limit foods that contain refined sugar.

● **Positive energy:** Self-esteem begins with the body. When healthy foods are ingested by the body, children are able to work with positive energy.

💎 SOCIAL BENEFITS

● **Confidence:** When your child/children eat well, they feel better physically and emotionally. This, in turn, helps them to speak up in a group setting and also be enthusiastic about meeting new people. If your children are prone to social anxiety, try and limit their caffeine intake. Instead, teach them to stick to an eating pattern rich in nutrients, staying hydrated with beverages such as water, low-fat milk, and herbal tea.

● **Improved self-esteem:** Higher self-esteem can also result from having a good body shape. This helps them to be comfortable in public spaces and meeting new people.

💎 PHYSICAL BENEFITS

● **Energy Boost:** Foods like yogurt, fruits, and nuts give a quick energy boost. Healthy food provides children's bodies with the nutrients that are needed for their cells to survive and regenerate.

- **Improved metabolic processes:** Without nutritional food, metabolic processes improve dramatically, and their physical health enhances.

- **Improved weight loss:** Another healthy social benefit of eating healthy is that it can help in weight loss.

CONCLUSION:

When children lose a healthy amount of weight, they are able to avoid being the object of body shaming, ridicule, and bullying in school or at playgrounds.

It is your responsibility as a parent to ensure your child/children are in the right shape in body, soul, and mind, as this will help them to be physically fit in the long run. When someone is physically and mentally fit, there is no limit to what they can achieve in the long run.

PRACTICAL STEPS TO EATING HEALTHY FOOD

It is natural for your child/children to want to eat snacks, fatty hamburger and soda. However, if a child is constantly eating this kind of meal, it can cause a health concern. To get a child to eat healthy foods, you can follow the following steps:

1. START BY ELIMINATING ADDICTING FOODS FROM THEIR DIET

Try as much as possible to remove certain foods like chocolates, fried foods, cookies and ice cream. They may get cookies once in a while, but it should not be in the main diet. The foods should only be provided occasionally during holidays, festivals or special days like birthdays.

2. SHOW THEM WHAT IS IN THE PROCESSED FOODS

There are an incredible amount of sugar and fats in processed food, and when they are too much in the body, they can be harmful. Make them read the ingredients' list and recognize the unhealthy and disgusting components. If they are too young to understand, enable them to know basic nutritional facts.

3. FIGURE OUT WHY THEY ARE NOT EATING ENOUGH HEALTHY FOOD.

Could it be that they do not like the taste or they simply prefer to eat unhealthily? The answer to this will help you in developing the right approach to helping them eat healthy foods.

4. DO NOT FORCE THEM

It is important to get them involved in the process of eating healthy foods. If you force them to eat healthy at home, they may go to school and purchase all the chocolates out there. It is important to make them want to eat healthy than force them to swallow vegetables.

5. ALLOW THEM TO PICK OUT FOOD FROM THE VEGETABLE AND FRUIT SECTION

If the children pick the type of healthy food that they want, they will be more likely to continue eating them. You can encourage them to eat more fruits by purchasing "fun" fruits and vegetables, such as a banana with a face on it or an apple with a sticker. One of the reasons children eat cookies is because they look fun and exciting. When you make the food fun and exciting, they are more likely going to like eating them.

6. EAT HOMEMADE FOODS WITH THE CHILDREN

When you take your child/children out, you are exposing them to foods that have hidden fat and sugar and also contain a lot of processed junk that makes the food extremely unhealthy. Instead, try and make your own foods at home. Cook your own peanut butter with the children. Not only are you going to be eating healthy, but you will also be spending quality time with them.

TEACH THEM HOW TO COOK SIMPLE HEALTHY MEALS

If your child/children learn how to cook healthy foods on their own, they will be more inclined to eat what they cook. If your children are able to cook their own food, they won't beg you to take them to fast-food restaurants. You will save a lot of money if you teach them how to make simple meals like breaded chicken cutlets, meatballs and even pies.

Eating healthy is a major requirement for a healthy living in children. Your children need your help in maintaining a healthy eating lifestyle. Ensure that they fully understand the benefits of eating healthy.

 ## ALLOW THEM TO DO SHOPPING WITH YOU AND SELECT THE HEALTHY FOOD THAT THEY LIKE

When children are allowed to choose their healthy foods, they are more likely to stick to such meals.

# Habit Thirty-six
BE COOPERATIVE

WHY IS IT IMPORTANT?

When Nelson Mandela left prison to become the first black president of South Africa, many thought he would punish the English masters who put him in jail for many decades. Instead, he put an end to apathy and racial discrimination in South Africa. He put some of these men in his cabinet and gave them official appointments in his government. He went a great deal to restore cooperation among the blacks and whites in South Africa. Today, the Blacks and Whites live together in South Africa.

Cooperation is an essential skill that future leaders must possess. It helps them to be able to diffuse conflicts, gain the respect of others, and drive societies forward.

The first place where children develop the virtue of cooperation is in the home. Cooperation is what makes a family one, and when children are able to be cooperative with family members, they would be able to demonstrate this good habit with others. In the past, humans lived in clusters, so it was easy to enforce such good habits like cooperation. In those days, a child was raised by the entire village. Today, children move from school to entertainment centres, and to home. They do not have a substantial stay in a place where they could get to know about the benefits of being cooperative. In this section, we are going to discuss the intellectual, emotional and social benefits of being cooperative.

BENEFITS:

INTELLECTUAL BENEFITS

● **Having more ideas from the others:** Being cooperative takes massive creative confidence from children. They must be able to come up with more positive ways of diffusing a conflict and maintaining peace.

- **Solving problems quickly:** One of the huge benefits of cooperation is that it enables children to be able to solve problems quickly.

- **Contributing personal ideas:** Cooperation helps children to be able to contribute personal ideas. They are able to make others see things from their perspective.

💎 EMOTIONAL BENEFITS

- **Assertiveness:** Cooperation helps children in developing assertiveness, tolerance, and self-confidence. These are vital skills to have in children.

- **Emotional Intelligence:** Children who are cooperative are emotionally intelligent, and are able to diffuse emotionally tensed situations. If they are able to develop these emotional strengths as children, they would have less difficulty surviving and thriving as adults.

💎 SOCIAL BENEFITS

- **Effective family bonding:** Cooperation is needed for effective family bonding, and team building. It takes cooperation for a family unit to fully bond. If your children want to eat at a restaurant while you plan cooking a healthy meal at home, there is going to be discontentment and dissatisfaction. It could even get worse if there are differing opinions on the choice of physical activity and house chores. It is therefore important that you let your children understand the importance of being cooperative.

- **Respect:** It does not always mean compromising. Instead, children must be able to respect authority figures, express their opinions and cooperate towards a common positive goal.

- **Conflict management:** Cooperation helps children deal with conflict. Where there is cooperation, there is less room for conflict. Your children will be able to avoid unnecessary conflicts with bullies and authorities if they are able to agree on common positive goals. As highlighted above, cooperation helps children to develop assertiveness which is necessary to confront bullies and act as an ally to emotionally weaker children.

- **Facilitating:** Cooperation helps your children to be able to make group decisions and anchor a meeting. If your children are going to be social leaders in the nearest future, they must be able to handle objections positively while cooperating with others.

💎 COMMUNICATION BENEFITS

- **Communication skills:** Cooperation helps your children build communication skills. A child who is cooperative is going to be well versed. In truth, it takes an excellence in communication to be able to cooperate with others.

- **Cooperation:** Children do not have to know all the words in the dictionary to cooperate with their peers and family members. However, when they choose to take the path of cooperation, they are going to be able to understand each individual's language.

CONCLUSION:

Cooperation is always a positive attitude to imbibe in children. It ensures that there is less conflict which may lead to physical injuries. Being cooperative will help your children to navigate the terrains of life without experiencing avoidable conflicts. Hence, help them to see the importance of being cooperative in everyday life.

PRACTICAL STEPS IN BEING COOPERATIVE

Cooperating with others involve living in harmony with others. For children, it is easier said than done, especially in a world filled with catastrophes, conflict, and differing opinions. Your children may struggle to feel in sync with people close to them and with society at large. To be cooperative, they should start by connecting with family, friends, partners, and neighbours. They should focus on dealing with any disharmony in their life in a generous and compassionate way.

1. VOLUNTEERING AT SCHOOL AND COMMUNITY EVENTS

By volunteering to help at the local library, they are going to feel more connected with others. This will help them practice being more cooperative. They can volunteer at community events and donate goods or money to local events. Also, they can check the local community boards for postings about events like a block party or a community garage sale.

2. CONNECTING WITH NEIGHBOURS

Your child/children should actively reach out to the people who live around them.

- They can randomly say "hello" to them.
- They can also invite your neighbours over for dinner or a drink to connect with them.
- They can also offer to help their neighbours. If, for example, there is an elderly neighbour, they can offer to help them with yard work or a chore, like cleaning out the gutters.
- Your children should be friendly and sociable with the neighbours.

3. HANGING OUT WITH FRIENDS

Your child/children should actively spend time with good friends. This will help them stay connected with them and not lose touch. In order to have regular hangouts with their friends, they should schedule regular hangouts once a week or once a month with different friends. Your child/children should try to keep your friendships alive and active. For instance, they can create traditions with their friends—this may include anniversaries of special events or taking an annual trip together.

4. SPENDING

To help foster cooperation, your child/children should spend time with the family in creating meaningful and memorable experiences. These may include: planning a trip with the family or having regular dinners. By sharing life events and remembering shared moments, they create a sense of belonging and foster cooperation.

HELPING A NEIGHBOUR OR FRIEND OR FAMILY IN NEED

To show cooperation, your child/children should show assistance to those around them. They should do this without expecting repayment. This helps them to connect in a more generous way. For example, they may go see a family member who is feeling ill or unwell and bring food for them if they are too sick to cook. Also, they can help the neighbour by trying things like taking care of their pet or shovelling snow for them while they are away on vacation.

 **Habit** Thirty-seven

BE ABLE TO ADMIT TO THE MISTAKE.

> *To err is human...*
> Alexander Pope

WHY IS IT IMPORTANT?

Children make mistakes with who to trust. Sometimes, they do things that hurt them. When children know what is morally right, they feel ashamed to admit their mistakes.

Research suggests children will learn better if they can see the beauty in spilled milk.

We all make mistakes; more so do children who are exploring the world on the borders of new morals and rules. Sometimes, the fall, but they have to rise. It is the duty of the parents to ensure that they are big enough to admit their mistakes, so they can move on. We have seen over and over again when people get prosecuted not for their initial offences, but for trying to cover up. Nothing spells confidence more than being able to own up to one's mistakes. It is therefore important that you imbibe this important virtue in your child/ children.

Making mistakes is part of growing up—when children make mistakes, they are able to know what is good to focus on and what is bad to discard. The only people who do not make mistakes are those who do not attempt new endeavours—children are naturally curious, so they always engage in new things which sometimes cause mistakes.

BENEFITS:

💎 INTELLECTUAL BENEFITS

Intellectual integrity: You need to make your child/children know that admitting to mistakes do not make them weak, it actually makes them strong. It takes intellectual integrity to admit to mistakes. Many children will cave in, but those who are of superior intellect are going to admit to their mistakes.

Enhanced Learning: Socrates is widely regarded as one of the wisest Greek philosophers. This is because he admitted to not knowing much. When children do not admit to their mistakes, they exude arrogance which may inhibit their learning and knowledge.

Learning to focus on the right choice: When children are able to admit their mistakes, they are able to focus on what truly matters. This is healthy for their mental health.

💎 EMOTIONAL BENEFITS

Emotional relief: Mistakes can be as painful as physical injuries. However, when they are accepted and corrected, it is like taking an analgesic—there is almost an immediate relief.

Enhanced self-image: Acceptance of one's error is a soothing balm to one's crushed ego. When children make mistakes and they admit to them, they are able to quash feelings of doubt, fear, insecurity, and regrets.

As a result, when your child/children are able to admit to their mistakes, they grow up to be emotionally healthy adults.

💎 SOCIAL BENEFITS

Social acceptance: When your child/children admit to their mistakes, they are able to find acceptance within their social structures. This is because they have first accepted themselves. Children who do not admit to mistakes end up being bullies because they do not correct wrongdoings.

- **Trustworthiness:** Mistakes are never secrets. When children make mistakes, they need to know that there are others who are watching them. If they are able to admit to their errors, they would be regarded as trustworthy, sincere, and responsible. These are the qualities that endear children to their peers. It makes them leaders, spokesmen, and influencers.

- **Meaningful connections:** When children admit mistakes, they help establish a culture of open communication and a willingness to improve by demonstrating an attitude growth mindset.

CONCLUSION:

Admitting mistakes helps in building peer trust, provides an atmosphere for growth, and improves collaboration in children. This is very important in having a healthy child. Children make a lot of mistakes, and the faster they are at admitting these mistakes, the better adults they will become.

PRACTICAL STEPS IN ADMITTING TO MISTAKES

Your child/children may find it difficult to admit to making a mistake, especially if they want to avoid "losing face". However, in the eyes of other people, a person who can admit to mistakes and move on from them is more likely to garner respect, than someone who blusters and pretends they weren't responsible. Ultimately, continued refusal to face up to being wrong or causing a problem can take a toll on your child/children's reputation and relationships, later in life.

As difficult as it may seem, if they are not already used to admitting to mistakes, this skill can free them and allow them and others to move on to better relationships and outcomes. Your child/children should get ready to own up to their errors!

1. EXAMINING THE FEELINGS

One of the first things that your child/children can do after making a mistake is to examine their feelings. If they are perfectionists or have a strong inner critic, they may be terrified about making mistakes. This may cause them to want to cover up for their mistakes or blame others. Yet, these actions cause their own problems and end up making the mistake worse, or even having greater ramifications than they would have, had they faced the mistake openly.

2. REIMAGINING A MISTAKE

First up, your child/children have to understand that mistakes are bound to happen; and these mistakes are going to keep happening even after they have "learned their lessons." Life is very generous with mistakes, just as it is very generous with learning opportunities, love, and a chance of fulfilment, if they choose to take them.

Second, mistakes teach your child/children what they are capable of by showing them what doesn't work. They should remember Edison's 1,000 attempts at getting a light bulb to work when they feel like calling their efforts a mistake.

Third, quite a large number of mistakes have resulted in creations and inventions of a scientific, business, architectural, creative, or other nature. Indeed, mistakes can even reveal breakthroughs in self-understanding. Mistakes have their place in life.

3. ACCEPTING MISTAKES

One of the best and most effective responses that your child/children can have towards making a mistake is to take responsibility for having made it, especially where it harms, upsets, or disturbs other people. And owning up to their mistake is also good, as it would've simply bothered their own sense of who they are striving to be, so as to avoid the blame game. They shouldn't try to run away from the mistake, or it will continue to chase them.

They should concentrate on how to deal with the underlying reason rather than on belittling themselves. For example, they could tell themselves something like: "In future, I could ensure I've eaten before going to school."

 **Habit** Thirty-eight

BE EMOTIONALLY OPEN AND QUITE SENSITIVE.

WHY IS IT IMPORTANT?

The world's problems stem from not being emotionally open and quite sensitive.

Research studies suggest that early social and emotional competencies are linked to later academic achievement, whereas, social and emotional problems or challenges are linked to academic difficulties.

Children are often timid when it comes to communication. As a result, they are not often heard when they are emotionally open and quite sensitive. When they open up, they are called childish.

However, this is not appropriate. Children are to be encouraged to be emotionally open and quite sensitive. There are huge benefits associated with being emotionally open.

BENEFITS:

💎 INTELLECTUAL BENEFITS

- **Enhanced awareness:** Emotionally open children are quite sensitive and intuitive. When your child/children are emotionally open, they are more likely to be able to notice a slight change in the environment. This information can prove vital in preventing crimes and disasters. Sensitive children are more likely to notice someone who is upset or sad. Again, this crucial detail can help avert an event of suicide or depression.

- **Quality goal setting:** Another intellectual benefit of having children that are emotionally open is that they pursue meaningful projects. Sensitive children seek meaning and purpose; they want to work on projects that connect with their inner core. Whether it is choosing a physical activity or helping a friend, your child/children will be drawn to activities that bring meaningful stimulation to their life.

⬢ **Allowing the mind to distinguish the different feelings:** When children become emotionally open and quite sensitive, they become more self-aware. Thus, they are able to distinguish between different feelings, and are able to know what to do when they feel in certain ways.

💎 EMOTIONAL BENEFITS

⬢ **Meditation:** When your child/children are emotionally open, they are going to think and feel deeply. They will process events, changes, and situations more thoroughly.

⬢ **Empathy:** Emotionally open children are empathetic, service oriented, and good-natured. When children are emotionally open, they care more about others. Hence, they are good-natured and are more inclined to help others.

⬢ **More meaningful connections:** They connect more with family members and friends because they are in tune with the needs of others.

⬢ **Allowing the true feelings come out:** Children who are emotionally open allow their true feelings to come out. They are genuine and real.

⬢ **Controlled conflict:** This helps them foster healthy relationships and avoid conflict.

⬢ **Trading back positive feelings:** There is no way children can flourish in the happiness of friendship, understanding, care, harmony, satisfaction, and love; without having being exposed and experienced anger, anxiety, doubt, weakness, embarrassment, disappointment, and despair.

💎 SOCIAL BENEFITS

⬢ **Being true and honest to self:** When children are emotionally open and quite sensitive, they become more self-aware and can identify what resonates with their being. This makes them more attuned with nature.

- **The ability to adapt to an environment:** To thrive in any environment, your children must be able to adapt to changes in the environment. For instance, your family may have to leave your country for another country. If your child/children are not emotionally open to new opportunities, it will be a hard task for them adjusting to a new culture, environment, and life.

- **Social integration:** It takes a child who is emotionally open to explore the beauties of the society. For your child/children to be able to stick to a physical activity like sport, they have to be able to enjoy and catch fun. In doing so, they create positive energy that attracts others to them.

- **Being sympathy:** It takes an emotionally open child to be sympathetic. Children who are quite emotionally open are often sensitive to the feelings of other children. Hence, they are able to offer a helping hand and support to another hurting child.

CONCLUSION:

The world is looking for men and women who have large hearts and feel deeply for people. To help your child/children foster a harmonious relationship with people, you need to help them a lot in the area of emotions. You need to help them manage their emotions positively and help them spread love and not hatred.

The benefits of having children who are emotionally open and quite sensitive cannot be overemphasized. Intellectually and socially, they are able to derive joy in their openness. The future is going to be a shared world, and it is going to take adults who are ready to bridge the gaps to thrive. By all means, encourage your child/children to take pride in their emotional sensitivity. They will grow up to become adults who are able to adapt and thrive in their generation.

PRACTICAL STEPS IN BEING EMOTIONALLY OPEN AND QUITE SENSITIVE

The word "open" is used a lot. A lot of children would like to be more open than they are right now. They know it feels good to share with others. It's really a nice feeling for your children to get things off their chest, and out in the open. They sometimes use their friends and families for this purpose. It feels good for your child/children to talk to somebody about things they are concerned about. It is good for your child/children to be able to trust somebody. In this section, we are going to explore the practical steps they can follow in being emotionally open.

1) IGNORING FEAR OF REJECTION

Your child/children might get their feelings hurt or even become angry when they attempt to be emotionally open and sensitive. Instead of being afraid of getting a rejection, they need to understand that they are still the same person with the beautiful traits and characteristics. It is imperative that your children let go of the fear and simply open up so that others can understand them, their points of view, and their feelings.

2) FORGIVENESS

Since they are only children and human, your child/children will make mistakes, hence, they should learn to forgive quickly. When they get hurt emotionally, they should walk through the pain, learn a lesson, and forgive as soon as possible.

3) COMMUNICATION IS A PRIVILEGE

By seeing communication as a privilege instead of a burden, they are able to open up emotionally and share personal stories. When people open up to them, they should be able to keep their personal information private.

4 HONESTY

No matter how hard it is to be honest, your child/children should imbibe it. The truth always seems to come out in the end and if it has been covered with lies, there is always more pain associated with its revelation. To avoid unnecessary regrets, your child/children should learn to be honest. They should tell the truth about their emotions and help others cope with the truth of the situation.

5 ASK QUESTIONS

To remain interested in others, they should ask relevant questions. Communication is a two-way street. If your child/children are able to open up to others, it will be easier for them to be emotionally open and quite sensitive.

6 EVERYTHING DOESN'T HAVE TO BE EMOTIONAL

When there are important decisions to make, they should try to step back out of the situation and re-evaluate all aspects. Everything does not have to be emotional. They should try to keep the emotions out of the decision so that rational thought and discussion can occur.

7 CONGRUENCE

Your child/children should make their outside behaviour the same or congruent with their inside feelings and thoughts.

8 FOCUS ON FEELINGS.

It is usually easier for your child/children to share opinions or thoughts about something. Every child has an opinion. It is harder to share feelings. Your child/children should get in touch with how they feel and share openly the feelings as much as they can. Some feelings cover or come from other feelings. Anger may come from hurt; that's why they might find it easier to show the anger. However, they should work really hard and try to understand the hurt. If they share the hurt and are open about it, they are actually being more open at a deeper level.

By all means, encourage your child/children to take pride in their emotional sensitivity. They will grow up to become adults who are able to adapt and thrive in their generation.

4. SELF-WORTH

▶ **SELF-WORTH AND ITS IMPORTANCE TO CHILDREN**

Self-worth, also called self-esteem is how children think or feel about themselves, both inside and out. Children with good self-worth have a positive mindset, accept themselves as they are and feel confident always.

It also has to do with the feelings people go through that stems from their sense of worthiness or unworthiness. People with high self-worth are also those who are inspired to take care of themselves and to strive towards the achievement of personal goals and aspirations consistently. People with lower self-worth don't seem to regard themselves as worthy of happy outcomes. They may have the same types of goals as people with higher self-worth, but they are generally less inspired to go after them.

Your child's self-worth affects how well he/she does in his day-to-day activities and tasks. It takes a toll on his/her relationships with you and with others and affects how he/she performs at school and in social situations. Later in life, it might affect how he/she fares in the workplace, or in a relationship.

Positive self-esteem helps children:

- Have the confidence to live their own life.
- Believe in their own worth and value.
- Make informed decisions under pressure.
- Interact with others, and develop a good rapport with them.
- Handle stress and life's challenges effectively

- Make healthier choices.
- Be strong enough to say no in some situations.

As your child gets older, providing him with the right structure and guidance will help him feel confident that he is cared for. Gradually provide him with opportunities to make choices for him/her to feel more independent. This will go a long way in giving the child/children a sense of positivity and high self-esteem.

| HABITS TO BENEFITS |

 **Habit** Thirty-nine

TAKE PRIDE IN SELF

WHY IS IT IMPORTANT?

Children must learn to take pride in themselves while they are still young. The society at large is a battlefield of cultures and beliefs. It is important for them to understand their core competence and what they bring forward to the table. You should let them understand that a valueless life is a miserable life and being proud of oneself is one of the best parts to be adored anywhere.

Low self-esteem is a recipe for disaster. It makes children embrace vices and habits that are bad for their health and wellbeing. It stops them from speaking up. Children must be able to take pride in their selves. This is the starting point for confidence, courage, and charisma. This habit is very important and must be cultivated early in children.

Teach them how to be valuable among peer groups, schools or home. All these will shape their mentality as they are growing up.

BENEFITS:

💎 INTELLECTUAL BENEFITS

Independent thinking: Children who have pride in themselves are able to think independent of a group. They do not succumb to peer pressure and group thinking. As a result, they are able to generate original ideas that dignify their thought process.

Purposefulness: It takes pride in oneself to be able to live a purposeful life. This is not less true for children. Children, like adults, want to be able to identify the object of their creations. They want to be able to point to things and say, "I did that." When your children have pride in themselves, they are more purposeful.

- **Intellectual energy:** When your child/children have pride in their self, they have boundless intellectual energy to explore creative activities as well as physical activities.

💎 EMOTIONAL BENEFITS

- **Self-love:** Self-pride leads to self-love. Children who take pride in themselves are more inclined to love themselves more. Hence, they will not be seeking love in things as this may lead to depression.

- **Confidence:** A moderate pride in their dignity can boost their confidence in all social settings. This confidence helps them to be able to function effectively.

- **Joy:** When your children take pride in themselves, they manifest boundless joy. As a matter of fact, confidence leads to joy. A child who is not confident may find it tacky to be joyful. And, joyful children are brilliant children.

- **High Self Esteem:** When your children are confident and joyful, there is a huge spike in their self-esteem.

💎 SOCIAL BENEFITS

- **Positive and healthy relationships:** People associate with others who are like them. It takes pride in oneself to be able to associate with positive and empowering people. This is why it is important that your child/children take pride in themselves.

- **Self-acceptance:** When your child/children are confident as a result of taking pride in themselves, they are able to accept themselves for who they are. This helps them to deal with the labels that others and society may give them.

- **Charity:** Children who take pride in themselves are more charitable and fun to be with. They want to offer helps in order to make others happy.

💎 COMMUNICATION BENEFITS

● **Assertiveness:** Children who take pride in themselves are assertive. This assertiveness helps them to explore their creativity. Assertive children are able to express themselves in public and among peers.

● **Knowing to choose the right language for representing self-worth:** Children who take pride in themselves use positive and empowering words. They have a can-attitude, and their words are inspiring.

CONCLUSION:

It takes people who have developed full pride in themselves to survive and thrive in society.

The society won't value you if you don't value yourself and express that value always. To be respected in life, you need to have shown a certain level of value in you over time. As parents, you need to build up your child/children's confidence and let them know the world only celebrates people that distinguish themselves. Show them examples of past leaders that have been celebrated because of what they did during their life and use it to inspire them to do more.

PRACTICAL STEPS YOUR CHILDREN CAN TAKE IN TAKING PRIDE IN THEMSELVES

Many people mistake pride for selfishness. However, it's okay for your child/children to have pride in what they do. They are a valuable person, and this section will teach them how to have pride while being humble and accepting the fact that there will be some people that are better than them. In developing a healthy self-pride, there are a few practical steps that your child/children can take, and we are going to be analysing a few of them:

1. ALLOW YOUR CHILD/CHILDREN TO TAKE HEALTHY RISKS:

For children to take pride in self, they have to make choices, take chances, and take responsibility for them. Parents have to desist from rescuing their children from failure all the time. Children who have a healthy self-pride are able to solve problems on their own.

2. TALK A LITTLE ABOUT ACCOMPLISHED GOALS.

This doesn't mean they should boast about themselves, but just to say that they are very pleased they completed those goals.

3. CONFIDENCE

This is an essential ingredient in developing a healthy self-pride. They should not allow others to put them down. Instead, they should just walk away. There are some things that they are better at than others. However, they should always be friendly to everyone, including those they hate. They should respect others exactly the way you wish to be respected.

4. ACTING LIKE THE PERSON THEY WANT TO BE.

They should smile, have a positive attitude, and find a mentor or role model of who they want to be. In addition, they should find out how they can implement things that their role models do into their daily life. Self-pride is an essential ingredient of your child/children's confidence. By all positive means, they should develop self-pride.

 **Habit** Forty

HAVE INTEGRITY.

WHY IS IT IMPORTANT?

The world is currently struggling with integrity. The masses are losing faith in their leaders. Now, news sources are no longer authority sources on information. Even journals have to be verified several times. The world is plagued with lack of integrity.

Honesty, character, and goodwill are some of the values that are often associated with integrity. These character values set children apart from others. It makes them more trustworthy and reliable.

When your child/children have integrity, they are going to be true to their words. Integrity distinguishes them from other children and set them on a course for greatness. Children who are clear and straightforward are generally respected and celebrated by their peers. In this section, we are going to explore the various benefits of having children who possess this key virtue.

Integrity is more important in today's world because of the impact of technology on the society. There are new ways of doing things. Children must not be caught up in the confusing terrains of societal influence. They must be able to maintain their identity while they navigate life. It is the character that they have built while they are young that will help them to go through life successfully.

BENEFITS:

💎 INTELLECTUAL BENEFITS

Integrity: This means staying true to one's values, principles, and ideas. It is an outright honesty in the way children do things and carry out their daily routines.

● **Leadership:** To lead, your child must be able true to himself. When your child/children have integrity in their dealings with other children, they are able to lead others effectively.

● **Improved decision making:** When there are no rough edges to smoothen, children have clarity, and they are able to make better decisions. Lack of integrity thwarts the thought process of children.

● **Self-awareness:** Integrity ensures that your child/children are who they say they are. As a result, they will be more self-aware if they have integrity. This is good because self-awareness leads to better decision making and self-improvement.

● **Vision:** For your child/children to develop a solid vision, they need clarity in their thought process which can be obtained from integrity. Children who have visions are more proactive and deliberate in their attitude towards life.

💎 EMOTIONAL BENEFITS

● **Confidence:** If there is nothing to run away from, it is easier for children to be confident. However, if there are flaws in their personality, action, and words, they may have a significant drop in their confidence. Therefore, it is important that your children take integrity seriously.

● **Peace:** When your child/children demonstrate integrity on a consistent basis, they experience inner peace. This is important for their health as well as other significant areas like academics.

💎 SOCIAL BENEFITS

● **Influence:** Integrity makes children demonstrate massive influence in a group setting. This is because they are not afraid to express their ideas which are usually an extension of what they stand for.

● **Respect:** Integrity makes your child/children more respectable by their peers. They are revered for their words, actions, and identities. It takes a lot of courage to put oneself out there. As a result, others will respect the courage of your children to be of high integrity.

- **Trust:** Also, your child/children are going to be more trusted if they have integrity. Money and other valuable resources are going to be trusted to them for simply displaying the virtue of integrity.

COMMUNICATION BENEFITS

- **Communicating effectively:** Children who have integrity are able to communicate effectively because there is no discrepancy between their personalities and their words. They are able to commit themselves in every situation. This is an ideal trait to have as a child.

CONCLUSION:

The social benefits of integrity in children include influence, respect, and trust. As parents, you should endeavour to raise your child/children in a way they will imbibe integrity as their hallmark. As it is pointed above, Integrity enables them to have a lot of influence over their peers and help them build up their reputation. Integrity also brings respect to an individual as such a person will be trusted with important things and won't be subjected to any scrutiny.

Anyone with a stainless integrity is set for a life of peace, and as parents, it is our duty to do all it takes to foster this trait in our children.

PRACTICAL STEPS YOUR CHILDREN CAN TAKE TO HAVE INTEGRITY

Personal integrity requires children to be honest with themselves and others. Also, it is exemplified when children live a life that is aligned with their moral principles. Developing personal integrity requires children to evaluate their belief systems and take conscious steps to behave in ways that are consistent with their personal moral code. Here are some of the ways children can develop personal integrity:

① IDENTIFY AREAS OF BEHAVIOUR THAT REQUIRES A CHANGE:

Often, not all areas of a child's life need an overhaul. There will be things (a lot of things) that they get right. The goal then is for your child/children to be able to reflect on their interactions with other children and adults at the school, home and in social situations in order to identify specific areas that require improvement. For example, if they are always not doing their assignments and feel guilty about creating excuses for this behaviour, this may be an opportunity to develop greater personal integrity.

② IDENTIFICATION OF REASONS FOR NOT BEHAVING WITH GREATER PERSONAL INTEGRITY

For example, they may be pushing unpleasant work tasks on to their siblings instead of being honest with you about their inability to do the tasks. They may be afraid to admit to themselves or to you that the assignment is not the right fit for them.

③ FACING THE OBSTACLES

To conquer their failings and achieve a high standard of honesty, children must be able to face obstacles that weaken them to excuse themselves, lie or violate their moral code. They should get involved in finding a more suitable use of their talents and skill sets.

④ BUILDING RELATIONSHIPS THROUGH CANDIDNESS

To effectively develop integrity, your children should be encouraged to build relationships at home and work through greater truthfulness, being candid. For example, when interacting with other children, they should be honest and direct with each person about their expectations while avoiding backbiting or gossiping. They should also refrain from causing unnecessary harm. Part of developing personal integrity is gauging when and how to deliver the truth. They should be careful not to confuse truthfulness with anger-driven and brutally honest confrontation.

5. DEVELOPING AN INTEGRITY LIST

Your children should make a list of tasks and behaviours in which they will become more trustworthy doing them. The list may include basic tasks, such as remembering to take out the trash as promised.

6. RESPECTING OTHER'S DECISIONS

One of the essential aspects of having a personal integrity is listening to and respecting the opinions and decisions of others. Children who have personal integrity protect the human rights of others. Openness to other people's opinions and decisions enable them to be able to maintain their personal integrity.

 **Habit** Forty-one

ALLOW THE PAST MISTAKE TO GO

WHY IS IT IMPORTANT?

Many children grow up in a society that pressures them to be perfect – to get good grades. In fact, studies have found that learning from mistakes enhances children's confidence.

Holding onto past mistakes hinders progress.

The formative years of children are the period of fastest growth. When they hold onto past mistakes, it is hard for them to progress as much as they should. This is why it is very important that children ensure that they allow past mistakes to go, so they can move forward and do excellent things.

Peace of mind and letting go, work together harmoniously. Children should always endeavour to let go of past memories or happenings in order to embrace positive changes. Children who refuse to let go of the past remain stuck on less important things and leaving their present important things to be suffering. Often time, this affects their state of mental health, peace of mind, and general wellbeing.

By letting go of past mistakes, children are able to forge ahead in life. They are able to embrace life's circumstances without budging.

BENEFITS:

INTELLECTUAL BENEFITS

Focus: There are several things trying to battle for the attention of your child/children. These distractions affect the focus of your child/children. If your child/children are able to let go of past mistakes, they will have fewer distractions to deal with and have improved focus.

Clarity: When your child/children keep relaying mistakes that have occurred in the past on their mind, it may severely impair their clarity. They may begin to see life from a distorted lens. This can affect their decision making.

- **Improved decision making:** There are several cognitive biases that leverage on a child's inability to focus on the present. Primacy effect may come in and impair the decision making of the children. As a result, they may be unable to make accurate decisions. However, if they are able to let go of the mistakes they have made in the past, they will be able to enhance their decision-making process.

EMOTIONAL BENEFITS

- **Courage:** It takes courage to leave the past behind and move ahead. When your child/ children are able to let go of the memories of past mistakes and stay in the present while making plans for the future, they will exude such courage that will be admired by their peers.

- **Passion:** True passion is unadulterated. If your children are clinging to what must have transpired in the past, they may find it hard to truly identify their passions and follow them wholeheartedly.

- **Positive Thinking:** The first step to developing positive thinking is letting go of past mistakes. If your child/children forgive themselves and move ahead, they will have a positive outlook towards life.

SOCIAL BENEFITS

- **Positive relationships:** It takes a healthy child to develop a positive relationship. And, one of the best ways of developing a healthy mindset is by letting go of previous mistakes. Your child/children will be able to see what's possible and the good in others.

- **Enterprise:** There are several factors that contribute to a child's entrepreneurial passion—letting go of the mistakes in the past is absolutely one of the great factors. Your child/children will be more enterprising if they let go of past mistakes.

CONCLUSION:

Everyone makes mistakes, and children are not exceptions. Children have their own ways of manifesting the guilt of their past mistakes—sometimes they cry about it. Making mistakes at school, or at home can be demoralizing for children, especially if they are trying their best to stay on top of their responsibilities and abilities.

PRACTICAL STEPS YOUR CHILDREN CAN TAKE TO ALLOW PAST MISTAKES TO GO

Children may make mistakes because they are feeling overwhelmed, overly tired, or simply due to forgetfulness. Rather than beating themselves up over their past mistakes, they should learn how to bounce back and recover from them. More importantly, they should consider how they can prevent making mistakes in the future so they can feel confident and in control. If you find your child/children unable to let go of past mistakes and regrets, here are a few practical steps that they can take:

1. CHANGING THE MINDSET

If your child/children are having trouble getting over a mistake, there may be a reason they can't let go. The first thing they should do is spending some time in identifying the underlying emotions behind the regrettable behaviour. In order to let go of the past, they need to be able to release certain emotions tying them to a mistake.

Do they feel like they did wrong by a family member or classmates?

What do they associate with this mistake?

Do they feel like they missed out on something?

For example, maybe they feel it is a mistake for not showing up at a friend's birthday party. They feel regret over what fun it could have been. They should try to deal with feelings of regret head-on; work on accepting that everyone has regrets, and they're a normal part of life. This will help them let go of a perceived mistake.

2. SEPARATION FROM THE MISTAKE

Your child/children must understand that poor behaviour does not define their character. Understanding this will help them in moving on. Every child makes mistakes and engages in poor behaviour, and such behaviour does not necessarily reflect their values and worth as a child. Your child/children should learn to see themselves as a separate entity from the mistakes they've made.

④ LOOKING FOR A LESSON

It is easy for your child/child to let go of past mistakes if they see them as valuable. Instead of ruminating over what could have happened, they should be focusing on the lessons. They cannot change the past, but they can learn valuable lessons from past mistakes that can help them in making better choices in the future. For example, if they feel frustrated when they are told to engage in an assignment, they can use that opportunity to be grateful for having parents and loved ones who deeply care about them and are trying to make them successful adults.

③ ACCEPTANCE AND EMPATHY

To allow past mistakes go, your child/children have to be able to accept what they did wrong. They should be able to do this without making excuses, especially if they have hurt someone in the process. To overcome past mistakes, your child/children must be able to acknowledge their wrongdoings.

In fostering empathy, your child/ children should be able to put themselves in the shoes of others. They should be able to imagine how the other person felt being on the receiving end of their behaviour.

 **Habit** Forty-two
BELIEVE IN HIM/HER

WHY IS IT IMPORTANT?

Nothing will work if children do not believe in themselves.

Children have the ability to believe in themselves. They are not too young to have a healthy self-belief. They can do a whole lot of things when they believe in themselves.

There are a lot of sports and events that are targeted at showcasing the brilliance in children. Children can at a little age begin to attain greatness.

Children must get rid of our fears and self-doubt in order to build self-esteem and self-confidence. Everything they'd have later in life is a result of their belief in self.

Without self-belief, children are going to be docile and extremely lazy. They won't have compelling reasons to attain excellence. Lack of self-belief has led to many colossal failures.

Muhammad Ali is an example of someone who had a massive self-belief. He had this healthy habit since he was a child. He would go on to become one of the greatest sportsmen in history.

BENEFITS:

💎 INTELLECTUAL BENEFITS

- **Clarity:** When your child/children believe in themselves, they are able to gain clarity in forging out their identity.

- **Better memory and increased cognitive functioning:** It can be hard for children to focus if they think their parents don't believe in them. This can seriously impair their reasoning. Children who do not have faith in themselves are regularly beset by groupthink.

⬢ **Focus:** When your child/children are fully convinced in themselves, they are going to be more focused and have increased attention span. This will greatly improve their academic and intellectual performances.

💎 EMOTIONAL BENEFITS

⬢ **Lowered stress:** It can be really stressful for children trying to please others. Children are more relaxed when they have self-belief.

⬢ **Positive Thinking:** Positive thinking is an emotional benefit that children derive when they believe in themselves. Positive thinking helps your child/children to develop a healthy outlook towards life. It dispels depression in children as well as improve brilliance.

⬢ **Confidence:** Children who are self-believing will naturally be more confident. Self-esteem is developed at a very early age. When children are young, they develop a self-image based on how they perceive themselves.

💎 SOCIAL BENEFITS

⬢ **Positive relationships:** Positive relationships are developed from a strong sense of self. By believing in themselves, they are affirming their identity and giving themselves permission to explore their curiosities and identities.

⬢ **Enterprise:** Your child/children will not take into entrepreneurship if they don't believe in themselves. From young ages, they will begin to explore creative ways to leverage on your belief in them.

💎 COMMUNICATION BENEFITS

⬢ **Having a strong independent belief** Your child/children will become more assertive and expressive in their interactions with peers and older people because they have developed a strong belief in themselves.

CONCLUSION:

When your child/children begin to grow in self-belief, they are going to improve socially. It spurs them on to continue giving their best to all their doings. Children are not different. This will go a long way in taking care of their mental state while growing up.

Children who believe in themselves will go the extra mile in achieving success. They will not stop at the heights that others stop. They will go ahead to become great men and women.

PRACTICAL STEPS IN BELIEVING IN YOUR CHILD/CHILDREN

At times, it can be really hard for your child to believe in himself/herself. This can be as a result of several factors, such as moving to a new environment. They can take stock of all the things they have already accomplished and set goals for the future, can make new friends, get a fresh perspective of things, have good discussions, and look for opportunities to use their skills—by doing so, their self-confidence will rise. In this section, we are going to explore the ways in which you can believe in your children.

1. BRAG ON THEM IN PUBLIC.

The easiest way to display your belief in your child/children is by showering your adoration for them in public. It boosts their self-esteem and confidence.

2. GIVE THEM RESPONSIBILITY EARLY AND OFTEN

Part of believing in your children is giving them responsibility early in life. This shows that you trust in their abilities to get things done. It doesn't matter how old your child is, there's something he can do to help.

3. DON'T OVER HELP

There is always this tendency to over help your child. However, this has proven to be counterintuitive. It affects their self-confidence and makes them not to be self-reliant.

4. DEMONSTRATE TRUST

There are several ways of demonstrating trust in your child/children. You can allow them to keep a huge amount of money or let them lead their siblings. The purpose is to engage them in acts of responsibilities that enable them to know that you trust in them.

5. BE EMPATHETIC

When dealing with your child/children, it is important to always see things from their perspectives. They are children and would often have needs and desires that are alien to adults, so before you criticize them, you have to understand things from their perspectives.

6. COMMUNICATE WITH RESPECT

Even though they are your child/ children, they deserve your respect—respect for their human dignity. By so doing, you help them to see the dignity in their being.

7. GIVE UNDIVIDED ATTENTION

Whenever they want to tell you about an event that happened in school on the playground, it is important that you give them your undivided attention. By sacrificing your time to focus on their needs and desires, you are assuring them of your belief in them.

8. ACCEPT AND LOVE YOUR CHILD/CHILDREN FOR WHO THEY ARE

Part of parenting is accepting your child/children for who they are. Love them regardless of their personalities.

9. GIVE YOUR CHILD/CHILDREN A CHANCE TO CONTRIBUTE

When making vital decisions at home, give your children the chance to contribute their ideas and opinions.

10. TREAT MISTAKES AS LEARNING EXPERIENCES

Your child/children are going to make some mistakes early in life. Do not beat perfectionism into them. Help them to treat mistakes as learning experiences.

 **Habit** Forty-three

RETAIN A GREAT BREAKFAST

WHY IS IT IMPORTANT?

Without breakfast, children get tired easily. This is because they won't have sufficient energy to push through the day.

Research studies have shown that children who regularly skip breakfast become obese. This is because they try to quench hunger later in the day with snacks and fast foods.

Skipping breakfast can make kids feel tired, restless, or irritable. In the morning, their bodies need to refuel for the day ahead after going without food for 8 to 12 hours during sleep. Their mood and energy can drop by midmorning if they don't eat at least a small morning meal.

It is very important that children take breakfast seriously. Not only have they not eaten for about 8 hours over the night, but because they need energy to ride the morning. In addition, eating breakfast has been linked to improved concentration, better test scores, increased energy, a higher intake of vitamins and minerals, and even a healthier body weight.

BENEFITS:

INTELLECTUAL BENEFITS

Brain Health: When children wake up in the morning, they have less oxygen and nutrients in the bloodstream because they have probably gone several hours without food overnight. Oxygen and the right nutrients are needed for proper brain development. A healthy breakfast will ensure that your children are well-prepared for the day's activities.

Improved memory: One of the signs of a healthy brain is improved memory. Children who regularly miss breakfasts may find it difficult to remember things and names.

● **Clear thinking:** When the brain is healthy, thinking becomes clear. A proper and healthy meal for breakfast ensures that oxygen and the right nutrients are supplied to the children's brains. This enhances clarity in thinking. Children who can think clearly find it easy to perform well in their academics.

💎 EMOTIONAL BENEFITS

● **Happiness:** Research has proven that regular breakfasts improve the happiness of children. Children who are well-nourished in the morning are going to be more focused on the beauties of the day than children who regularly skip meals. Indeed, "a hungry child is an angry child."

● **Thrive to learn:** When children eat breakfasts, they have more energy to pursue learning activities. Children who are deprived of energy won't have the mental concentration to learn.

● **Sleep quality:** It has been proven that children who start the day with good breakfasts sleep well at night. This is because their energies are properly managed during the day. As a result, they are able to sleep well and wake up relaxed in the morning.

💎 PHYSICAL BENEFITS

● **Preventing weight gain:** When your child/children skip breakfasts, they are going to eat a lot of junks throughout the day to satisfy their hunger and get energy for the day. However, this will make them gain lots of calories which may make them add more weight than necessary. Therefore, to prevent these problems, your child/children need to have a proper breakfast to start their day healthily.

● **Remains high energy:** When children start the day with breakfast, they are able to start the day with high energy which they will sustain throughout the day.

● **Reduces hunger and tiredness:** Children who eat early in the morning are not going to suffer from hunger, which leads to the tiredness.

CONCLUSION:

If they take breakfast, they are going to avoid junks and intake fast food later in the day. They are going to lose unnecessary body weight. As parents, you should endeavour to pay a lot of attention to what your child/children eat to make sure they are taking everything in the right proportions.

A balanced diet, they say give rise to a balanced life.

PRACTICAL STEPS CHILDREN CAN TAKE IN RETAINING A GREAT BREAKFAST

It is a common nutrition education that breakfast is the most important meal of the day. Breakfast fuels the children for the day. It gives them energy and makes them focused on the day's work. Here are a few suggestions on how children can retain a great breakfast.

1. ENOUGH SLEEP.

Sleep deprivation or a bad night's sleep can make children feel bloated or nauseated. This will starve off feelings of hunger until later in the morning when tiredness begins to be mistaken for hunger. They are more likely to eat candy bars and fatty baked goods later in the day to quell the queasy stomach if this is why they skipped breakfast.

2. MAP OUT A VARIETY OF CHOICES FOR BREAKFAST.

Some of your children may dislike having the same breakfast food on their plate every morning. If the thought of pop tarts, cornflakes, or toast has them jumping out of the house with an empty stomach, it's time to vary their choices. They can consider the following possibilities:

- Cereals
- Fruits - sliced into your cereal, smoothies, tropical platter, etc
- Bread - bagels, scones, French toast waffles, crumpets, homemade biscuits

- Eggs - add sauces such as soy sauce, salsa, and Tabasco for variety
- Drinks - freshly squeezed juice, smoothies (fruit/milk/soy), vegetable juices, blended drinks
- Beans - beans and rice, baked beans and sausage, refried beans in a breakfast burrito, etc.
- Meats - bacon and eggs, ham and eggs, sausage, chorizo, smoked fish, etc.
- Leftovers or foods that are more typically thought of as dinner foods can be good options if they are not a fan of breakfast foods.

3 EXERCISE BEFORE BREAKFAST

Exercising before breakfast can help your children to work up their appetite. At the very least, they can drink a multi-fruit juice or a smoothie to give your body some vitamins and a small amount of fibre.

4 AVOID SNACKS AT NIGHT

If your child/children tend to have bedtime heartburn, it is advisable that they stop eating a few hours before they go to bed. This may make them hungry enough to eat breakfast, and may also help them cut back on "empty" calories. However, if they need to eat late snacks, they should try small portions such as apple slices, cheese cubes, a banana or hot drinks.

5 DRINKING PLENTY OF WATER BEFORE BED

Your child/children should drink at least two to three cups of water two hours before they go to bed and remind them to go to the toilet to prevent bed wetting. By drinking at least two hours before they go to bed, they are going to be able to urinate before sleeping.

By drinking the right amount of water before they go to bed, their stomach acid is diluted, and the queasiness that some children experience early in the morning is removed.

 **Habit** Forty-four

ENJOY DINNER/ MEALS WITH THE GUESTS.

WHY IS IT IMPORTANT?

Children who eat regular family dinners with guests also consume more fruits, vegetables, vitamins, and micronutrients, as well as fewer fried foods and soft drinks.

The dinner atmosphere with guests is also lively. This makes children happier and charismatic.

Your child/children should be encouraged to enjoy meals with guests. They should not be left to themselves when an opportunity to share a meal with guests arises. Children who share meals with guests have been shown to have immense intellectual, social, emotional, and physical benefits.

Dinners with guests provide an opportunity for family members to come together, strengthen ties and build better relationships, especially with outsiders. It helps children to be able to know how to relate with guests. They build a sense of belonging which leads to better self-esteem. Dinners offer children a chance to pick role models. They can set an example of healthy eating and polite table manners.

BENEFITS:

💎 INTELLECTUAL BENEFITS

- **Mindful eating:** When children have meals with guests, they begin to watch their eating habits. This helps them to drop lousy eating habits and embrace a more matured approach to eating.

- **Better grades:** Children who enjoy their meals with guests have been proven to have better grades. This is because they are able to explore subjects and issues from various perspectives through their relationships and interactions with guests.

- **Learning good habits and attitudes:** Dinnertimes are excellent times for children to learn good eating habits. They are also able to watch others as they talk and behave while eating.

EMOTIONAL BENEFITS

- **Happiness:** Children are generally social beings. Even those who keep to themselves will be happier when they meet guests who share several commonalities with them.

- **Fun:** When your child/children begin to enjoy their meals with guests, they have more fun. This is good for them as it helps to improve their outlook towards life.

- **Enhanced identity:** When your child/children interact with others, they will begin to see how they differ from others and how they are unique. This understanding helps them to enhance their own identity while exploring other perspectives.

SOCIAL BENEFITS

- **Strong parent-child bond:** When children interact more with guests, they are able to appreciate their parents more. This helps them to develop a stronger parent-child bond.

- **Opportunity to practice gratitude:** Dinners with guests often avail children the opportunity to be grateful for life and resources.

- **Obtain good manners:** Children are able to obtain good manners when they watch others—guests and family members eat.

- **Learning social expectations:** They are also able to learn what social expectations are ideal for them. They are able to develop the right etiquettes.

◈ PHYSICAL BENEFITS

◉ **Feeling important:** When children are constantly invited to dinners with guests, they will feel more important, and as a result, they will be thriving to grow.

◉ **Less harmful habits:** From their conversations with guests, they will drop many harmful benefits like poor eating habits as well as several childish attitudes.

CONCLUSION:

Dinners with guests are fun. Hence, your children will often look forward to enjoying their meals. This will help them avoid fast foods containing fat, sugar, and calories. Eating together as mentioned above helps to foster good rapport between your child/children with guests and also help them to pick up a lot of healthy table manners along the line. This will contribute a great deal to social skill now and later in their lives.

PRACTICAL STEPS CHILDREN CAN TAKE IN ENJOYING MEALS WITH GUESTS

If your child/children are shy, getting them to enjoy their meals with guests can be a tough task. However, there are lots of things that they can begin to do to let loose and enjoy their dinners with guests. They can make some new friends by talking to people and getting to know them through conversation. The following are practical steps that they can follow in enjoying their meals with guests.

1. LOOKING APPROACHABLE

Your child/children should pay adequate attention to their body language. A lousy body language may turn off a guest. They should notice if they are crossing their body and try to uncross their arms and legs. When having meals with guests, they should smile, look friendly, look up and try to make eye contact with other people.

2. INCLUDING OTHERS IN GROUP CONVERSATIONS

. If children are initiating conversations, it is easy for them to focus only on familiar members. This may alienate the guests. Instead, they should invite guests to join them in their conversations. They should let them know what everyone is discussing or invite them to contribute to the discussion.

For example, they can say, "Alex just got a puppy, and we're discussing dogs. What do you think about having a puppy?"

Dinners are a great time for children to meet people. While it's cool for them to be with their friends, they should make efforts to meet other people as well. This will help them make new friends who they can hang out with at future parties.

3. BE COURTEOUS

The children should be courteous and let others speak before them. By making eye contact and acknowledging the guests when they speak, it will engage the children with the guests, and open them up to more conversation.

4. CONTINUE EATING

While they listen to the conversation between members on the table, they should continue eating and try to enter into the conversation by injecting a thought and a smile and friendly chatter and laughter.

5. COMPLIMENTS

To effectively enjoy their meals with the guests, children should also appreciate the family member who made 'this delicious dinner,' mention that the soup was great. The best parts of a dinner are the sociable aspects.

 **Habit** Forty-five

OBTAIN A SENSE OF BEING HIM/HER

WHY IS IT IMPORTANT?

Without a sense of identity, the world will be messy.

Identity and self-esteem are closely related. Developing self-esteem and a strong sense of identity are very important for children to have good mental health. Their sense of identity has to do with who they think they are and how they perceive themselves.

> Most people are other people. Their thoughts are someone else's opinions, their lives a mimicry, their passions a quotation.
>
> **Oscar Wilde**

Perception is believed to be of immense importance than knowledge. How your children perceive themselves is very significant in expressing who they are. This also brings the benefits in the sense of being enough and self-worth. Therefore, it is important that your child/children obtain the sense of being who they are. It is your duty as parent/parents to point them in the right direction so they can discover who they are and leverage on it perfectly to know their value and importance.

BENEFITS:

INTELLECTUAL BENEFITS

Focus: When your children know who they are, they are able to focus on what truly matters. A child who has a healthy self-esteem will not focus on pleasing others at the expense of his own interest or integrity.

- **Intellectual energy:** There is a boundless intellectual energy that a child obtains when he or she obtains the sense of being himself or herself. This intellectual energy enlarges the cognitive bandwidth of children, which makes them able to engage in quality creative thinking.

- **Clarity:** A healthy sense of oneself enables children to have clarity in their streams of thoughts. This increases their mental power and focus.

- **Critical thinking:** To think critically, your children must have a reference point. If your children are able to obtain a sense of being themselves, they will be able to anchor their thinking on a solid reference point.

- **Better grades:** Consequently, children who think clearly, have focus and are intellectually energized are going to have better grades and perform well in their academics.

EMOTIONAL BENEFITS

- **Self-love:** Identity leads to self-love. When children have a strong self of identity, they are able to find love in themselves, and their self-esteem will skyrocket.

- **Confidence:** The confidence that a child who has obtained a sense of himself or herself is massive. He or she walks with a sense of purpose. They know themselves, and they are able to approach everyday life with confidence.

- **Emotional stability:** Your child/children are going to be emotionally stable if they have obtained a solid sense of themselves. They will desist from seeking people's approval and focus on being themselves.

SOCIAL BENEFITS

- **Healthy relationships:** Your children will be able to network with the right people if they have a healthy perception of being themselves.

- **Strong sense of cultural identity:** Children who have obtained a good sense of themselves are able to identify with their heritage. This helps them to carve out their identity in a world filled with diversities.

💎 COMMUNICATION BENEFITS

- **Having confident with any kind of conversation:** A strong sense of identity will help children to have confidence in any kind of conversations. This is because they are aware of who they are and are not ashamed to be themselves.

- **Speaking effectively and interact effectively:** If your child/children have obtained a solid sense of being themselves, they are going to be able to speak effectively. Since speaking is simply an expression of oneself, it takes a child who has a right sense of himself or herself to be able to complete and interact effectively.

💎 PHYSICAL BENEFITS

- **Feeling important:** They will engage in less harmful habits. People who have not obtained a sense of their being themselves often engage in harmful behaviours to feel good about themselves.

- **Less harmful habits:** Your children will consume fewer junks if they have a perception of who they are. As a result, they will consume less fat, sugar, and calories to keep them healthy.

CONCLUSION:

Your children will engage in less harmful habits when they obtain a sense of being themselves. It is important as parents to guide our child/children towards the right path through helping them stay clear away from harmful habits. We should nurture them in a way that they will understand the right things to engage in and the ones to stay away from. This brings long term benefits for your child/children's lives in many ways.

It is important to be yourself at all times and be the perfect lesson for your child/children to learn from.

PRACTICAL STEPS CHILDREN CAN TAKE IN OBTAINING A SENSE OF BEING HIMSELF OR HERSELF

"Be yourself" is probably the most popular advice you have ever given to your child/children. However, it is such a vague adage. Children do not often know what it means for them "to be yourself." With the steps below, your child/children can begin to obtain a sense of being themselves:

1 **DEFINING HIMSELF/HERSELF ON HIS/HER TERMS.**

Your children cannot be themselves if they don't know, understand, and accept themselves. Finding themselves and defining themselves on their own term should be the first step in obtaining a sense of being who they are. For your child to discover himself, there are steps he or she can take:

i. He or she can take personality tests. However, your child/children should be careful when taking personality tests, so that these tests do not define them. Instead, they should focus on defining themselves on their own terms. They may feel self-conscious, but by associating themselves with positive people, they are going to feel right to be who they are.

ii. They should take time to learn the things that they value. In addition, they should also know why these values are important to them by contemplating their choices. They should figure out what they like or enjoy doing.

2 **THEY SHOULD AVOID FIXATING ON THE PAST.**

One of the unhealthiest approaches that your child/children may take is to try to maintain an idea of who they are based on a decision they made a long time ago. They should not decide that who they are is defined by a moment or period of time, after which they spend the rest of their lives trying to still be that person from the past rather than someone who is still them but grows with the passing of each season and decade.

3. THEY SHOULD NEVER STOP LOOKING FOR THEIR OWN STRENGTHS.

With time, they will grow, and life will happen. However, they must never stop discovering new strengths in themselves. They should allow themselves the space to grow, to improve, to become wiser.

4. THEY SHOULD RELAX ABOUT THEIR IDENTITY

It can be really overwhelming for a child trying to obtain a sense of being who he or she is. They should not take everything seriously. They should learn to have fun, turn experiences into a fun story that they can share with others. And, if people make mean or insensitive judgments, they do not have to take it personally.

 **Habit** Forty-six
MAINTAIN SELF-LOVE.

WHY IS IT IMPORTANT?

Self-love is the basis for all love. If your children can't love themselves, they will find it hard to love others. Teaching them to maintain a healthy self-love is teaching them to be a healthy person to themselves and to the others.

> The most terrifying thing is to accept oneself completely.
>
> C.G. Jung

Self-love is an essential part of confidence. Having good self-esteem implies accepting and feeling positive about yourself. Confidence is not just feeling good but also knowing you are exceptional at something. Specific ways of thinking are very important for building confidence.

When children begin to show self-love, they become more confident and courageous. This is good for excellence in children.

BENEFITS:

💎 INTELLECTUAL BENEFITS

- **High achiever:** When children are full of self-love, they are going to go for excellence. They will become high achievers.

- **Having ideas to offer to the others:** Self-love is the beginning of self-expression. When they show love for themselves, they are going to be able to have ideas to offer to others.

- **Focus on tasks:** A healthy self-love helps children to be able to focus on the right tasks. This improves their focus and concentration.

⬢ **Being able to find solutions for problems:** Self-love makes children more creative. They see challenges as an opportunity to find solutions to problems.

⬢ **Pursuing in interests and passions:** Self-love helps children to focus on activities that excite them. They are able to handpick passions that are productive and beneficial.

💎 EMOTIONAL BENEFITS

⬢ **Confidence:** It takes immense self-love for children to feel confident. Children who do not love and respect themselves are going to find it hard to feel confident. They will hide when they are supposed to express their talents and nature.

⬢ **Joy:** Joy follows children who maintain a healthy self-love. They are able to find the positives in everyday interactions. They are happy and make others around them happy. They find humour in everything and do not miss opportunities to find fun.

⬢ **Tranquillity:** They are calm, cool, and collected. They rarely get upset as they find joy within. Your children are able to navigate the courses of life effortlessly because they have maintained self-love.

💎 SOCIAL BENEFITS

⬢ **Healthy relationships:** Beyond the emotional benefits of self-love, your child/children are able to develop healthy relationships and experience confidence in social gatherings.

It takes a huge amount of self-love for children to have a healthy relationship with others. Children who do not love themselves are toxic. They cause harms to others, and as a result, good children do not associate with them.

⬢ **Comfort in social gatherings:** One of the benefits of a healthy self-love is confidence. Children who display self-love are able to feel secure in the presence of other children without feeling inferior or overly sensitive.

💎 COMMUNICATION BENEFITS

● **Assertiveness:** When your child/children have healthy self-love, they are more assertive in their expressions. They know what personal values that they will not compromise on. As a result, their peers will respect them for who they are. This also helps them to have more self-love.

● **Articulation:** They are able to articulate their thoughts in a healthy and convincing manner. This helps them to be able to be more proactive and initiative.

💎 PHYSICAL BENEFITS

● **Less harmful habits:** It takes a healthy dose of self-love for children to avoid harmful habits. Children who love their bodies will not engage in smoking or mindless eating that may result in weight issues.

● **Prevents addiction:** Self-love also protects children from addictions that can easily beset children.

● **Thriving to grow physically:** Self-love helps children to thrive to grow physically. When they love themselves, they are able to take care of their physical health.

CONCLUSION:

Drugs, food, TVs, and internet are some of the common addictions in children. When your children maintain self-love, they are able to overcome common addictions. Maintaining self-love is important for children. it helps them to focus on activities that are good for them.

PRACTICAL STEPS YOUR CHILD/CHILDREN CAN TAKE IN MAINTAINING SELF-LOVE

Maintaining self-love is essential to a child's development. It helps your children as they forge their path in this world.

1. STOP CARING ABOUT THE LOOK.

This decade is filled with many beauty influencers who want to teach your child/children the definition of beauty. Your children should understand that beauty is first innate. Beauty is largely a function of character than of the shape of a child's nose or the colour of their hair.

2. LET GO

In order for your children to fully love themselves, they must be able to let go of previous ideas of themselves. They must be willing to redefine the love in their lives. They must let go of previous mistakes and maintain a positive outlook towards life.

3. WIN HIMSELF/HERSELF OVER.

Maintaining self-love will require your child/children continuing pressing on their areas of strengths. They have to be able to have fun, take on challenges, and seek experiences on their own. They must be able to surprise themselves and win themselves over and over.

4. AVOID COMPARISON

Comparison with others leads to discontentment, jealousy, and bitterness. It makes a child feel insecure. It is therefore important that your children do not derive satisfaction from comparison with other children. They must be able to love themselves wholly enough and strive to be better every day. They do not have to compare themselves to others; they are unique, and people love that.

5. SELF-BELIEF

Even if they do not believe that they deserve certain things, they should act as if they do. They have to truly believe that they are lovely, loving, and loveable.

6. HAVE FUN

They should have a good time with whatever they do. In whatever they do, they should seek creative ways to have fun and do the things that make them laugh. This is good for their self-esteem and helps them to enjoy the time they spend alone.

7. DOING THINGS THEY LOVE

There are a lot of things that your child/children can do, but their greatest source of joy will form the things that they love doing. It will spike their confidence, and people will notice their talents. Also, they should attempt to do things that they have never done before. It fuels their dopamine and makes them feel alive.

8. PAYING ATTENTION TO APPEARANCE

Even though it is advisable that children do not focus on how they look, there are certain aspects of their appearance that they have control over. They should wear clothes that make them feel good. For girls, heels are a major confidence builder. For boys, they like to strut their stuff in the latest jacket.

9. REMEMBERING THE SMILE

This is very essential. It projects a confident attitude and an appearance of positivity. When children smile, people are drawn to them, and this makes them more confident. Your children should not forget to smile.

 **Habit** Forty-seven

CARRY OUT GOOD PERSONAL HYGIENE

WHY IS IT IMPORTANT?

Good personal hygiene will help your kids stay healthy, ward off illnesses, and build better self-awareness.

Personal hygiene habits such as washing of hands and brushing and flossing the teeth will help children in keeping bacteria, viruses, and illnesses at bay.

This is an essential habit that your children should develop. This habit alone could help them in developing several good habits. Children who have excellent personal hygiene tend to be more conscientious and smarter than their peers. It is important for young children to develop the habits of good personal hygiene as early as possible as it will help them develop a fantastic adoration for cleanliness.

A good personal hygiene is very important in children. It keeps them away from dirt and other germ-causing messes.

BENEFITS:

💎 INTELLECTUAL BENEFITS

- **Critical thinking:** Would you have thought that personal hygiene helps improve your child/children critical thinking? But it does. Research studies have proven that children who are tidy are more logical and analytical in their thoughts pattern. As a result of keeping good hygiene, they are more critical in their thinking.

- **Focus:** If your child/children are able to pay attention to the little details of what they wear and how they wear them, they will be more focused in all other areas—academics, sports, etc. Getting a child focused can be tedious work. However, when your child/children begin to incorporate proper hygiene in their day-to-day activities, they are able to stay focused and smart.

● **A Better Environment for Learning:** Without good hygiene, the learning environment becomes messy. A messy environment is not an ideal place for children to learn.

● **High efficiency:** One of the characteristics of efficiency is good hygiene. Children who are hygienic are more efficient than their peers. This is because when they keep proper hygiene, they are able to stay focused on the right things instead of worrying about what else they got wrong in their appearances.

💎 EMOTIONAL BENEFITS

● **Confidence:** A hygienic child is naturally more confident. His sense of confidence comes from his appearance and proprietary—which is his correct behaviour.

● **Peace:** There is an internal peace that your child/children enjoy when they know that they have done everything right in keeping the proper personal hygiene. Peace from fear of germs and other perils of poor hygiene.

💎 PHYSICAL BENEFITS

● **Growing properly in physical:** Children who are focused on improving their hygiene are more inclined to grow properly. This is because they are going to watch what they put into their mouth.

● **Balancing the functions of the entire body:** A good personal hygiene is essential in having proper bodily functions in children.

● **Prevention of diseases:** When your child/children keep proper hygiene, they are able to stay off several diseases that easily beset children who are unkempt.

● **Prevention of domestic injuries:** By putting the right things in the right place and taking care of their bodies, children are able to avoid several domestic injuries in the home.

CONCLUSION:

There are significant benefits that your child/children can obtain by carrying out good personal hygiene.

Good personal hygiene will help your children to be healthy, fight off illnesses, and build improved self-awareness.

It's never too early to start teaching hygiene to your children. You can help clean your child's hands after changing their diapers or before eating, brush their teeth and gums before bed, and set them a daily bath routine. This helps you start the process and slowly teaches them as they grow and take over the process. This is a fundamental process that needs to be paid attention.

PRACTICAL STEPS YOUR CHILDREN CAN TAKE IN CARRYING OUT GOOD PERSONAL HYGIENE

Having good hygiene is an important aspect of staying healthy and clean. Maintaining good hygiene can also improve your child/children's appearance to others. When they have bad hygiene, there's a greater chance of spreading bacteria to other parts of their body and it increases the likelihood of getting sick. Luckily, maintaining good hygiene is easy as long as they take the right steps to keep their bodies clean and build good habits that they stick to.

1 TAKING A SHOWER DAILY

This has to be a non-negotiable for your child/children. They must be able to take showers daily, use soap and hot water when they shower and concentrate on their face, feet, hands, underarms, groin, and bottom. They should also remember to shower after sweating a lot, especially after a physical activity or sports.

2 WASHING HAIR REGULARLY:

If your child/children have dry, coarse, or very curly hair, they may not want to wash it every day because it could dry it out. However, if the hair is overly oily, greasy, or fine hair, they should do it every day to prevent oils from building up.

3. REGULAR BRUSHING AND FLOSSING

To keep healthy gums and teeth, your child/children should brush two to three times a day. Each time they brush, they should make sure that they are scrubbing all of their teeth and take their time. The toothbrush should be replaced every two to three months.

Also, it is good that they floss at least once a day. This helps them keep their mouth clean and smelling good.

4. CLIPPING OF NAILS

Keeping shorter nails will help your child/children maintain good nail hygiene. They should cut their nails whenever they are getting along with manicure scissors or clipper. They should also keep them clean by washing them when they wash their hands.

5. CHANGE YOUR CLOTHES DAILY.

Wearing dirty clothes can cause microorganisms and bacteria to build upon your children's body. It's especially important for them to change clothes that are closest to their body, like undershirts or underwear. Doing this daily will prevent their clothes from smelling bad and will keep them clean.

6. APPLYING UNDERARM DEODORANT.

If your child/children sweat a lot, they should try using underarm antiperspirant. It will prevent them from sweating. You can buy some deodorant for them at the store. They should apply the deodorant every day when they wake up so that their underarms smell fresh throughout the day. It is important that your child/children do not replace showering with deodorant.

7. KEEPING THE FEET CLEAN

Your child/children will have smelly feet if they wear dirty socks or no socks at all. If they are wearing clean socks but still have bad feet odour, they should concentrate on cleaning them when they shower or bathe and rotate which shoes they wear during the week. In addition, they should ensure that their feet are completely dry before putting on socks and shoes. For their feet to smell better, they can put talcum powder on their feet after the shower.

8. STICKING TO DAILY HYGIENE ROUTINE

The best way for your child/children to maintain good hygiene over a period is for them to make it a routine that they do every day. They should alter their schedule, so they are leaving enough time to take care of their hygiene.

- A simple morning routine would include waking up at 7 a.m. to brush their teeth, wash their face, and put on deodorant before going off to school.

- Once they get home, they could take a shower at 6 p.m. and brush and floss their teeth right before bed.

9. READING PICTURE BOOK, HEALTH MAGAZINES, ARTICLES

Reading picture book, magazines, and articles will help children to develop and maintain personal hygiene.

10. WATCHING, LISTENING GOOD HEALTH TV SHOWS, RADIOS PODCAST

These are also additional ways that children can develop and maintain personal hygiene.

 **Habit** Forty-eight

KEEP THE BODY SAFE AND SAFETY AWARENESS.

WHY IS IT IMPORTANT?

At an early age, your child must be security conscious. He or she must be able to keep his or her body safe and develop an awareness for safety.

Self-awareness is a skill that helps your child/children understand his feelings, thoughts, and actions. It's more than just being able to recognize these things. It means understanding that how he acts on his thoughts, feelings, and actions affects him and others.

Kids who have self-awareness do an improved job when self-monitoring. This means your child/children are able to monitor what they are doing (either in learning or socially) and discover what's working and what's not. Self-awareness also leads to self-reflection—thinking over things that happened so as to find avenues to make things work better next time.

BENEFITS:

💎 INTELLECTUAL BENEFITS

- **Less distraction:** The fear and distractions that come from the lack of safety awareness can impair the cognitive functioning of a child. However, a child who keeps his or her body safe has one less thing to worry about —safety. The awareness of safety helps children to be able to take trips and enjoy their plays on the playground without fear.

- **A Better Environment for Learning:** When your child/children begin to pay attention to their safety, they are, as a result, priming themselves for proper learning. It is hard for a child to stay focused if everything around him or her poses issues concerning safety.

● **High efficiency:** For there to be high efficiency, children must be able to keep their bodies safe.

● **Improved cognitive functioning:** When your child/children begin to develop an awareness of their environment, they develop a higher cognitive functioning. They are able to relate to their environment and others in a way that is higher than others. As a result, they are able to overcome the usual cognitive biases that children have.

COMMUNICATION BENEFITS

● **Nonviolence communication (NVC):** Children who are aware of their bodily safety engage in nonviolence communication in expressing their concerns without causing any violence. Through the power of words, they are able to diffuse the tension in a place.

● **Assertiveness:** It takes assertiveness and volition for children to speak up when there are issues concerning safety. When children begin to focus on bodily and environs safety, they develop confidence and assertiveness.

SOCIAL BENEFITS

● **Healthy relationships:** When children begin to focus on bodily safety and security awareness, they are able to make the right choices in friendships. This allows them to develop more meaningful and healthy relationships.

● **Comfort in social gatherings:** It takes absolute trust in a group for a child to be comfortable. However, when a child is able to decipher the security measures of a group, he or she is able to feel comfortable in social gatherings.

PHYSICAL BENEFITS

● **Prevention of domestic accidents:** When your children are adequately aware of their environment and their body, they will have fewer domestic accidents.

- **Prevention of illness and possible contamination:** Children like to explore things. It is important that they do their exploration in a safe and healthy way.

CONCLUSION:

When children are bodily safe and security conscious, they are able to prevent illness and possible contamination.

Australia is mostly a safe place to nurture our child/children. We also need to understand that there are some people around who can pose a danger, especially to kids. Most of the people who hurt kids are people the kid knows, including people in their families and bullies at school, but a few of these people are strangers to them. It is important for you as a parent to always teach your child/children the skills of self-awareness and how they can always hold their own whenever an emergency arises.

PRACTICAL STEPS CHILDREN CAN TAKE IN KEEPING THE BODY SAFE AND MAINTAINING SAFETY AWARENESS

Young children are often taught all types of ways to keep themselves safe. They are taught to watch the hot stove, check both ways before crossing the street, but more often than not – body safety is not taught until much older. In this section, we are going to explore practical steps that your children can begin to take in keeping the body safe and maintain safety awareness.

1. TALKING ABOUT BODY PARTS.

Your child/children should be encouraged to talk about their body parts early on in life. They should be able to call each of their body parts by their appropriate names. This is very important especially when a child is lodging a complaint. When a girl calls her vagina her "bottom," it can be very confusing.

2. BODY PARTS ARE PRIVATE

Your child/children need to understand that their body parts are private and only their parents can see them because they are still young. No other person is allowed to see them naked especially outside the home. In addition, they have to further understand that the doctor can see them naked because mommy and daddy are with the doctor.

3. UNDERSTANDING BODY BOUNDARIES

Your child/children should know matter-of-factly that no one should touch their private parts and that no one should ask them to touch somebody else's private parts.

4. NO PICTURES OF PRIVATE PARTS

Your child/children should know that no one is allowed to take pictures of their private parts, nor should they look at the pictures of the private parts of others.

5. UNDERSTANDING HOW TO GET OUT OF SCARY SITUATIONS

If your child/children feel uncomfortable with telling people "No" – especially older peers or adults. They can make up excuses to get out of uncomfortable situations. This helps them to be safety conscious.

Your child/children can use code words when they feel unsafe. This will be more effective at home if there are visitors at home who make your children uncomfortable. As your children get older, code words will enable them to be able to effectively communicate any appearance of danger without getting themselves in trouble.

KNOW WHEN TO SAY NO.

WHY IS IT IMPORTANT?

Your children have to know when to say NO. They cannot just say yes to everything. The world is filled with manipulators and abusers who want to prey on innocent children. By being assertive, your children are able to express themselves with respect without being demeaning.

Children must be able to say NO to things that destabilize their moral compass. They must be able to be assertive when they voice out their concerns.

Learning how to say "no" when you emphatically mean "no" is a life skill. For some children, it comes quite naturally. For others, it needs to be groomed habitually and practiced over time. It is essential that children are able to say NO to things that they do not approve of. They must learn not to submit to intimidation.

It may not feel ok at first, but it's essential for living life truthfully and a skill that will improve your child/children overall emotional health. When children are able to say NO, they avoid doing or consenting to bad things.

BENEFITS:

INTELLECTUAL BENEFITS

Carte blanche: Today, carte blanche means that your child is free to do or say whatever he or she pleases. Note that it is a mistake to say "a carte blanche" unless you are talking about a piquet hand or a blank signed contract. It is a French phrase, meaning "unlimited discretionary power to act. When your children are able to say NO to things that do not please them, they are able to act within the context of their schedule, skill set and goals.

- **Independent thinking:** It takes a child who can think independently of others to say no. independent thinking is good for a young child as it helps him or her to be able to identify what he or she wants early in life. Hence, it saves unnecessary wastage of time in an attempt to find purpose.

- **Critical thinking:** When the word no is uttered, a statement of reason may be required. In cases like this, it will require critical thinking for your child/children to be able to come up with creative explanations without sounding defensive.

- **Focus:** In addition, the power of saying NO is the power of focus. It helps your child/children to be able to focus on their priorities.

EMOTIONAL BENEFITS

- **High Self Esteem:** Your child/children will have an enhanced self-image when they begin to say no to people who seek out to manipulate them. Self-esteem is good for children.

- **Charisma:** They also have charisma. They are cheerful and fun to be with. This may sound counterintuitive, but it is true. By saying no to people, places, and tasks that they do not want, they are able to focus on activities and relationships that inspire them.

- **Positivity:** When your child/children have mastered the art of saying no, they are generally more positive. This is because they are able to avoid passive aggressiveness which generally accompanies children who are door-mats for others.

SOCIAL BENEFITS

- **Courage:** There is so much courage in saying NO. The mere uttering of those words will make the children appear more courageous and bolder. Courage and boldness are essential social skills that children need in interacting with others.

Authenticity: Saying no means that your child/children have identified what they want and what they do not want. It brings out the authenticity in them. As a result, people are going to love and respect them more.

COMMUNICATION BENEFITS

Expressive: Your child/children are going to clearly show their thoughts or feelings in all situations without any feeling of shyness or fear.

Assertive: Also, they are more assertive in their expressions. Their communications are full of energy and purpose. People are able to deduce purpose in their conversations. They will generally be regarded as leaders.

Persuasive: In addition, your child/children who say NO to things that they do not want are going to be more persuasive. They will be able to convince about their choices and decisions without causing any feeling of animosity.

CONCLUSION:

Finally, they are going to accept themselves for who they are. This is good for their self-image and confidence.

The faster a person understands him or herself, the better for their peace of mind. By being able to say NO a lot of times, they place priority on themselves and will understand that you don't give what you don't have. They need to be happy first before they can share happiness, they shouldn't help people at their own detriment, and it will help them understand who their trusted friends are.

PRACTICAL STEPS YOUR CHILD/CHILDREN CAN TAKE IN KNOWING WHEN TO SAY NO

Like most people, your child's natural instinct is probably to help others when he or she can. However, there are times when he or she just need to say "no." It is okay to say no. They can say no while still being respectful. If they feel it's necessary, they can also provide a reason for their answer. Whatever the situation, they have to be clear, polite, and firm when saying no.

❶ UNDERSTANDING WHEN TO SAY NO

Little children of about two years of age are quick to say NO because they've only recently learned that such a thing is possible, and the new chances for independence it provides are fun and exciting. Two-year-olds are also known for being selfish and thoughtless. However, they're on to something: it's okay to say no. However, your children cannot just say NO to everything. They have to know when it is appropriate for them to use the word.

1. They can learn to say no because they don't have the time to meet a commitment.
2. Saying no when they just don't feel like doing something is okay, as long as the thing they are being asked to do won't reflect on their school performance. There's nothing wrong with wanting time for himself or herself instead.
3. Saying no to a situation that makes them uncomfortable is perfectly okay. They never have to step outside their personal comfort zone to accommodate the wishes of anyone else.

❷ STICKING TO PRIORITIES

They can't do everything, so it is important for your child/children to be able to give a respectful "no." To effectively do this, they must schedule their time wisely, account for all their activities, write down their priorities each day, and commit to getting them done. If someone asks them to do something, not in line with those goals, they can say no. Of course, if something important comes up, they can always be flexible and make an exception. For example, if they need to visit the dentist, they might have to cancel going to the playground on Saturday morning.

③ COMING UP WITH A THOUGHTFUL RESPONSE

When they say no, they do not have to give excuses. Instead, they can give a short explanation. It is within their rights to not give any excuse or reason when they decline to do things. They can simply respond, "no," but if they feel like adding more, they can still be respectful while keeping it simple.

- Another way to say no is simply, "No, I can't do that."
- They could say, "I'm sorry, that just won't work for me."
- If someone asks if they can buy them a drink, they should feel free to just say, "No, thanks."
- They should think before saying no. if they say no immediately, it might seem like they didn't even consider the request. In order to be respectful, they should take a moment to think about your answer-- even if you already know what it is going to be. Take a pause, and then kindly say no.

Habit Fifty

HAVE COURAGE

WHY IS IT IMPORTANT?

Courage helps children overcome the fear of rejection.

It also helps them to engage well with others. Courage allows children to attempt things that they have not tried before, despite the fear of looking foolish.

In this fast-paced technology world, children must have the courage to pursue their interest in order to stay relevant when they grow up.

For children, courage can be standing up to a bully or restraining an urge to eat an unhealthy meal. Real courage requires wisdom. Courage comes in a lot of little ways for children. It affects the way they interact with others and with themselves. Courage help children to shake off childishness and pursue worthwhile goals. It helps them to be able to take on ambitious projects and achieve them. Courage is the essence of living. It lights them up and makes them enthusiastic.

Leadership requires making bold and often unpopular decisions. Leadership takes courage. If children are going to grow up to become leaders, they have to be able to be courageous.

BENEFITS:

INTELLECTUAL BENEFITS

- **Leadership:** To lead other children, your child/children must be courageous. When your child/children have a courageous disposition towards life, they are able to lead others effectively.

- **Improved decision making:** Courage allows children to think on the borders of cognitive limits and make wise decisions. As a result, courage helps children to be able to avoid personal and cognitive biases. This not only improve their decision making, but it also helps them to be able to avoid prejudices.

- **Self-awareness:** True courage involves the learning of oneself. When your child/children are courageous, they are going to have an enhanced self-awareness which is important in personal development.

- **Vision:** True vision is a product of courage. It makes your child/children see things farther than their peers. Hence, they are able to make decisions that do not lead to regrets but are well thought-out.

EMOTIONAL BENEFITS

- **Confidence:** Courage makes your child/children feel more confident. When your child/children begin to dare their limits, they begin to have an increased belief in their strengths and talents. This is significant for their self-esteem and personal perception.

- **Peace:** It is counterintuitive to think that courage brings peace, but it does. When your child/children know that they have the liberty to pursue their goals, they feel a sense of tranquillity that very few can have.

SOCIAL BENEFITS

- **Influence:** Influence follows the child who demonstrates the acts of courage consistently. People will naturally gravitate towards him/her. They will admire him/her and want to like him/her. Influence is good for a child. It helps him/her aspire for lofty heights and act in a way that is proprietary.

- **Helping and protect the right of others:** Courage makes children help and protect the right of others. It takes courage to stand up for others.

- **Not being manipulated:** It helps them to stop being manipulated.

♦ COMMUNICATION BENEFITS

● **Gestural:** In their speeches and communication, they are more gestural. This gives the impression that they know what they are doing. This is really good for their confidence and esteem.

● **Public speaking:** Courage destroys shyness. They are more likely to take on projects that involve public speaking because they are courageous in the expression of their ideas.

● **Assertiveness:** In addition, they are generally more assertive. They do not compromise on their basic values, and they are empathic.

CONCLUSION:

In addition to influence, your children gain the respect of their peers. This helps them to be able to reinforce their self-image and develop a positive outlook towards life. Courage is everything in life. To take any productive step, you need to be courageous. To start a business, start a course, take a swimming class or even light up your gas, you need a little bit of courage. Since the importance of courage is not in doubt, why not take all the time you have to imbibe the spirit of courage in your child/children?

PRACTICAL STEPS YOUR CHILDREN CAN TAKE IN HAVING THE COURAGE

Courage is a personality trait that every child possesses, but it sometimes falters because of bad experiences or memories. Having courage is necessary for your child/children's success early on in life from meeting the fellow classmates to setting audacious goals. By identifying the source of any lack of courage and actively changing their behaviours, your children can build confidence in any aspect of their lives.

1. IDENTIFYING SPECIFIC FEARS

Children are often reluctant to admit that they are afraid of something and this may be undermining their confidence and courage. In order to begin building courage, they need to determine their specific fear. They may not be aware of their specific fears until they talk about what causes their lack of courage. They can write a list of their fears as soon as they begin to emerge or are known. This may help them in developing the appropriate strategy in overcoming them and building courage.

2. RECOGNIZING COURAGE

Just as it's important for your child/children to take an inventory of their fears, they should also recognize that they also possess courage in many situations. Taking the time to acknowledge that they are courageous can help them to figure out how to apply this quality to situations in their life that cause timidity. Your child/children have courage in some ways even though it may not always be obvious. Recognizing their courage can help them to develop their behaviour and begin building courage in every aspect of their lives.

3. DEVELOPING A CONCRETE PLAN TO BUILD COURAGE

Once they have identified their fears, your child/children should develop a strategy to build concrete courage. Having an explicit strategy that they can follow may help them stay on track if they have setbacks or see their progress over time. They should update their plans regularly. Having a tangible list will help in keeping them motivated. In dealing with situations that elicit fears, your children can conceptualize a game plan or "script" for a specific situation and follow through with it. For example, if they are scared of speaking to a classmate in school, they can write notes and develop a plan that will allow them to have to know what they could say in response to any questions or contingencies that may arise in your interaction.

4. FRAMING FEARS WITH SIMPLER TERMS

If they are confronted with something that causes them to fear or to lose courage, they can frame it in simple terms. Framing is a behavioural technique that can help them shape how they think and feel about specific situations by making them seem commonplace or banal. Working with smaller and more manageable units of anything will help build their courage. In addition, they should focus on seeking out the positive in any situation as this will help build their overall courage. Even in the most fearful situations, there will always be some aspect of courage. The ability to see these aspects will help them to build courage and confidence.

5. EXPOSING TO BOOKS, MAGAZINES, ARTICLES, TV PROGRAMS FOR ROLE MODELLING

This is another excellent way by which children can develop and maintain courage. This is actually easier as they watch and learn about the courageous acts of others. There are reports of people who are engaging in courageous acts daily. This will inspire them to build confidence and courage.

 **Habit** Fifty-one

DRINK PLENTY OF FRESH WATER

WHY IS IT IMPORTANT?

A child's body is made up of more than 55% of water. It is a circulatory system, and fresh water has to be regularly introduced into the system. Beyond the necessity of regular fresh water intake, there are several benefits of fresh water that we are going to explore in the following section.

Water helps keep the temperature normal, and you can be sure that water is the primary ingredient in perspiration, also known as sweat. Besides being an essential part of the fluids in your body, water is needed by each cell to work correctly. Your body doesn't get water only from drinking water; it gets a whole lot of benefits which will be talked about in the next line.

You should ensure your child/children drink enough water every time to prevent dehydration from happening.

BENEFITS:

💎 INTELLECTUAL BENEFITS

● **Increase in Brain Power:** In a study of young children, mild dehydration can impair brain performance, concentration, and mood, and increase the frequency of headaches. Hence, it is important that children take water regularly to improve their brain power.

● **Improved decision making:** When there is clarity in their thinking, your children are going to have enhanced decision making. Water provides the body with the necessary fluid needed for digestion and supply of nutrients to your children's brain.

💎 EMOTIONAL BENEFITS

Confidence: Studies have shown that children who drink lots of water appear more confident than their peers.

Self-esteem: A study showed that fluid loss of 1.59% was detrimental to working memory and increased feelings of anxiety and fatigue.

💎 COMMUNICATION BENEFITS

Clarity in voice: Water has been recommended for public speakers to help improve the clarity of their voice and intonation. This helps prevent breaks in voice and coarseness. In addition, water adds breaths and richness to the speaking voice of your children.

Assertiveness: The natural result of clarity in voice is assertiveness. To be assertive, your children must be able to speak once and clearly. If they had to repeat every word they say because people couldn't hear them, their assertiveness quota goes on a decline.

💎 PHYSICAL BENEFITS

Maintain the Balance of Body Fluids: Your child's body is composed of about 60% water. The functions of these bodily fluids include digestion, absorption, circulation, the creation of saliva, transportation of nutrients, and maintenance of body temperature.

Weight loss: A 1-3% fluid loss equals about 1.5-4.5 lbs (0.5-2 kg) of body weight loss for a 150 lbs (68 kg) person. This can easily occur through normal daily activities, let alone during exercise or high heat. This kind of weight loss is not ideal for children. However, when they take fresh water, they are able to digest their food properly, and eat less food. This results in a healthy weight loss.

Prevents Kidney stone: Regular intake of water helps prevent kidney stones and other kidney diseases in children.

CONCLUSION:

Drinking enough water also helps produce more urine, which helps to flush out infection-causing bacteria.

Your body monitors the volume of water in your system. The body holds on to water when you don't have enough or gets rid of it if you have too much. If your urine is very light yellow, you are well hydrated. But when your urine is very dark yellow, then you have to drink enough.

You can help your body by drinking whenever you are thirsty and drinking extra water when you work out, and it's warm out. Your body will be able to do all of its wonderful jobs, and you'll feel great if you always drink the right volume of water. You should ensure this applies to your child/children too.

PRACTICAL STEPS CHILDREN CAN TAKE IN DRINKING PLENTY OF FRESH WATER

Water is essential for your child's health; over 70% of the body consists of water, and the effects of dehydration can be life-threatening. Your child/children should consider replacing high-calorie sodas or alcoholic drinks with plain water. This will help them control appetite and weight, improve sleep and energy levels, reduce the likelihood of dental cavities or tooth decay, and help manage chronic conditions. If you would like to know how your child/children can increase their fresh water intake for dietary, athletic, or health purposes, there are many safe and effective ways to do so.

 ## UNDERSTANDING HOW MUCH WATER SHOULD BE TAKEN DAILY

Keeping in mind that 20 percent of daily water intake typically comes from food and 80 percent of water intake typically comes from a combination of plain water and other beverages, the amount of fresh water that your child needs to drink every day for optimal hydration will vary.

Perhaps the most important factor in successfully increasing their daily fresh water intake is making it easier for them to drink water. Try some of these suggestions to make it a cinch to up their daily consumption of water.

- **Carrying water with them**. Having their own water supply on hand makes drinking water very easy. When your child/children have easy access to water, they are more likely to drink water instead of soda.
- **Developing reminders.** They can try setting alarms to remind them to drink water once per hour. They can also include triggers that will remind them to drink water. Triggers to drink more fresh water include hearing someone say their names, watching the TV, or stretching during a physical activity.

2 SUBSTITUTING WATER FOR SWEETENED BEVERAGES

Your child/children need to understand that sweetened beverages cannot replace water. If they routinely drink soda with their evening meals, they should consider swapping water for the drink of their choice. Even though these beverages are high in water content, by drinking fresh water, your child/children are able to avoid the side effects of taking caffeinated or sweetened drinks.

3 DRINKING WATER BEFORE, DURING AND AFTER LUNCH

Your child/children should make it a habit to drink a quick glass of fresh water around mealtimes. By drinking a glass of water — or at least a few sips — before, during, and after eating any meal is a great way for them to up their daily water intake. In addition, drinking water during and after each meal can help them feel full longer after eating and aid in the digestion of their food.

4 PLAYING WATER DRINKING GAMES

Your child/children can motivate themselves by playing water pong. When playing water games, care must be taken so that they do not drink excessive amounts of water. To play water pong, your child/children are going to need the following: a large stable table with a durable flat (and waterproof) surface, 20 cups, and 2 ping pong balls. These are the steps in playing water pong:

- *Clear everything off your table.*
- *Fill each cup with 4 oz. of water. Make sure all the cups are equally filled.*
- *Arrange 10 cups at each end of your table. You'll want to position the two groups of cups as far away from each other as possible, so if your table is rectangular, set them up at the long ends of the table.*
- *Align 4 cups in a row at the edge of the short end of the table.*
- *Line up 3 more cups in a row in front of the line of 4.*
- *Place 2 more cups in a row right in front of the row of 3 cups.*
- *Place a final cup in front of the row of 2 cups. You'll notice that you just formed a flat pyramid out of the 10 cups.*
- *Arrange the remaining 10 cups at the opposite end of the table in the same pattern. Both peaks of the pyramids should be facing in, pointing in toward the centre of the table.*
- *Take turns trying to throw your ball into one of your cups at the opposite end of the table. When you get a ball into a cup, you get to drink the water in that cup. The person who finishes all their cups of water first wins!*

With the steps highlighted above, your child/children will be able to drink a lot of fresh water.

 **Habit** Fifty-two

EAT FRUITS AND VEGETABLES

WHY IS IT IMPORTANT?

Fruits and vegetables are an excellent source of dietary fibre, which can help to maintain a healthy gut and prevent constipation and other digestion problems in children.

Today, children eat a lot of fast foods and unhealthy snacks that have little to no nutritional value.

Research has shown fruit and vegetables are a good source of vitamins and minerals, including folate, vitamin C and potassium.

Fruits and vegetables are important for a child's overall development. They contain the necessary vitamins needed for your child/children's development. Children who eat more fruits and vegetables as part of an overall healthy diet are likely to have a reduced risk of some chronic diseases. Fruits provide nutrients vital for health and maintenance of your body. Fruits and vegetables are very important for the overall development of a child.

BENEFITS:

💎 INTELLECTUAL BENEFITS

- **Increase in Brain Power:** Fruits and vegetables provide the needed vitamins and nutrients needed for brain development. Thus, there is a significant increase in the brain power of your child/children.

- **Critical thinking:** It takes an enhanced level of critical thinking to be able to follow through the process of active listening. The child must be able to ask the right question at the right time. This helps develop their ability to think critically before making any decision.

⚫ **Improved decision making:** When there is a significant increase in brain power, and your children get involved in critical thinking, their decision making will be highly improved.

⚫ **Focus:** Fruits and vegetables provide the useful body sugar needed for your children's brain to be focused.

💎 EMOTIONAL BENEFITS

⚫ **Confidence:** When your children eat fresh fruits and vegetables, they feel better physically and emotionally. This, in turn, helps them to speak up in a group setting and also be enthusiastic about meeting new people.

⚫ **Self-esteem:** Higher self-esteem can also result from having a good physical health. This helps them to be comfortable in public spaces and meeting new people.

💎 PHYSICAL BENEFITS

⚫ **Physical fitness:** If your child/children eat a lot of fruits and vegetables, they are going to stay in good physical conditions for a long time. This will prevent them from getting sick or having ailments.

⚫ **Weight loss:** The easiest way for your children to lose unnecessary body weight is by putting them on a diet of fruits and vegetables.

CONCLUSION:

Your children are going to benefit greatly when they eat a lot of fruits and vegetables. Not only will they appear stronger and healthier, but they are also going to adopt healthier habits. Fruits and vegetables have been proven to supply children with all the necessary nutrients needed to grow at such a tender age.

PRACTICAL STEPS YOUR CHILD/CHILDREN CAN TAKE IN EATING FRUITS AND VEGETABLES

Of course, every child loves to take a bite out of a fatty hamburger and chug a bottle of Fanta. However, if a child is constantly eating like this, serious health risks could become a reality. To get your child to eat fruits, there are certain steps you must follow.

1. FIGURE OUT THE REASON WHY HE OR SHE DOES NOT WANT TO EAT FRUITS AND VEGETABLES

There are several reasons why your child may prefer not to take mangoes, oranges, and banana. He or she may not like the taste of them, or simply prefer to eat unhealthy foods such as fast-foods. By knowing the right reasons, you will be able to choose the right fruits that solve the problem of colour, taste, shape or smell.

2. ALLOW THEM TO PICK THEIR OWN FRUITS AND VEGETABLES

By allowing them to pick their own food in the grocery section at the store, they are more likely to eat fruits and vegetables. You could also try purchasing "fun" fruits and vegetables, such as a banana with a face on it or an apple with a sticker. Children actually love to eat foods that look fun and exciting.

3. SETTING BOUNDARIES

To further encourage the consumption of fruits and vegetables, your child/children can set boundaries. For instance, your child may have to eat at least a fruit or a certain amount of vegetables before leaving the table or getting dessert. Parents should be supportive and provide plenty of praise and encouragement as they eat.

4. EXPOSING TO BOOKS, MAGAZINES, ARTICLES, TV PROGRAMS FOR ROLE MODELLING

Books and quality magazines help children to get informed about healthy eating habits. Also, when they watch TV programs for right role modelling, they are able to pick up healthy eating habits such as eating fruits and vegetables.

 **Habit** Fifty-three

DEVELOP THE INTEREST

WHY IS IT IMPORTANT?

When children do not have interests, they get bored.

Naturally, children are creative. By having an interest, they are able to explore their curiosities. Hence, they are constantly engaged. This makes them happier and fun to be with.

Your child/children need to develop personal interests. Personal interests invigorate them to be positive and cheerful. It makes them feel unique. It makes them exciting and joyful to watch. Most children naturally develop a personal interest that suits them. In this section, we are going to look at the various benefits of developing interests.

Interests are part of a child who is developing self-identity and can help them connect with peers. Children gain many benefits from trying out different activities and selecting interests that really excite them.

BENEFITS:

💎 INTELLECTUAL BENEFITS

- **Brain Health:** When children pursue their passions, they are able to have more flow of oxygen and nutrients in the bloodstream. Oxygen and positive outlook are needed for proper brain development. A focus on their passions will keep them engaged in other areas of their lives.

- **Improved memory:** One of the signs of a healthy brain is improved memory. Children who are passionate are more likely to have improved brain functioning than the rest of their peers.

- **Clear thinking:** When your child's brain is healthy, thinking becomes clear. This enhances clarity in thinking. Children who can think clearly find it easy to perform well in their academics.

💎 EMOTIONAL BENEFITS

Another aspect of the benefits we will be considering is the emotional benefit. When your children pursue to engage in activities that catch their interests, they are going to be happier, and have an enhanced sleep quality.

◉ **Happiness:** There is the pure joy that comes from children who focuses on their interests. It is a joyful thing to behold. They leap in joy and happiness. They are excited and positive about life. It is what interests them that make them come alive.

◉ **Sleep quality:** Your child/children will be free from worries and sleepless nights when they are able to do what pleases them. By engaging in activities that catch their passion, they are able to give out positive energy. They feel relaxed and calm—these are the ingredients of a good night sleep. In addition, they feel fulfilled. This is what childlikeness is all about.

💎 SOCIAL BENEFITS

Your child/children will have more healthy relationships and a strong sense of cultural identity if they focus on their areas of passion.

◉ **Increased energy levels:** Children are attracted to other children with high energy. This will help them to be able to develop more positive and meaningful relationships that may even go on into adulthood.

◉ **Enterprise:** They are also more enterprising. This is good for business and relationship building.

💎 PHYSICAL BENEFITS

The physical benefits include weight loss and reduction in hunger.

◉ **Having ideal weight:** Children's interests keep them energized. They are not feeding on junk foods and unhealthy drink with high calories; they are able to keep ideal body weight.

◉ **Reducing hunger:** When your child/children are focused on tasks that they resonate with, they are going to feel less hunger which may make them eat junks and feed on snacks.

CONCLUSION:

Overall, what is most important is that we, as parents, should stop worrying too much about our children's future, and stop rushing them as well. We all want to give our children the best chances for success. However, we need to understand that the definition of success is really when our kids are happy and doing what interests them most.

We need to stop treating our kids as adults and allow them to grow up in proper ways, more cooperative, peaceful and natural way with their interests. We need to stop forcing some selected activities on them and enable them to have more free time, relaxation and play — or at least maintain a better balance. You never know which of your children's interests may lead them to very big success in the future.

PRACTICAL STEPS YOUR CHILD/CHILDREN CAN TAKE IN DEVELOPING AN INTEREST

Aside from their innate talents and their training, there are certain activities and things that are going to interest your children. Interest makes them come alive. It invigorates them to be positive and cheerful. It makes them feel unique. Even though interests are largely peculiar to children, they may need a little help in developing their interests.

1. DEVELOPING INTERESTS

Your child/children have to evaluate what currently takes their spare time and check if they enjoy it. It may be reading a book or drawing still objects. By evaluating what they currently like, they can begin to focus more on them. There is no point in your children focusing on activities that do not inspire them. They have to be able to develop their interests and enjoy them.

2. IDENTIFYING WHAT THEY VALUE MOST

To identify what they value most, they have to begin by asking themselves such vital questions as, "Do I admire artistic expression?" "What traits do I prize?" "Do I value wisdom or courage?" "Do I feel drawn to people who give back?" For example, they may volunteer at the local library because they value education.

Certain interests require certain skill sets and personality traits. Before your children begin to pursue an interest, they must evaluate their personality traits to be sure that they are the right fit for such pursuits. This will help them avoid frustration.

3. GIVING CHOICES

Sometimes, children are not aware of their interest because they have not been exposed to many options. Hence, they should be given choices, so they can select an interest.

4. SHOWING YOUR APPRECIATIONS TOWARD THEIR INTERESTS

Whatever choice they make, ensure that you appreciate their interests.

5. JOINING WITH YOU CHILD/CHILDREN THE ACTIVITIES THAT THEY INTEREST

One way of showing interest in their choice is to join them in the activities they have chosen.

 **Habit** Fifty-four

OBTAIN A HOBBY

WHY IS IT IMPORTANT?

Without hobbies, the world is going to be a boring place.

Hobbies are Healthy. Hobbies benefit children in many ways. It gives a child an opportunity to express themselves, and it allows them to discover themselves and build self-esteem. Hobbies teach children to set and achieve goals, solve problems and make decisions.

Several research studies have shown that children who have at least one hobby and are dedicated to enjoying them are less likely to consume fat, sugar, and calories.

Hobbies help sharpen the minds of these children. It also provides a fun way for them to stay clear of boredom during the long, hot summer days, or the cause of the depression doing the cold of the winter time.

Children must be allowed to choose hobbies that make them happier.

BENEFITS:

INTELLECTUAL BENEFITS

- **Self-discipline:** Many children find themselves stuck in a daily or weekly routine that offers little more than a "rinse and repeats" type life. These are often the ways of life for families who settle in a communal environment or when there are issues in the family. When your child obtains a hobby, he or she is able to find a way out of being sucked into the unproductive routines of life.

- **Competence:** Having a hobby improves the competence of your child/children. It makes them smarter and more intelligent when making decisions.

- **Goal setting:** Hobbies are a great way of sticking a schedule and setting quality goals. Hobbies help children to know what to expect, and this makes life easy for them to live.

- **Critical Thinking:** Another benefit of having a hobby is that it helps children to engage in creative and relaxing puzzles which help them to increase their intellectual energy and their critical thinking.

💎 EMOTIONAL BENEFITS

- **Happiness:** Spending time doing an enjoyable activity that is not attached to work or other commitments will help increase the happiness of your children and satisfaction with life. It will allow them to spend time doing something that is only for their own personal benefit, and not the benefit of others.

- **Fun:** One of the benefits of having a hobby is that it helps children to relieve stress while allowing them to do something that they enjoy.

- **Enhanced identity:** By working on a hobby that is of their own choice, they are able to have an enhanced identity. They are able to express their identity.

💎 SOCIAL BENEFITS

- **Strong parent-child bond:** When you join your children in their hobbies, they will develop a stronger parent-child bond with you. This is essential for a beautiful and harmonious family. It also helps the children to have a connection.

- **Opportunity to practice gratitude:** When your children engage in one or more hobbies, they will be more grateful for life and everything in it.

- **Building healthy friendships:** Aside from parent-child bonding, your children are going to have more healthy friendships.

◈ PHYSICAL BENEFITS

● Less harmful habits: By focusing on their hobbies, they will have less time engaging in harmful habits. Your children are going to have less time to learn harmful habits that may lead to regrets later in life.

● Produce good hormones to deal with stresses: Hobbies create good and positive-feeling hormones in children. Hormones like oxytocin make children happier.

CONCLUSION:

The actual importance of hobbies, in a child's life, cannot be underestimated. Hobbies help mould personalities which are creative and self-sufficient while providing them a sense of purpose and not while away their free time watching TV and surfing the web.

Parents must encourage their children in the formative years and help them pursue hobbies which they love. The true importance of pursuing a hobby consistently will be seen only once you watch your children develop along with their hobbies over time.

PRACTICAL STEPS YOUR CHILD/CHILDREN CAN TAKE IN CHOOSING A HOBBY

Hobbies allow your children to explore interests outside of their normal home and school activities. They let them be creative and try all kinds of new things. This helps your child to discover what he or she is good at before fixating on one. If they are bored with their old hobby, they can try picking a different one that can get their creative juices flowing again.

1. PAY ATTENTION TO WHAT EXCITES THEIR PASSION

The way they talk about events can also reveal a lot about them—their passions and those passions can be developed into a hobby. They should evaluate the topics they talk about endlessly. They can ask family members and their friends about what they seem to talk about the most. In addition, they should think about what it is about that subject that they enjoy so much and determine how it can be transformed into a hobby.

2. EXPLORING NEW TERRITORIES FOR IDEAS

Your child/children can visit a craft store to check what hobbies are available. At the craft store, they may find many things that they have never thought of. They can also visit the hardware store to explore different hobbies such as woodworking, or gardening. If they are old enough to read, they can use the library to explore a variety of topics on the how-to section, browse through them to find an interesting topic, which they can turn into new hobbies.

3. ENCOURAGE YOUR CHILD/CHILDREN TO PLAY WITH THE PETS

Children would want to play with toys and the computer. Instead, you can encourage your child/children to throw the ball for your dog, or play with the cat or look after a turtle, rabbit or goldfish.

4. THROW A FAMILY DANCE PARTY

The easiest way to introduce a new routine is by making it as fun as possible. Pop on some music and start dancing. To make your family dance party more fun and rewarding, ensure that you bear these points in mind:

a. Curate a playlist of favourite songs

b. Move furniture to create space

c. Wear fun costumes

d. Use fabric, ribbon and scarf s props

e. Learn new dance moves together

5. TAKE THEM TO PARKS AND PLAYGROUNDS

Taking your child/children with you to playgrounds and parks will allow them to make new friends based on the common interest of play. With these new friends, your children will be willing to play more and explore new physical activities.

6. THEY CAN CHECK HOBBY WEBSITES

These are websites that are dedicated solely to exploring hobbies, and they can use them to figure out what they'd like to do with their time. They should be willing to try more hobbies. The first one they try might not be the right fit.

7. ALLOWING CHOICES

Children should be allowed to have their choices. This will make them have a sense of autonomy and creativity. They will have a sense of being able to do what they want.

 Habit Fifty-five

HAVE BRAVERY

WHY IS IT IMPORTANT?

Bravery is an essential quality that your child/children must develop. It is so vital in their development that a lack of it may manifest in adulthood in several forms—social awkwardness, shyness or even laziness. Therefore, it is important that your children see the benefits of this important quality.

While we all want to be known or seen as a courageous person in a lot of ways during our lifetime, only a small fraction of the population is brave.

Bravery is important to our lives in a lot of situations. We need to be brave to leave our comfort zone and pursue new opportunities. Sometimes we need to be brave to make some decisions or contribute our quota to a discussion irrespective of whose ego will be bruised. Whatever we are doing, there is no denying the fact that bravery is important in everything and as parents, we should try hard to teach our children the acts of bravery.

BENEFITS:

◆ INTELLECTUAL BENEFITS

Focus: There are several things trying to battle for the attention of your child/children. These distractions affect the focus of your child/children. If your child/children are able to identify their fears and confront them with all bravery, they will have fewer distractions to deal with and have improved focus.

💎 INTELLECTUAL ENERGY

● **Clarity:** When your child/children brave, they have a clear mental state. They are able to see and reason clearly. This is good for their cognitive functioning.

● **Critical thinking:** When embarking on a daring task, it takes critical thinking to succeed. Critical thinking is one of those things that naturally follow your child/children when they choose bravery.

● **Better grades:** When they have focus, intellectual energy, clarity and are able to think clearly, they get better grades. This is good for their self-image.

💎 EMOTIONAL BENEFITS

● **Passion:** The biggest benefits that your child/children will cherish from choosing bravery are largely emotional. True passion is unadulterated. If your child/children are brave, they find it easy to identify their passions and follow them wholeheartedly.

● **Positive Thinking:** The first step to developing positive thinking is to be brave. Let's admit it, there will be situations at home and school that may bring reasons for gloominess. If your child/children are brave, they will have a positive outlook towards life.

💎 SOCIAL BENEFITS

● **Healthy relationships:** It takes a brave child to develop a positive relationship. People are naturally drawn to people who are courageous.

● **Strong sense of cultural identity:** In a world where civilization is redefining social and communal morals, a strong sense of cultural identity is required. A black child must not feel inferior because of his race, nor should a rich child have to apologize for his or her inheritance.

💎 COMMUNICATION BENEFITS

⚫ **Assertiveness:** True bravery brings assertiveness and eloquence in positive thinking. It makes your child/children be able to present their ideas in a way that is respectable and uncondescending.

⚫ **Public speaking:** If they choose bravery, they are more likely to take on public speaking opportunities.

⚫ **Eloquence:** When speaking, they will be more eloquent and articulate.

💎 PHYSICAL BENEFITS

⚫ **Less harmful habits:** From their pursuits of worthy goals, they will drop many harmful benefits like poor eating habits as well as several childish attitudes.

⚫ **Less consumption of fat, sugar and calories:** Bravery in areas of interest is fun. Hence, your child/children will often look forward to their next conquest. This will help them avoid fast foods containing fat, sugar, and calories.

CONCLUSION:

Children who are brave grow up to become healthy adults. They pursue worthy goals and become role models in the society. They also grow up to become successful in any field they choose as it takes a lot of bravery to produce results in generating decisions.

As parents, we should develop ways in which we can test the bravery of our children. This can be done by delegating tasks to them, or by assigning responsibilities and checking how they fare in them.

Bravery gives one a lot of confidence to take life-changing steps, and it is imperative as parents to always look out for ways to maximize our children's bravery and courage.

PRACTICAL STEPS CHILD/CHILDREN CAN TAKE TO HAVE BRAVERY

By many, bravery is considered one of the most important human virtues. For children, it means learning to do things despite their fears. The following are steps your child/children can follow in building bravery.

1. EMBRACING FEAR

Bravery means doing something despite the fear. Fear comes from the body's natural response to the brain's fight or flight response. The brain sends cortisol, a stress-inducing hormone, throughout the body's nervous system, making the body go into hyper-drive. Fearfulness is a learned behaviour, based on our brain chemistry, but strengthened by the world around your child/children that has trained them to be fearful. Learning to work through fear and step beyond it is about retraining their mind.

2. GETTING OUT OF THE COMFORT ZONE

Your child/children have to take unfamiliar paths. They have to step outside the little world they have known. This is a great way for them to grasp bravery. By doing the things they don't normally do, they will be able to cope with the unexpected, which is where fear often springs from. Learning to deal with that fear, in a situation they have chosen, can help them perform bravely when the unexpected happens.

- Starting small. They should start with the actions that induce less fear and require less courage to accomplish.
- Knowing the limits. There are certain things that they just cannot do. This may include picking up a spider or go skydiving. Instead, they should focus on building their courage for other things, like putting a glass over the spider so someone else can take care of it.

3. BUILDING BRAVERY

Having bravery allows your child/children to be able to trust in their abilities and themselves, and realize that they are more than their fears. When they have confidence in themselves, they will find it easier to take courageous action. For a child, learning to have confidence takes practice. There are a number of ways that your child/children can follow to build confidence:

- **Fake it until you make it.** This is fast becoming a popular cliché. They can trick their minds into confidence by pretending that they are confident.

- They should not let their failures or limitations dictate who they are. Failure simply means that they are trying; it is something to learn from, not avoid. They must be able to remind themselves that their failures do not define them unless they let them.

- Most importantly, they must have faith in themselves. Bravery involves trusting yourself and believing in yourself.

4. BUILDING BRAVERY FOR SPECIFIC SITUATIONS

It takes a different kind of bravery to volunteer for a project that a child is interested in, to confront a bully, or to say no. All of these scenarios require a show of confidence, whatever they actually feel. Confidence and bravery come through acting as if they are unafraid, even (and especially) when they are. When they are confronting a bully, they must remember to act as if they are feeling brave and confident.

This will trick the bully into thinking that the child is confident and unafraid. Bullies thrive on your child's emotional response, so he or she must be conscious of not giving them the pleasure of a reaction.

 **Habit** Fifty-six

KNOW HOW TO STAND UP FOR RIGHTS

WHY IS IT IMPORTANT?

Today, people are scared of speaking up. There is corruption in governments, terrorism in places, and human rights being abused. The world needs people who can stand up.

Research studies have shown that the ability to stand up for one's rights are being developed at a very tender age.

Just like with adults, it is important that your child/children stand up for their rights at school and at home. If the world is to be the land of the free and prosperous, it is important that future generations learn, understand and appreciate the freedoms they have, as there are many who are working to undermine those freedoms and our way of life. These days, it seems children hear less about their own rights.

BENEFITS:

💎 INTELLECTUAL BENEFITS

- **Critical thinking:** : When they stand up for their rights, they are going to have to think critically. This is because there will be other people (children and adults) who are going to challenge their stance. If they are not able to come up with strong arguments for their stance, they may not be able to continue focusing on their rights.

- **Focus:** They are also going to be seen as more focused and purposeful.

- **Vision:** By standing up for their rights, they are going to be able to develop their own vision—which is going to make them stand out from the rest of the park.

💎 EMOTIONAL BENEFITS

● **Confidence:** Through the act of standing up for their rights, they are going to appear more confident and have an enhanced self-confidence.

● **Joy:** They are also going to have more fun, joy, and cheerfulness. This is because they will be living based on their inner compass.

● **Tranquillity:** In addition, they are going to appear calmer and more relaxed. This will help them in being happier and able to recognize the good things happening around them.

💎 SOCIAL BENEFITS

● **Authenticity:** Your child/children are going to appear more authentic and original. In a world beset with groupthink, your children will be original and authentic. They will be able to stand up for themselves, be unique and become more proactive. As a result, people are going to be drawn to them.

● **Charisma:** This is the personal attractiveness that enables them to influence others. The leaders among children are those who understand their rights and responsibilities and are able to stand up for them. Others will want to look up to them.

● **Knowing right from wrong:** They will know their rights from wrong when they start standing up for their rights.

● **Self-protection:** Children who focus on standing up for their rights are going to be highly self-protected. They are going to be able to protect themselves from harms.

💎 COMMUNICATION BENEFITS

● **Assertiveness:** They are going to appear more assertive and confident in their communications. Even though standing up for one's right should be a normal thing. It isn't. When your children begin to show up and stand up for their rights, they will be met with stiffening oppositions; but, they will be able to develop assertiveness in the process.

- **Public speaking:** They are also going to be more interested in leading others through their oratory prowess. People are going to be drawn to them. This is good for their esteem.

- **Eloquence:** In addition, they are going to appear more eloquent and articulate in their use of words and expressing their ideas.

CONCLUSION:

When children stand up for the right of others, they are able to bring out their authenticity. In addition, they are more charismatic. Children must be able to start standing up for their own rights at a very early age. They must be able to exercise their rights without feeling bad. Not only will they become more confident, but they will also be able to avoid being overlooked in public. Their voices will garner weight.

PRACTICAL STEPS YOUR CHILD/CHILDREN CAN TAKE IN STANDING UP FOR THEIR RIGHTS

It can be really challenging for a child to stand up for himself/herself if they are used to letting others have their way, or they are a people pleaser. When they compromise on their values to suit everyone else, it can all be too easy for them to chisel away their self-esteem; learning to stand up for their rights is a good way of ensuring other people respect them and do not try to push them around or manipulate them. In this section, we are going to learn about the basic steps that your children can take to stand up for their rights.

1. MASSIVE SELF-BELIEF

Your child/children have to get it right from a very young age that if they do not believe in themselves, no one will believe in them. Developing a strong sense of self-confidence is the first step that your children can take towards standing up for themselves.

- Children who are lacking in self-confidence are easy targets for bullies and manipulators. If your children are confident, people are less likely to tease them or identify them as weak. Confidence has to come from within, so do whatever it takes to make them feel better about themselves— lose some weight, learn a new skill, repeat positive affirmations daily— these changes will not happen overnight, but their confidence will grow in time.
- Another way your child/children can build massive self-belief is by setting goals for themselves. Goals give children a sense of purpose. It gives them a sense of control and helping them realize what they truly want. It is an essential aspect that enables them to stand up for themselves and prevent others from walking all over them. They can set weekly goals, monthly goals, and annual goals. More importantly, when they achieve their goals, they must remember to reflect and celebrate what they have done.

② DEVELOPING A GOOD ATTITUDE

The first step to developing a good attitude is that your children have to first stop seeing themselves as a victim. This makes them blame others and shrink from responsibilities. Attitude is everything. It impacts how people relate with your children. As a matter of fact, it affects how they see themselves. Attitude sets the tone of their voice, the quality of their thoughts, and is reflected in their facial expressions and body language. They should remember that attitude is contagious. If they are happy, it will encourage those around them to be happy about themselves.

③ LEARNING TO BE ASSERTIVE

Assertiveness is the key for your child/children to standing up for themselves. Being assertive enables your children to express their needs, wants, and preferences in a way that shows they are prepared to stand up for themselves while still respecting the other person. It involves being open and honest about their thoughts and feelings while trying to work towards a mutually satisfying solution.

4. LEARNING TO SAY NO

This is perhaps the hardest thing for a child. However, it can be one of the most important ways of standing up for their rights. If they are a yes-person who wants others to feel good about them, they risk being a door-mat. By standing up for their rights, they will be able to demonstrate confidence and courage. This will help them to become more useful adults.

5. HAVING ROLE MODELS

When children have role models, they are able to stand up for themselves. The picture of who a role model is to them will determine how they will live their lives.

Part Three
CONCLUSION

This book has been a journey into selected habits for children's development.

These are habits that will help your child/children love and appreciate life; habits to help them become resilient, habits to build self-discipline and habits to build self-worth. In other words, this book contains habits to help young child/children become fruitful, happy and successful adults.

These four major sections are essential for having responsible and healthy children. There are many men and women in the world who have no identity or discipline. They might be seen as morally corrupt by the world's standards. They do not want to wake up to change their current actions or behaviour. It is because of lifelong bad habits that have been developed inside them. Many parents who rely on their "natural instincts" to raise their children often fall into the majority of statistics on failed parenting.

However, all hope is not lost. This book is developed in such a way that before each habit starts to be formed, parents are aware of the importance of such a habit. Then, a detailed how-to is written to help parents know what their children can begin to do to make them more successful and responsible.

According to results from several research studies, it takes more than 2 months before a new behaviour becomes automatic. To be exact, that is about 66 days. Of course, the period of habit formation varies based on several factors: the child, the circumstances around him/her and the nature of the habit. The essence of this habit formation is that, as a parent, you have to be patient with your child/children when implementing these habits. Since they have been acting one way all their lives up to now, they cannot just change in one day. However, by being patient with them, they will become successful and responsible adults.

In addition, it is important that these habits are not forced on children all at once. They must be taken one at a time. As parents, you should allow sufficient time for your child/children to learn, form, develop and crystallise new habits that you want to build up for the future. It is amazing to witness/see/observe how much improvement a child will make by incorporating one positive habit at a time. As a matter of fact, it might be noted that other factors are complementary. When a child begins to embrace one habit, other positive habits are also noticed in the child. For example, when a child becomes compassionate, he or she is going to enjoy little things, let go of past mistakes and maintain self-love.

Each habit is carefully and thoughtfully chosen to ensure that they are essential for the psychological, physical and emotional growth of the child. This explains why the emphasis is placed on the physical, emotional, social, intellectual and communication benefits of each habit. These areas are the most important aspects of a child's growth process. They are excellent determinants of who a child will turn out to be in the future.

It is my hope that these habits will help ease the burden of parenting and illustrate the directions and ways to equip your child/children at an early age. I must say as early as possible! I have spent time and done lots of research over the last 25 years. I've worked with more than a thousand young children. I can now confirm that I am giving you essential information that you need to equip your child/children as early as you can. I also hope that the content of this book, will provide you a chance to change your own habits to match with the habits you want your child/children to have in their lives. You also can add on to your knowledge, learning and research on habit building to enrich the benefits of the above mentioned 56 habits. I hope you will go with the 'one-by-one habit' steps and put your full commitment to achieve the best benefits and outcomes for your child/children's future.

I look forward to a world in which there will be more and more successful and responsible adults. It's possible if today's parents do their jobs with excellence, to ensure that the child/children in their care are being properly brought up and given the best chance for success.

REFERENCES

Adriaanse, Marieke A.; Kroese, Floor M.; Gillebaart, Marleen; Ridder, De; D, & Denise T. 2014. *Effortless inhibition: habit mediates the relation between self-control and unhealthy snack consumption.*
Switzerland: Frontiers in Psychology.

Anthony Dickinson 1985. *Actions and Habits: The Development of Behavioural Autonomy.* Philosophical Transactions of the Royal Society B: Biological Sciences. http://rstb.royalsocietypublishing.org/content/308/1135/67 Retrieved on 10/12/2018.

Baars, B. & Gage, N. 2010. *Cognition, Brain and Consciousness: Introduction to Cognitive Neuroscience* (2nd ed). Oxford: Elsevier.

Bas, V. & Suzanne, F. 1999. *Good intentions, bad habits, and effects of forming implementation intentions on healthy eating.*
United Kingdom: European Journal of Social Psychology.

Bill, B. 1996. *Making Families Work and What to Do When They Don't.*
New York: Haworth Press.

Bodrova, E. & Leong, D.J. 2007. *Tools of the Mind: The Vytgotskian Approach to Early Childhood Education.* New Jersey: Pearson Education Inc.

British Journal of General Practice 2012. *Making health habitual: The psychology of 'habit-formation' and general practice.*
London: British Journal of General Practice.

Dean, J. 2013. *Making habits Breaking habits.*
London: Da Capo Lifelong Books.

Dockett, S. & Fleer, M. 1999. *Play and Pedagogy in Early Childhood: Bending the Rules*. Australia: Harcourt Brace.

Duhigg, C. 2012. *The Power of Habit: Why we do what we do and how to Change*. New York: Random House Trade Paperbacks.

Durham, C. 2001. *Chasing Ideas: The Fun of Freeing Your Child's Imagination*. Sydney: Finch Publishing.

Erikson, E. H. 1950. *Childhood and Society*. New York: WW Norton & Co.

Gardner, B & Lally, P & Wardle, J; 2012. *Making health habitual: the psychology of 'habit-formation' and general practice.*
London: British Journal of General Practice.

Herbert, F. & Jean B. 1975. *Don't Say Yes When You Want to Say No*. New York City: Dell.

James, T. & Flores, L & Scholber, J. 2000. *Hypnosis: A Comprehensive Guide. Producing Deep Trance Phenomena*. UK: TJ International Ltd

Jay, S.L. & Ellis, A. 2010. *Rational and Irrational Beliefs: Research, Theory and Clinical Practice*. Oxford: Oxford University Press.

Karpov, Y.V. 2014. *Vygotsky for Educators*.
Cambridge: Cambridge University Press.

Krashner, A.M. 2001. *The Wizard Within*. Santa Ana: American Board of Hypnotherapy.

Lahey, J. 2015. *The Gift of Failure: How to Step Back and Let Your Child Succeed*. New York: Harper Collins.

Lally P. 2009. *How are habits formed: Modelling habit formation in the real world*. United Kingdom: European Journal of Social Psychology.

Lally, P., & van Jaarsveld, C. H. M., Potts, H. W. W., Wardle, J. 2010. *How are habits formed: Modelling habit formation in the real world.*
United Kingdom: European Journal of Social Psychology.

Lally P, Wardle J & Gardner B. 2011. *Experiences of habit formation: A qualitative study.* England: Psychology, Health & Medicine.

Mariana, V 1998. *Disease or Habit? Alcoholism and the Exercise of Freedom.* Cambridge: Cambridge University Press.

Muthu, M. & Sivakumar, M. 2009. *"Oral Habits", Paediatric Dentistry: Principles and Practice,* Elsevier.

Nash, J. 2011. *Lose Weight, Live Healthy: A Complete Guide to Designing Your Own Weight Loss Program.* Bulls Publishing Company: England.

Neal, D., Wood, W., Labrecque, J., & Lally, P. 2011. *How do habits guide behavior? perceived and actual triggers of habits in daily life.* Journal of Experimental Social Psychology. http://dornsife.usc.edu/assets/sites/545/docs/Wendy_Wood_Research_Articles/Habits/neal.wood.labrecque.lally.2012_001_How_do_habits_guide_behavior.pdf Retrieved on 11/12/2018.

Pearson, S. 2017. *Ultimate You.* Melbourne: Global Success Institute.

Scheck, S. 2014. *Stages of Psychosocial Development According to Erik H. Erikson.* Munich: GRIN Verlag.

Suzanne, L. & Gary, R. 2001. *The Complete Idiot's Guide to Breaking Bad Habits.* Kindle DX Version. Retrieved from Amazon.com.

Vygotsky, L. 1978. *Mind in Society.* Cambridge: Cambridge University Press.

Vygotsky, L. 1987. Thinking and Speech. In *The Collected Works of L.S. Vygotsky: Vol. 1. Problems of General Psychology*, eds. R. Rieber & A.S, Carton, trans. N. Minick. 37-285. New York: Plenum.

Wise, A.L. 2015 Habits: *The Power of Habits – Creating Habits for Success to Change Your Life.* Kindle DX Version. Retrieved from Amazon.com.

www.ingramcontent.com/pod-product-compliance
Lightning Source LLC
Chambersburg PA
CBHW031405290426
44110CB00011B/269